D0835912

ROOTLESS

ROOTLESS

Bruce Oldfield

with Fanny Blake

HUTCHINSON

LONDON

First published by Hutchinson in 2004

1 3 5 7 9 10 8 6 4 2

Hutchinson
The Random House Group Limited
20 Vauxhall Bridge Road, London SW1V 2SA

Random House Austria (Pty) Limited
20 Alfred Street, Milsons Point, Sydney
New South Wales 2061, Australia

Random House New Zealand Limited
18 Poland Road, Glenfield
Auckland 10, New Zealand

Random House (Pty) Limited
Ebdulini, 5a Jubilee Road
Parktown 2193, South Africa

The Random House Group Limited Reg. No. 954009

www.randomhouse.co.uk

A CIP catalogue record for this book is available from the British Library

Papers used by Random House are natural, recyclable products made from
wood grown in sustainable forests. The manufacturing processes conform to
the environmental regulations of the country of origin

ISBN 0 09 179997 X

Typeset by SX Composing DTP, Rayleigh, Essex
Printed and bound by Mackays of Chatham Plc, Chatham, Kent

ILLUSTRATIONS

1. My Mother, Betty Eileen Oldfield
2. A very white looking me – on the Strays in Harrogate, 1951
3. Me, George and two foster brothers in the back yard at 18 West Street, Hett village, 1952
4. Violet – with obligatory fag washing dog at Hett, c. 1950
5. Violet, Marie Lambert and chums, late 1940s
6. Group of local kids in Hett village
7. Victorious at sports day, 1957
8. Linda, George, me, Christine at Crimdon Dene, c.1958
9. Summer hols – Linda, me, George, Barry
10. Janet on tricycle, Christine, Mum and me, c.1962
11. The Lally sisters: Christine, Joan, Betty and Enid, c.1940s
12. Holiday snap. Christine, George, Barry and me with Linda in the front row with offensive smelling seaweed or am I just squinting into the sun?
13. Auntie Carol, Barry, me and George in Whitby, 1959
14. George, me and Barry
15. Family picture taken in Spennymoor, 1965. Me, Barry, George, Linda. Front row: Janet and Mum
16. Me and fellow inmate at West Mount, 1964
17. Alistair and Ann Lambert, c.1957 – my first wedding dress!
18. Janet and Mum outside Number 8, Tweed Road, c.1964
19. Me with afro in cemetery in Sheffield, 1969
20. My Student Union ID card
21. Carina Fitzalan-Howard, now Lady Carina Frost at the Revlon Fashion Show to launch the fragrance Charlie, 1973. My tutors, Lydia Kemeny and Bobbie Hilson in the front row
22. One of the models in my St Martin's leaving show

23. Charlotte Rampling, wearing a smocked jersey dress and cape for Jackpot, 1974

24. Work in progress on a piece of smocked jersey, Ravensbourne, 1972

25. Me, looking sultry for my modelling portfolio

26. Su Suter after my Berkeley Hotel show, 1975. 'Oh Bruce you've done it again!'

27. Ninivah at Campden Hill Square in front of the Colin Barnes drawing with a missing sleeve

28. Me at Campden Hill Square, Christmas, late 1970s © *Harpers & Queen*

29. Tim Lamb's original artwork for show invitation mailer, *c.*1977. Jerry Hall photographed by Eric Boman

30. Marion

31. Redcliffe Gardens – Mock Last Supper. Michael Roberts, Robert Forrest, Bill Reed, Rifat Ozbek, unknown and Raymond Paynter

32. Michael Roberts photographing Jacques Azagury at Redcliffe Gardens

33. Colin Barnes and Pauline Denyer (now Lady Smith)

34. Victor working on a sample in Walton Street, 1977

35. Anita at home during a party she gave for my 31st birthday

36. Another party at Redcliffe Gardens – David Reeson, Anita, and Colin Barnes

37. Romilly, Lady McAlpine

38. St. Martins. Back row: Joe Casely-Hayford, Andrea Sargeant, me, Ninivah Khomo and Alistair Blair. Front row: John Flett, Nick Coleman, John Galliano and Rifat Ozbek. Photograph by Eamonn J McCabe

39. Reception at the Barnardo's Gala 1985. HRH Princess of Wales, me, Joan Collins, Charlotte Rampling, Jean-Michel Jarre, Barry Humphries. Photograph by Desmond O'Neill

40. Shirley Bassey, Dame Edna Everage, Charlotte Rampling, Christopher Reeve – all in BO except Superman! Photograph by Barry Swaybe

41. Charlotte Rampling. Photograph by Eva Sereny

42. Joan Collins and me in Beverly Hills. Photograph by Alan Davidson

43. HRH Prince Charles and HRH Princess Diana, polo at Smiths Lawn, Windsor, 1988

44. Diana and Nancy Reagan in Washington 1985. Photograph by Tim Graham

45. Diana (in cream satin and lace suit) at Sadlers Wells 1990. Photograph by Tim Graham

46. Diana at the Birthright Ball at the Albert Hall in 1985. Photograph by Tim Graham

47. Ultimate red carpet occasion 1989. Photograph by Tim Graham

48. Me and Mrs Thatcher at Downing Street, c.1986. © News International

49. Me and HRH Princess Margaret at a fashion show in Guildhall, 1979

50. Scott Barrie in San Lorenzo, New Year's Eve, 1989

51. Ralph Steadman distressed Polaroid, Aspen, 1987

52. David Bailey photograph of me and Marie Helvin for *Ritz*, 1970s

53 Me with Barnardo's children at a Christmas party given in the canteen at Marks & Spencer, Baker Street during my stint as consultant

54. Two decades of fashion shows. Photographs by Niall McInerney

55. Me with chairs at the Design and Decoration Building, 1991

56. One of the couture chairs at the 'Decoration, Haute Couture' exhibit, 1991

57. Jemima Goldsmith and Imran Khan, 1995. Photograph by Harry Page

58. Francesca Fisher marries John Jermyn to become Marchioness of Bristol at Ickworth Hall. Photograph by Norman Parkinson

59. Susanne Bond

60. Rania Al-Yassin marries HRH Prince Abdullah, now HM Queen Rania and HM King Abdullah of Jordan

61. Me and Marie Helvin at Versace opening party on Bond Street. Photograph by David Koppel

62. That Kiss. Joanna Lumley and me at the wedding of the decade in *Absolutely Fabulous*

63. Noemi Cinzano and me
64. Susan and Fiona Sangster wearing my hand painted pareos at Jane's Harbour, Barbados, 1994
65. Me repairing Fiona's zip in a dress to be worn that night. Melissa Lilley, Sue's daughter looks on
66. Me and Guy Sangster at Cobbler's Cove drinking an infamous Cobbler's Cooler with disastrous results
67. Caroline Charles and Malcolm Valentine at my 50th birthday at San Lorenzo's. Photograph by Hugo Burnand
68. Sarah Reed and Desmond Biddulph. Photograph by Hugo Burnand
69. The late Robert Sangster, Kevin Carroll in background. Photograph by Hugo Burnand
70. William and Annabel Astor. Photograph by Hugo Burnand
71. George Sinclair. Photograph by Hugo Burnand
72. Lizzie Walker, Barry and Anita. Photograph by Hugo Burnand
73. Christine Lambert and partner George. Photograph by Hugo Burnand
74. The other family. Cousin Jennifer and behind her, husband Stuart, Aunt Enid, me and Aunt Joan with husband, Len Collier. Photograph by Hugo Burnand
75. Linda and Amy Li. Photograph by Hugo Burnand
76. Romilly McAlpine. Photograph by Hugo Burnand
77. Babe looking regal at home in London
78. Staff and friends at lunch party at the Mill

To Violet

ACKNOWLEDGEMENTS

Many thanks to the following who have helped me dredge the dimmest corners of my memory: Linda Hall, Christine Lambert, Winnie Watts, Roger Singleton, Sarah Reed, Annette Worsley-Taylor, Marie Helvin, Georgina Alexander Sinclair, David Reeson, Rosalind Wolfson, Kevin Carroll, Romilly, Lady McAlpine, Marie Todd, Ninivah Khomo, Judith Wolkenfeld, Charlotte Rampling, Fanny Blake, Lis Mcleod, Ted Emerson, Monica Scott, Jan Rowsell, Anna Watson, Ivor Montlake, Tina Shingler, Constance Gilbey, Enid Goodall, Victor Herbert, Noemi Cinzano, Guy and Fiona Sangster, Su Suter, Susan Sangster, Annabel Astor, William Yeoward, Colin Orchard and the Barnardo's Files.

And to absent friends: Violet Masters, Edith Blair, Anita Richardson, Colin Barnes, Diana, Princess of Wales, Robert Sangster, Sheila Wetton, Joan Collier, Scott Barrie and Betty Eileen Oldfield, who, for better or for worse introduced me into all of this.

PROLOGUE

I enjoy making glamorous clothes for women because I love glamour. I was brought up watching the films of Fred Astaire and Ginger Rogers in the 1950s, when my foster family and I would sit in front of the television, glued to the sophistication of Fred and the elegance and femininity of Ginger in those glittering routines. As far as I'm concerned, glamour and couture go hand in hand. As a clothes designer, I think my remit is to make a woman alluring and sexy, to make her look the very best she can by highlighting the best parts and camouflaging the less than perfect bits. That's what I've been attempting throughout my career.

To have survived for thirty years is unusual for a small British company but, somewhat to my amazement, I'm still here in the fashion business and gearing up for another push forward. I'm an eternal optimist and see exciting possibilities emerging out of the backlash against the globalisation of fashion. If you walk down Madison Avenue, the Faubourg St Honoré or Sloane Street today, you will see the same designers with the same boutique design, the same accessories and merchandise. A lot of people are put off by the fact that the exclusive labels they buy are not in fact exclusive at all. As a result, many women are now looking for something that little bit different. Exclusive, interesting and with word-of-mouth reputation. That's what I think the Bruce Oldfield label should be. I love the fact that we are able to make very beautiful clothes. The way things are finished and the care that goes into making every single garment is extremely important to me. I'm lucky not to have someone constantly looking over my shoulder but choosing to remain small has meant it has been far from plain sailing.

In the early years, I was pushy and had lots of energy. I moved from Ravensbourne College of Art to St Martin's then, again without completing my course, left for New York at the invitation of Geraldine Stutz, director of the prestigious store, Henri Bendel, who asked me to design a range of clothes for them. That was followed by a stint in Paris and the south of France before I returned to London to consolidate my own business. It could be called impatience that I didn't finish one thing before going on to the next but I was able to make those decisions for myself and just go with it. You stand or fall on those decisions in life. I've always had great ambition and never felt I was going to marry or settle down so the pay-off was that I was going to be successful. I worked hard, concentrating on ready-to-wear during the '70s and then in the '80s added couture to our business. We have focussed on the couture side of the business over the last decade but now I want to use the authority I have gained from my long involvement in the fashion world to spread my wings.

I have never felt I had unreasonable expectations in life, even when I was a teenager living in a Dr Barnardo's Home in Ripon. It's those expectations, the challenge and wanting things to happen that have kept me going. Not much has changed. The expectations continue to carry me forward. They may be scaled down somewhat but I'm happier keeping it small. It's about adapting to new situations.

Looking back, there was one day when all the strands of my life came together. March 26th, 1985 was a red-letter day for me. I was hosting a charity gala and fashion show at the Grosvenor House Hotel, Park Lane, to raise money for Barnardo's. It was perfect. It marked the tenth anniversary of the opening of my business, the Princess of Wales was the President of the charity and guest of honour, as well as being a friend and client of mine, and I was an ex-Barnardo's boy made good. My career and credibility rested on that evening. Months of planning had gone into it. At the end of the previous December we had been told officially by the Palace that the Princess would attend. As a photo opportunity it suited everyone: an ex-Barnardo's boy – poor, black and illegitimate – sitting next to the future Queen.

Despite the heart-stopping moments that are typical of putting on a fashion show with everything arriving at the last minute, half-pinned and half-tacked, it all went smoothly. I received Princess Diana, who appeared very relaxed, wearing the long ball gown in pleated silvery blue lamé that I had designed for her. She had wanted a dance dress with sex appeal, something a bit outrageous, so she liked the fact that her back was bare. It certainly caused something of a stir. She wanted to be the glamorous princess and that's what we made her. I introduced her to the line-up of celebrity guests including Joan Collins, Charlotte Rampling, Shirley Bassey and Dame Edna Everage (all of them sporting Bruce Oldfield dresses). The cameras popped and everyone was happy. Leading the Princess down to dinner was an especially proud moment. Being with the most idolised woman in the world made me feel pretty grand. As we walked down the steps, she whispered she had a present for me. When we got to the table she opened her bag and gave me 20 Benson and Hedges. I hadn't brought mine, since Royal Protocol prohibited smoking. Exactly what I needed to calm my tattered nerves. We always got on well and sat together chatting over dinner about quite private things. The atmosphere was fabulous. Every table was intimately lit with candles and decorated with simple displays of white tulips. After dinner, there came the fashion show followed by speeches. Mine was made with the Princess surreptitiously pinching my bum to make me keep it short so we could get to the dancing more quickly. Dame Edna orchestrated the tombola and then encouraged the guests to up their bids in the auction. Afterwards the Princess and I led the dancing to Kid Creole and the Coconuts. The plan had been for everyone else at the top table to follow our example after a minute or two but within five seconds the floor was packed. However, as we danced, a halo of space opened up around us, as everyone made sure they were far enough away to get a good look. When the evening ended and the Princess had left somewhat reluctantly, I went to join a party at Annabel's where I received a standing ovation. By the next morning we were on the front page of every newspaper.

In contrast, some months afterwards, I travelled apprehensively on the tube to Barkingside in Essex on the way to Barnardo's head office, a grim, grey concrete building that is the centre of the whole operation and where all the archives are housed. I had finally asked Roger Singleton, the chief executive if I could see my files. And after 35 years I was to be allowed to do so. As far as I'm aware this was unprecedented. Presumably, up until then it had been felt that giving Barnardo's children access to their personal records would be disturbing for the child, breach some confidentiality or provoke a legal action. The old system dictated that three files were kept on each child, one at Headquarters, one at the York office and one at the residential Home. Roger explained that when the Home closed, the file there was probably destroyed in the belief that everything of importance would be at Headquarters where they were obsessional about filing every report, letter and memo. When I arrived, I was led up to Roger's office and he showed me to a room off to the side.

It was starkly furnished with just a table with the files on it and a chair. It felt familiarly institutional. I spent ten hours reading everything. Roger stayed in his office, occasionally going out to buy me more cigarettes or to bring me another cup of coffee, until I had finished. I absorbed all the information in a very methodical, cold-blooded way, and the only thing I felt when I'd finished was exhausted. I was upset about some of the things said about my foster mother but I don't think I felt any more warmly towards my birth mother. I didn't go there looking for revelations. I was just curious.

I never knew my mother or father. I was born on July 14th, 1950, and by the time I was six months old my mother had signed the agreement entrusting me to the care of Dr Barnardo's Homes which we always knew as DBH.

For twelve years, I lived in a foster home with three, then four other children. To me that was home and our foster mother, Violet Masters was my mother. Of course we knew we were different. It was quite clear because of our colour (we were all mixed-race) and our situation. So we were odd, but we weren't that odd because we lived at home with our mother and were a family. There were, after all, plenty of children around who were missing one or other of their parents for one reason or another.

It was only when I was taken to West Mount, a DBH Branch Home in Ripon that I gave my parents any thought at all. Every child in my situation wants to find out about their real parents. I was in a very strange situation with twenty-four kids of varying ages, all quite different to me and from very different back-grounds. I'd pick up little snippets of other people's stories either from their parents or their brother or sister visiting, or when they came back from a weekend with a relative.

I hadn't felt that sense of disconnection until I went to Ripon because until then it was difficult for me to think of my foster mother as anything other than my mother. I was very fond of her and she of me, so it was hard to be any more than academically interested in my birth parents. Number one, it felt disloyal and number two, it just wasn't high on my list of priorities. Being in a Home prompted questions, however I can't remember talking to anyone outside the Home about what it was like being there or about my background. In fact I wanted to try and ignore the whole thing. I was certainly drip fed the minimum information about my mother while I was there, but that was part of the Barnardo's routine.

Most children left when they were fifteen or sixteen, after their CSEs, and were presented with the obligatory suitcase, birth certificate and Bible. Unlike the others, I was doing GCEs and staying on until A Level so the only thing I was told was her name, Betty Eileen Lally and the fact that she'd been married when she had me. They deliberately omitted to mention that the marriage was not to my father. Then at eighteen, armed with my suitcase and a copy of *Gerald Manley Hopkins: Man and Poet* (no Bible for me, thanks), they gave me my birth certificate and told me my father was a Jamaican boxer.

On my birthdays I occasionally used to think fleetingly about my parents but nothing more than that. When I first came to London in 1971, I did think I might trace them, but I've got the attention span of a gnat, so after one morning's research and a few telephone calls, I gave up. I once went to Hammersmith Hospital where I was born, but I went to the wrong department in the wrong place. That was the end of that. There is an address on my birth certificate, 61 Crowndale Road, but the house had been pulled down a long time ago.

Then in 1974, when I was becoming known and had the front cover of *Vogue* as well being featured a number of times in the national press, I did think I might get a telephone call. But it never came. I was conscious that nothing happened, but I was so busy with my career that I didn't have much time to dwell on it and besides, I was having fun.

So it was finally in 1985 that I sat down with my files. I wasn't looking for my parents. I was more concerned about what the people responsible for me had thought about me. It is a unique thing to have a detailed record of your life – a reminder of past events and a fresh perspective on old memories. But not only that, it gave me the details of my young life and my true origins.

CHAPTER ONE

I was born in Hammersmith Hospital on 14 July 1950. According to the file, my mother was 'mentally and morally weak, an epileptic who gave birth to a child with negroid tendencies'. Me.

Most of my pre-history is carefully documented in a Dr Barnardo's Homes (DBH) *Officer's Report re Application for Admission or Help* dated 11 October 1950, which refers to me as 'the candidate'. Reading it, it's hard to relate the events and personalities to my own life. These are the people responsible for my existence but the only way I know them is through impersonal records, so I can only relay the bare bones of the story as reported there.

My mother, Betty Eileen Lally, was the daughter of a railway worker and his wife. They were a 'respectable' couple who, by the time I was born, lived at 44 The Curve, Hammersmith. One of their daughters and her husband lived upstairs, and another was married to a doctor in Kent with two children. I was later to find out that they had four children, three girls and a boy, but for some reason this isn't recorded accurately. Betty was a teenager when she met Lawrence Oldfield at the Hammersmith Palais de Danse. He was something in the RAF but, for reasons not elaborated by DBH, both her parents disliked him and did everything they could to stop the match. Eventually she took matters into her own hands, left home when she was twenty and married him, against their wishes, in Pershore, Worcestershire in 1944. She was soon pregnant and it was during her pregnancy that she developed epilepsy. Their first child, David, was born on 18 August 1945.

Three years later she walked out on Oldfield and her baby, because, she claimed, her husband hit her. Indeed, her mother later reported to the welfare officer that she suspected Betty wasn't happy, '. . . although she has not spoken much about it'. Oldfield defended himself, saying he only did it because she didn't care for the child. He kept David and took responsibility for his upbringing. Betty kept the Oldfield name and did not press for divorce. 'The grandmother said that the mother never sees the child and does not seem to mind,' reads the report. The following year she had an illegitimate son, William, on 25 March 1949. Only a week or two later, a nun from the South Street Mission in London is recorded writing to a sister at Hammersmith Hospital explaining that Betty's parents are 'greatly distressed' and worried over her future, so much so that they blamed her father's illness on his anxiety over her behaviour. She concluded, 'Certain it is that the girl should not be let loose. She needs control and protection from herself and the temptations of these present days.'

Betty was sent to a Moral Welfare Home in Derby but she soon returned to London to live with William's father; '. . . this did not last long as she neglected and ill-treated the child . . . and the man finally turned her out.'

The records seem to contradict themselves here because another report relates that while still in a Mother and Baby Home in Chalk Farm she somehow gave the authorities the slip and met my father, a Jamaican trainee boxer, round the back of the Hammersmith Odeon. It was 'evident it was the most casual contact'. By the time she realised she was pregnant again, he'd done a runner. When she visited the address he had given her, there was no sign of him and he had left no forwarding address.

She apparently discharged herself from the home and 'drifted about' until she was finally housed in an institution. After I was born, she was placed in a home again but again discharged herself and went to live in Norwood House, a London County Council institution.

By now the sister at Hammersmith had apparently known my mother for some time and had already expressed concern for her. 'It was thought at one time, that she might be certified as morally defective and Sister took her to County Hall to try and arrange for her to go into a home but this could not be arranged.'

This may seem an outrageous infringement on her liberty now but I suppose it was 1950 and she had been a bad girl. A woman who left her husband and child was almost a pariah. To have one black illegitimate child might be regarded as a dreadful misfortune; to have two looked like moral turpitude. This was a terrible lapse that could socially stigmatise a family almost irrecoverably. The files make this clear over and over again.

After a conversation with the maternity almoner at Hammersmith Hospital, the report states:

> The mother is a great problem . . . She appears to be thoroughly irresponsible and quite unaware she is doing anything wrong . . . She was self-willed and uncooperative before the birth of the child.
>
> The mother is said to be a thoroughly amoral character without any sense of responsibility to herself or her children.

In a letter to the secretary of DBH, the almoner for Great Ormond Street Hospital writes about Betty: 'The maternity almoner now informs me she is due to be admitted shortly for sterilisation, for in addition to the epilepsy, she is of very low mentality.'

Betty had offended the authorities and they took action. Later the same year, she was sterilised. She had no choice. All that was needed was the permission of her husband and parents. Both were readily granted.

By this time, one of Betty's sisters had arranged through the courts for the second son William to be privately adopted by a friend. The family were equally adamant that they wanted nothing to do with me. 'Her family is . . . very upset by the mother's behaviour, but the grandmother is not willing to take responsibility of the candidate. I found her to be a very respectable and pleasant woman and her home is a good one, being a council house and clean and well-furnished,' reads the report. But Mrs Lally made it clear that while she would take Betty back home until she found other accommodation, they would not take me, a little coloured baby. Nor were she or her husband in any position to contribute financially to my upbringing. Her other three daughters could not help either, one being at work all day, another already with three children of her own and recovering from an operation. Whatever reason the third one had is unrecorded.

While she was pregnant with me, Betty had already applied to the National Adoption Society to have me adopted but had heard nothing from them by the time I was born. I developed gastro-enteritis shortly after my birth so the lady almoner of Hammersmith hospital decided I should go to a private nursing home to be cured. She believed my mother was neither suitable nor capable of taking care of me. I was sick enough to be sent to Great Ormond Street Hospital for Children and then to a convalescent home in Bognor Regis for something like seven months. That was how my life began.

The moral welfare officer then applied to DBH to have me put into a residential home. From the outset the authorities had made up their mind about how little Betty cared for me.

> The mother appears mentally quite normal, in that she is
> not deficient, but her attitude is easy going and unaware
> and I had no feeling that she would mind in the least
> parting with her child. She showed me a photograph of
> the candidate but it was more like a child showing the
> photograph of her doll, rather than a mother her child.

When I saw photos of her forty-seven years later, my reaction to her was much the same.

On 7 November, 1950, Betty signed the agreement entrusting me to the care of Dr Barnardo's Homes.

The arrangement was for her to return to her parents' home, where she was to take up her work as a packer in the Osram Lamp Factory in Australia Road, Hammersmith. She agreed that as soon as she was earning she would contribute regularly to the cost of my care.

Meanwhile I was transferred to Milton Lodge, Bognor Regis, a private convalescent home for up to eight babies run by a Miss Bates and partner who had trained at Great Ormond Street. They decided that, because I was prone to digestive disorders, I should be transferred directly from there to a DBH Branch Home to avoid too many upsetting changes. A vacancy came up in Roberts Memorial Home, Tewit Well Road, Harrogate, but the transfer took a long time, judging from the amount of notes and letters that went backwards and forwards between Roberts Memorial Home and Bognor Regis. First of all they didn't have anyone who could carry an infant from Bognor to Harrogate and then I was ill again. So I didn't move until 1951. It was 16 January. All the reports of that year have me as a chubby, healthy and happy baby who soon became the 'boss' of the nursery. 'He gets on well with the other children if he doesn't take all their toys.'

My earliest memory dates back to then. It resurfaced when I was sixteen and at a DBH reunion that for some reason was held at Roberts Memorial Home. As we walked in I immediately remembered so many things about the place that I couldn't possibly have known without having been there before. I remembered there was a railway line at the bottom of the garden that ran up along the side of the Strays, the green stretch of grassland to the south of the town. The nurses used to take all of us babies in prams up to the Strays and I remembered perfectly the bandstand near the end of Tewit Well Road.

That year, there is another report concerning Betty who by March was back home and had been employed by Osram's for nine weeks, earning £3 and 13/-. Rheumatoid arthritis in her knee was giving cause for concern and she had had time off to visit Hammersmith Hospital where she would eventually have an operation. Not only that but her financial obligations to the London County Council and to DBH were worrying her considerably although she is reported as being willing to meet her contributions to them as best she could. Her social life was severely curtailed too so that she rarely went out except with her mother or another female relative. Her mother thought that it would do her good to have the additional responsibility of me and promised to try and see that she kept up her future payments of 5/- a week. Despite Betty's alleged lack of care, the files contain a number of letters from her, usually sending money or explaining why she can't, but always asking for news of me, whether I'm toddling, have teeth, have recovered from measles and if she can have photos. In April 1951, she wrote: 'I should be glad to know how Bruce has been getting on. I hope he has been good.' The tone and content of the letters didn't seem to me to equate with a woman of 'low mentality' at all. Two weeks later she received a reply: '. . . Bruce is progressing well. He is a good baby, sits up and takes notice of all that goes on round him. He has gained weight and is chubby and happy.' Impressively, DBH replied to every one of her enquiries, passing them from one department to another until the answers were supplied.

At the end of 1951, the first mention is made of Violet Masters, the woman who effectively became my mother. She was living at 18 West Street, Hett, in County Durham and had applied to DBH for an under-school-age boy to be a companion for George Creighton, the youngest of the three foster children she had at the time.

> She is quite willing to take another little half-caste – in fact before I [the welfare officer] left she seemed quite thrilled about another little coloured child.

As there wasn't a school in Hett, DBH thought it preferable to send two coloured children among strangers in a neighbouring village school rather than isolate one to fend for himself.

On 18 February 1952 I went for a month's trial holiday with Violet Masters. She already had three other boys, two white and one black in a little cottage in Hett village. After a month it was decided that I should stay on because I got on very well there. In the background, Betty was agitating, applying to the Children's Society to have me adopted. DBH soon put paid to that by explaining to the Society's Miss Percy that I was 'half-caste' and a potential problem thanks to my mother's epilepsy and 'low mentality'. Realising she was not going to escape her payments that way, Betty wrote explaining that she was hoping to marry but that her future husband was refusing to contribute to my upbringing. 'This seems to be my only chance of happiness in the future and I sincerely hope you may be able to enable me to take it.' (14 July 1952 – my second birthday!)

Later the wedding was set for September, when the happy couple would move to Acton. The welfare officer reported that Betty planned to give up work and her husband was demanding that she must 'forget' me. Another attempt at having me adopted, this time through the League of Coloured Peoples, failed after DBH met the prospective adoptive parents and persuaded them it was a bad idea both because of my background and because I was happy with my foster mother.

After that, there are no other mentions of the marriage and any letters continued to come from Betty's parents' address in Hammersmith. I don't know. Certainly she seemed to find it increasingly difficult to meet the payments. In 1955, DBH tried to establish her whereabouts in case her permission was ever needed for me to have an operation and of course asking for the money that was owed them. They were told sharply by her family that Betty had left the country, first to Paris and then to the other side of the world. That is the last time she appears in the files.

Reading about her in 1985, I felt very little. It was quite gloomy reading but interesting too. I wasn't looking for my mother but she came over in the reports as I'd always imagined her and when I came out of that room she had not gone up in my estimation one little bit. It wasn't until I read the files again in 2002 that I thought more about her and did feel much more sympathetic to her predicament and the way she was treated. By then I also had the information gleaned from having met the rest of her family. They all say she was a generous, fun-loving, misunderstood woman.

Meanwhile my life was with my foster mother, Violet Masters, who looked after me until she gave me back into care twelve years later. To all of us foster children, she was known as 'Mum'. We don't know a great deal about her life before us but I have pieced together her history from the snippets that she told me or my foster brothers or sisters over the years.

Born on 19 January 1901 or 1902 (she consistently fudged her birth date), she was the tenth or eleventh of twelve children, six boys and six girls. She remembered being told how their mother visited the doctor in desperation after her birth to ask where all these children were coming from. Their father was a monumental stonemason who ran his business from their large middle-class family home. They were able to afford servants to help with the considerable cleaning, washing and laundering generated by all the children. The many photographs of Mum and her family show that they were reasonably well to do. Post First World War families can be measured by the number of records they kept of occasions like picnics and weddings, all of which look quite grand in the Masters' case. Because her mother was often ill, Mum looked after her next youngest brother and bonded closely with him although she later remembered feeling resentful about being restricted from doing the things she wanted. All the children had jobs helping around the house and I remember her telling us how scared she was of fetching and carrying things from the basement where her father stored his work when it was ready for collection. It was dark down there with shadowy shapes of carved figures and angels looming out of the darkness. Near the door stood a cherub with a pointing finger that always caught at her ringlets, terrifying her before she shot back upstairs. Our picture is of an Alice in Wonderland look-alike, dressed in a pinafore and button boots, her ringlets kept off her face with a ribbon. She didn't enjoy school but although she was not academic (her handwriting on the letters in my files is sometimes barely legible) she was very creative. We think that as soon as she left at fourteen or fifteen, she must have been encouraged to take up a trade and that's when she may have learned her dressmaking and sewing skills.

The next fifteen years or so of her life go unrecorded. None of us can remember her reminiscing about what she did in that time. The next we know is that she moved to London when she was about thirty. I've always thought she must have had some sort of disagreement with her family because I don't recall them being particularly supportive of her when she was struggling to make ends meet bringing up all of us. There's certainly barely a mention of them in my files. She ran a lodging-house in South London. My memory is of her talking about it being a theatrical boarding-house in Stockwell. I remember her reminiscing about Marie Lloyd and being a fund of theatrical folklore, including the story of some diva who died on stage when the curtain fell down in the middle of her singing 'I dreamed I dwelled in marble halls'. Whether this was one of her lodgers, I have no idea. My sister Linda's memory is that she ran lodgings in Dulwich for the medical students at King's College Hospital. Perhaps she ran more than one lodging house over the years or perhaps she changed her clientele. We'll probably never know the truth. Nor will we know why she never got married although, in her later life, I'm sure she would not have given us up for a man. We have a dim memory of hearing her talk about a romance with a man who was killed during the Second World War. However, Linda remembers Mum telling her she was abused in her childhood by one of her older brothers. She described how he had held her trapped by her ringlets and how, as soon as she respectably could, she had them cut off for ever. After confiding this once, the matter was never mentioned again although Linda remembers Mum's angry refusal when the brother wrote asking if he could come and see her. Perhaps this had frightened her off any close sexual relationship. Certainly I only recall seeing her with a man once. They were necking in the backyard. We giggled about it for weeks.

It was while she was running the lodging-house that she met Marie Lambert, a young married woman whose husband was posted abroad and who was working as a secretary in an agricultural feeds company. A female colleague of hers was boarding with Mum and recommended that Marie should try to get a room there. Although Mum was wary of single women looking for lodgings, she was only too aware of her own status and was persuaded to agree. It marked the beginning of a life-long friendship. Together, they seem to have had quite a racy time of it in London, despite the fifteen-year age gap. Violet had clearly always been a bit of a rebel and she and Marie went out together, smoking furiously and becoming loyal followers of the Joe Loss band.

Eventually the house was bombed during the Blitz and because she didn't have a man fighting for the country, Violet was not entitled to any insurance repayment. So she and Marie left London on their Norton Commando motorbike to work in a munitions factory in Newton Aycliffe in County Durham. By this time, Marie's husband was stationed at Barnard Castle so after the war they stayed in the area, moving to the village of Hett, a couple of fields or so back from the old A1. Far from being the kind of picturesque village found in Herriot country, it consisted of three windswept rows of two-up two-down cottages, originally built for agricultural workers, that flanked each side of a huge bleak green. A small church occupied one of the north corners close to the village pond where white farmyard ducks puddled about. The village shop was bang in the centre while the local Hett Arms took pride of place in West Street with chickens scratching about between the two. Compared to London and even to Newton Aycliffe, Hett didn't have much to offer, but 9 East Street was all that Violet and Marie needed while they established their new dressmaking business. Marie looked after the business side of things, delivering the clothes, collecting the money and doing the book-keeping while Violet made the clothes. I've still got one of their business cards with its faded italic lettering.

It wasn't long before they were successful enough to be able to take over the old pet shop in Spennymoor, a short motorbike ride away, and convert it for their business. Eventually Marie was divorced from her husband who had been having an affair with a local girl. She then took up with a local farmer, William Lambert, after the death of his first wife. Violet had been making clothes for his son and Marie had been to their house with deliveries and collections. A property owner and on the local council, William was definitely a good catch. When he married Marie, she moved into the farmhouse across the green and Violet moved to 2 West Street, soon afterwards moving again to number 18. At the same time, they decided to close down their Spennymoor business.

Violet continued to make clothes privately but this was when she decided to apply to DBH to be a foster mother. None of us really knows what her motive was. A single woman of over forty-five (though she shaved off a few years for Dr Barnardo's benefit) with a small unpredictable income was hardly prime foster parent material. I'm not sure that the fostering she did at first wasn't instigated by financial need. The dressmaking trade seems to have been petering out and it's noted in a few correspondences that work was hard to find and her finances were poor. Certainly, my files make it clear that money played a considerable part in the arrangement. They are full of letters from her, asking for extra to cover expenses such as school uniform, holidays and so on and equally full of internal memos noting her extravagances or needs. However there is no doubt that after the war there was an unprecedented number of orphaned children and children whose widowed or single mothers couldn't look after them. Perhaps Violet genuinely thought it was a good thing to help someone less fortunate than herself. She may have replied in response to a Dr Barnardo's Homes campaign. She was obviously not going to have a family of her own by this stage and perhaps a bit of her wanted to recreate the atmosphere of her childhood in a big family. Without Marie for company, she would also have been suddenly lonely. Whatever her reasons, there's no doubt that she genuinely liked children and did her best to provide a good home for them.

By the time I arrived in 1951, she had already fostered fifteen or sixteen children over short periods, taking three at a time. It can't have been easy looking after troubled teenagers. There's a story of how one who had a terrible temper threw a pitchfork at Marie's small son, Alistair. Winnie Watts, who used to run the village shop back then, still remembers the frustration Violet felt when every time one of the children left school at earning age and was ready for work, a relative would appear from out of the woodwork and claim them back into their family. Tired of losing the children like this, Violet made up her mind. She would ask to foster younger children whom no one wanted.

'That's the finish, Winnie,' she said. 'I'm going to take coloureds.'

And that's where we came in. First George, then me, then Barry, Linda and Janet.

CHAPTER TWO

By all accounts I arrived at my new home at 18 West Street, Hett, a smiling happy baby, a charming little boy who could wrap adults round his little finger and, as a result, deemed by the authorities as in serious danger of being spoilt. It wasn't long before I was reported as having a 'stomach upset due to too many titbits from adoring villagers'.

Returning to Hett village now, I see how small that house must have been for Mum bringing up four children. Then it would have had just the front room, overlooking the green, used either for best (although no one ever visited) or for dressmaking, and a small back kitchen-cum-living room with two bedrooms upstairs between all five of us. Out the back was the block that housed the loos and coal sheds for four neighbouring houses. It was said in DBH reports that the place was unsuitable and it is surprising that they allowed four children to be brought up in such cramped conditions but they did so on the condition that Mum used the front room as her bedroom so we boys could sleep two to a room upstairs. But Mum knew how to get what she wanted. Having agreed to their demands she was allowed to foster me, the fourth child, but I remember quite distinctly that my cot was in with her while the other three slept in the other bedroom. I don't think she ever moved downstairs.

Twice a year, we were visited by our welfare officer who came to check on our progress and well-being and report back to DBH. The visits were casual affairs. Nobody wanted to rock the boat unless they absolutely had to. The reports are all preserved on file and frequently provide an alternative view on the status quo as we knew it. In 1953, the house was reported as 'untidy and a bit smelly' – hardly surprising with four children – with windows that wouldn't open and a landlord who wouldn't fix them. It describes the sewing machine and fabrics that were habitually spread over the table, and small children from next door running in and out while I was recovering from chicken-pox. The report is mildly critical of what sounds like a pretty normal chaotic family home.

At about this time Mum had a run-in with the landlord who gave her notice to get out of the house because he wanted it for a farm worker. Mum wrote to DBH explaining:

> I know they cannot turn me out but all the same it makes me feel uncomfortable and unsettled and I don't feel inclined to spend anything on decorating the house which needs doing. Secondly there's not much work in my trade and . . . I prefer the work I am doing for you.

She even asked if there was a chance that she might move to one of their Branch Homes so that she could continue looking after her boys, 'making and sewing for them and teaching them different hobbies etc.' She must have been at a low moment of confidence in her future for her to consider giving up her home. The dispute arose after a visit from the sanitary inspector who gave notice of necessary improvements to the landlord, who was incensed that his tenant had asked the inspector to visit in the first place. She insisted she wasn't responsible for his turning up. Eventually the crisis blew over, relations were restored and Mum was granted another 10/- for each child per month to make life easier. Later that year she is criticised in a report: 'Miss Masters is very extravagant on food and household bills and will only buy the best quality clothes'. In DBH's view it was pointless because we would quickly grow out of them. In my view, it shows she was trying to give us the best she could against the odds. I found a note in my file written when DBH were considering her application that I think gives an insight into Mum's character.

> I liked Miss Masters very much as a foster mother, once I got to know her, and I felt she always showed consider-able patience and understanding with the boys she had. But she is quite an individualist, I think, and I cannot quite see her fitting into an ordinary Branch Home set-up. In charge of a small group she would probably do very well if she did not have very involved dealings with members of staff . . . She is very used to going her own way, of course. But she would always be warm-hearted and unsparing of effort in her dealings with the children.

The highlights of those early years as recorded by the DBH welfare officers seem to have been, the quantity of hard-boiled and chocolate Easter eggs given us by the villagers – (eleven each!); the coronation party with its presents, sports and games; the regular visits across the village green to see baby chickens and lambs; and an incident where I had to be taken to hospital having jammed a stick into the roof of my mouth. I of course remember none of it. By 1954, the older two boys must have left because Mum was allowed to foster someone new. That was the year that Barry arrived, another cute little half-Jamaican boy exactly the same age as me who was to become my greatest friend and ally. Our family was eventually completed when Mum fostered our half-Jamaican half-sisters, Linda in

1955 and Janet in 1961, both babies when they moved into our lives.

1955 was the year we moved to 6, Barmoor, one of a row of eight two-up, two-downs just a walk away from Hett through the fields towards the busy A1, then the main artery from the North to London. The property was owned by Uncle Bill Lambert, Auntie Marie's husband, who let Mum have it rent free while they moved with their two children, Alistair and Christine, to a bigger house just separated from ours by a clinker track with a field beside it that, despite being dangerously close to the main road, was soon to be the scene of many games of Cowboys and Indians. I think that even then, when I saw the Lamberts had three bedrooms, a TV, a telephone, a fridge and an indoor flush loo, a dawning awareness began in me that there was a better life to aspire to than the one we had where there was no TV, no telephone, no fridge and a freezing outdoor ash closet (i.e., a loo without a flush) that was used for everything from potato peelings to ash from the grate as well. You shut the door behind you and climbed up a couple of steps to reach the medieval wooden seat and the gaping black hole beneath. I remember vividly the giant spiders' webs stretching across from wall to wall that would wrap themselves round your face in the dark and the spiders that would dive-bomb you, then scuttle away into hidden corners. It was not a place to linger in.

Mum's most distinguishing feature was the jet-black hair that framed her long thin face and the hawkish nose that made her look a bit like Dame Flora Robson. She took great trouble over her hair and had it regularly cut level with the bottom of her ears by Auntie Marie before she washed it with green Fairy soap and rinsed it through with vinegar and water to cut through the grease and give it a shine. When she was working she would cover it up with a scarf tied like a turban, just as they wore them in the munitions factory. Every month Marie would come round, put on the stained old cotton gloves put aside for the task and carefully mix the contents of two small brown glass bottles of black Inecto hair dye in a special saucer. Then, making sure not to get it on anything else, she would brush it through Mum's hair with the blackened toothbrush kept especially for the job. All the while they would be drinking hot sweet tea, eating Marie biscuits, smoking and gossiping. Occasionally the dye would stain Mum's forehead or else one of us kids would deliberately nudge her to make it run down her face, provoking a great flurry as she rushed to get it off before being permanently marked.

She was quite a short, frail-looking woman, probably about five feet three or four inches tall. We were very poor so she made almost all her own clothes. I do remember she had a skirt in a print that was a wash of browns, greens, mauves and pinks – very much like an Ivan Hitchens painting, though of course I didn't know that at the time. Usually, she wore a practical warm pinafore dress in tweed or flannel with a short-sleeved blouse or hand-knitted jumper underneath and a pinny on top. Any blouse would always have faggotting [ladder stitch] or some kind of 1920s' or 1930s' detail on it. The jumpers she knitted for herself and for us were made from old ones, sometimes other people's cast-offs that she painstakingly unravelled and washed before winding the wool into hanks and hanging them on the line or in front of the fire. Then she'd have one of us sit the wrong way round on a hard chair so that our outstretched arms could rest on the chair back to hold each skein as she rolled it into balls. Our aching arms made it feel as if we were there for hours. The important thing about the pinafore dresses was that they had to have enough pockets to carry her cigarettes, matches and tape measure. They were essential. If the tape measure wasn't in her pocket it could always be found hanging by her chair. Her best dress was only brought out for school open evenings or best. It was black with a faggotted black flower on the bodice and worn with a delicate necklace made of carved Whitby jet interspersed with small painted gold balls. This was the only piece of jewellery I remember her having apart from the gold band encircling her arm above her left elbow. The finishing touch was a tiny slash of ruby red lipstick.

What we all remember most is her cigarettes. Faded photos of the time rarely show her without one. She never inhaled and would let the ash build up in a long increasingly precarious column. We would watch it, riveted, having bets when it would drop off. She would suck Jermond's Black Bullets, boiled sweets in a black-and-white tin. They were briefly superseded by Mint Imperials, but not for long.

But her fragile appearance belied her character. She could be an obstinate and demanding woman who wasn't afraid to speak her mind. Her reactions were often of the knee-jerk variety – not much thought behind them but a lot of emotion. I never had the impression she was very happy with her lot and she certainly considered herself a cut above some of the local people whom she saw as being slightly riff-raffish. She had little time for others unless they had an honest trade, in which case they were treated with respect. Of course her southern accent set her apart even more. She managed us with a pretty firm hand, setting a routine that ended with us in bed by seven while she stayed downstairs listening to *The Archers*. The smell of frying bacon would drift tantalisingly up the stairs as we went to sleep. She loved her bacon sandwiches and those endless pots of tea.

Just as at 18 West Street, we had a front room that was kept strictly for best. It was almost never used, for visitors only called rarely. It was lit by a central light with an opaque glass bowl clear enough to let us count the dead flies scattered in the bottom. In the middle of the room was a large table where Mum did her cutting out. A tailor's dummy stood beside it with the sewing machine forever up in the corner, covered with a tea towel when it wasn't being used. It had an elaborate box cabinet with a lid that lifted up on hinges to form the table, revealing the machine which swivelled upwards and clicked into place, the doors on the front opening to reveal the treadle mechanism. She always encouraged us to sew and I remember Linda once getting her finger caught in the machine – the needle went right through the nail.

We were taught how to look after the scissors and pinking shears by keeping them carefully oiled and putting them in their right places. If she caught us daring to use them to cut paper, we'd get the sharp edge of her tongue. I would spend hours sitting beside her watching her work and asking questions. I was always messing around with her black bead box with its broken lid with an iris painted on it. Inside there were hanks of embroidery beads that I loved fiddling with. I learned all the techniques beginning with hemming, sewing on buttons and simple embroidery. I patiently brought to life the pale blue outlines of flower patterns on tablecloths and napkins with brilliant Sylko threads. I would practise on all the off-cuts left over from Mum's work and make clothes for Linda's Cindy doll. I remember making a simple shift dress with an empire line but soon moved on to more elaborate dresses and ball gowns, inspired by the Fred Astaire and Ginger Rogers films we'd watch on TV. Linda remembers at first being under the impression that Mum and I were making them together, then being amazed when she discovered I was doing the lot by myself, including the fur coats and especially her favourite long red dress. She ended up with the best-dressed Cindy in town with a complete wardrobe crammed into her red vanity case. When I was just eight, one of the welfare officers noted my interest.

His little foster sister Linda plays a great part in Bruce's life and foster mother says he is happiest when he is playing with her. She has a dolly's dressmaking set and Bruce has cut out and sewn the dresses for this without any help whatsoever. He says he wants to be a tailor when he grows up so that he can help foster mother to earn some money.

If I wasn't making clothes for her, I would dress the puppet that Barry had made for me. She was really just an excuse for me to have a doll of my own and by the time I'd finished with her she looked like Hinge and Brackett or some kind of ungainly Edwardian lady. In January of the following year, 1958, another report says: 'Foster mother is quite convinced he is going to be a dress designer.' Although perhaps an extraordinary prediction at the time, she did later change her mind, holding out hopes for me to become a radiographer after a stint in hospital. According to family folklore, when Auntie Marie's future daughter-in-law, Anne, came to talk about the wedding dress she wanted and to be measured up, to everyone's amazement I sat and drew the dress as she was describing it. Neither was I shy about suggesting alterations to the clothes Mum was making, though how much notice she took of me I don't know. I was definitely very tuned in to what women were wearing even then. There's no doubt that Mum encouraged me and was probably glad of the company.

She made most of our clothes and photos often show us three boys dressed in almost identical tweed suits with shorts. Underneath we wore the shirts she had also made as well as her hand-knitted tank tops. All of them were labelled with indelible ink from a little black bottle. Today, my favourite shirts are two or three striped ones from Etro that remind me of the ones she used to make. If not making clothes for herself or us, she would take private orders or be busy with piecework that was provided by Binns, a small chain of department stores in the North of England.

In 1959, I was reported as having asked Mum if it was silly for a boy to make doll's clothes, 'but she encouraged him and lets him dress Linda and take a pride in her. He is very interested in clothes and observant about what people wear.' At about the same time there's an awful lot made in the reports of me being 'effeminate' or 'cissy'. When we went on holiday, it was noted by the welfare officer we stayed with that there was 'an effeminate streak in his nature and this was very evident when playing with any toys as he always picked the dolls to play with. He was also very anxious to dress up in my clothes, whilst the other two tended to choose my husband's clothes.' We were only eight, for God's sake, and why on earth were we allowed to dress in their clothes at all? I can only assume that I was somehow made aware of these criticisms and became self-conscious about what, until then, had been a hobby I'd been encouraged to pursue.

Most of our family life went on squashed into the living room at the back of the house. Along one wall was the range, with an open fire burning under the chip pan. On cold winter mornings we would put our socks in one of the compartments to warm up before we had to put them on and venture outdoors. Mum baked a lot so the smell of bread competed bravely with the stink of the chip oil. We said grace before every meal and took turns washing up after it, whisking the water into a lather with a wire mesh container holding pieces of soap. She often made suet pudding, stews, brawn or pigs trotters, which we hated but we'd never turn up our noses at food. We either ate it or had nothing. I also remember the number of milky puddings especially the rice pudding that always came with a delicious thick brown skin over it. She was a stickler for manners and insisted we chewed the meat properly, used our knives and forks correctly and remembered our Ps and Qs.

'Good manners will open doors for you,' she would say. 'Bad manners will slam them in your face.' And how right she was.

She'd always have the home service on in the background so we also had a diet of *Mrs Dale's Diary, Take It From Here, Sing Something Simple* and all those other popular shows of the time. Auntie Marie and Christine were constant visitors. Auntie Marie may have given up the business with Mum but she helped her with us as much as she could, looking after us when Mum was ill or had to go out alone. Christine was in and out of the house all day, joining in all our games and squeezing in round the table at tea-time as we dipped our chips into our eggs.

In 1957, we got a TV, BBC only at first. It must have been at the beginning of the summer because I can remember it was tennis, tennis, tennis. It put me off Wimbledon for quite some time. Those were the days of Armand and Michaela Dennis, *Dixon of Dock Green, The Billy Cotton Band Show* with the glamorous Alma Cogan and the Saturday Matinée with all those fabulous old black-and-white musicals starring Fred and Ginger and the rest. We would sit glued to the screen with Mum in the corner hooking a rug or crocheting, using the bright central light to see. To this day, there are certain things I won't entertain. One is bare lino because it takes me back to those days and the other is bare light bulbs. I could never see the television screen. All I could see was the reflection of the bulb wherever I sat. Because Mum was busy, the light couldn't be turned off and there was no question of her using a lamp in the corner. There was the one central light and that was it. Another thing I can't bear is to see clothes drying. It immediately brings back washing day when the living room was turned into a steamy laundry, windows covered in condensation, wet clothes being pulled from the dirty water in the machine (I'd wonder how they could be clean) then, if it was raining, hung around the room to dry. As she worked, Mum would play games with us and sing, most memorably 'You are my Sunshine'. But for me, those days were unforgettably uncomfortable.

Once a week we would have to wash properly so the big tin bath that hung on the outside wall was brought in and filled with water heated on the range. Steam rose off the scalding water as we plunged in, having to sit on a tiny square of flannel so the hot metal wouldn't burn our backsides. It was always oldest first – George, Barry, Bruce then Linda – so by the time I got there, the water was scummy with soap and I had to hope nobody had peed in it. Each of us was scraped dry with our own towel that was the texture of cardboard, marked with our name inked on to a piece of sticking plaster.

One of Mum's weekly jobs was to cut the newspapers into neat squares for loo paper. She used a special bone-handled kitchen knife that was worn away in the middle from the rigorous sharpening she gave it. You knew when she was at it by the distinctive screech of the knife against the back step or the black sharpening block in the living room. When she had finished she would pierce the squares with a gimlet and thread them on a piece of string to hang by the wooden seat.

Throughout our lives we had pet dogs and there were times when I resented the attention that was lavished on the animals. At least one certainly met its maker by sticking its neck too far out into the path of a lorry hurtling by on the A1. He was buried in a sack on the allotments – good fodder for the peonies next spring . . . Well, we were in the country and life cycles were dealt with in a very matter-of-fact way. One winter's day, we were playing in the fields behind Bowstead's transport café when Topsy, another of our dogs, skittered on to the ice of the pond that promptly broke and in she went. Rather bravely, and much to my surprise, I went straight in after her, water up to my wellies and then my waist. We rushed her home to dry out in the warm and I scored many Brownie points from Mum.

One chore we loathed was to go to the local knacker's yard to get horsemeat for the dog. It was miles away. We'd have to walk through the fields to Tudhoe and catch the bus to Spennymoor near Defty's, the haberdasher's where Mum would buy lots of her sewing and knitting materials and patterns. Then there was another trudge to the yard. Long before you got there, you could smell the sour stench of bones being melted down for glue. It took a long time to rid your mind of the sight of recent deliveries of horses, either hurled on the floor intact or suspended on hooks, their insides exposed with the discarded bits in a steaming heap below. It was enough to make anyone a vegetarian for life!

One of the 1957 reports from DBH didn't mince its words about the conditions in which we were living. 'The house is dingy, the living room rather poorly furnished . . .' Yet, 'the boys bedroom is very smart, the pretty eiderdowns were not the sort that the average mother would keep regularly on boys' beds'. Mine was a quilt embroidered with a scene from Ali Baba. It looked like something from the 1930s. I don't think Mum can have made herself. It was appliqué with overstitching, running stitch and cross stitch. It was quite fantastical and totally out of place in such an environment. The report goes on: 'Foster mother did not speak in a very understanding way of other children she had had. She obviously devotes her time to her current children and they are her life.' Funnily enough, I don't remember it as a particularly loving or cosy household but perhaps we were always too busy to notice.

Mum loved making things herself and passed on her enthusiasm to us. Barry and I were quite creative and were good at the things she wanted us to be good at. George didn't always pick them up as easily and Linda was too young, so there was a lot of bonding between Barry and me. Apart from knitting and sewing, we boys learned how to use a fretsaw so we could make models and create marquetry work. Barry could do all these things perfectly. I would probably have been standing over him, getting him to make mine for me because that's the way I am. One year he and Mum successfully spent months making a guitar, wetting the wood and bending it, stringing it and playing it – only to have it smashed during a family row.

One year Mum ordered a garden shed that was delivered and put up in the backyard. It soon became 'The Boys' Den', the name carved on a wooden sign by Barry. He and I spent hours in there. I don't remember George being around so much so I think he must have been sent to board at Parkstone Sea Training School by then, a real Dotheboys Hall by the sound of it. Our prized electric Hornby train set was moved from its temporary home on the table in the front room so that it had its own place. We could stand in a hole in the centre of the track and watch the trains whizzing round us, making sparks rise and giving off a distinctive pungent metallic smell that made it seem even more real. Mum was great at expanding our imagination, suggesting we made tunnels out of papier mâché and bridges from fretwork. For a good eighteen months while our interest was at its height, birthday and Christmas presents would be a shining new Pullman coach or some other much-coveted item.

We made shelves to hold our much-used Meccano set and the Bayko house-building kit. In our imaginations we could make all sorts of things happen and would build fantasy worlds, including a saloon set so that I could re-enact the Marlene Dietrich western *Destry Rides Again*. In the evenings we were gripped by *Compact*, a television soap set in what seemed an impossibly glamorous world of magazines. Inspired, we produced our own magazine, *Denpact*, and I was the fashion editor – probably an excuse for me to draw yet more extravagant dresses. The shed was a central part of our childhood with its cold concrete floor, the sharp stench of its creosoted walls mingling with the distinctive smell of the paraffin stove that never quite kept the place warm. I think Mum got it for two reasons. One was to give the boys a place of our own but also to give her a break from us and to give Linda space too. I probably distrusted the move more than the others because I was always considered Mum's favourite. Being in the Den made me feel that Linda might be usurping my position in the forefront of her affections.

When I say 'favourite', I don't think that she necessarily singled me out to give me more than the others. But I possibly didn't get as much of her bad side. She had a sharp tongue and wasn't afraid to use it. I know I was considered to be the favourite by the others. The reports refer to my constantly climbing on to her knee and even mention Mum's realisation that she was spoiling me by letting me go to bed later than the rest, as well as her repeated resolve to treat us all even-handedly. But Mum certainly had her negative side and would often use the ultimate threat: 'If you don't behave, you'll go back to the home'. The other consistent cause of tension was money. We were given pocket money in small amounts, always strictly monitored by DBH and Mum had an allowance for each of us plus an equally restricted clothes allowance. 'I can't give you any more because I only get "x amount" for you per week,' was a regular refrain. I'm still saddened and irritated by the fact we were frequently reminded we were charity cases. I don't think it was intentional but it made for a level of unease in our otherwise good relationship. Even though I didn't know any different, it didn't feel right. There's a lot of correspondence in the files about money and Mum's demands for more, whether it's for school uniform or requesting enough for a holiday for herself and for us. It's interesting that she did receive more than the average foster mother was getting then. Maybe her tenacity on the subject is one of the reasons money motivates me so strongly now. I've always been money mad – only too aware of wanting it, keeping it and the danger of losing it.

CHAPTER THREE

When we weren't at school, pursuing our hobbies or busy in the Den, we would spend hours playing in the surrounding fields. It was all very *Darling Buds of May*. There's a spot on the dirt track between Hett and Barmoor where two trees bending over a little stream provided Linda and Christine and Barry and me with our separate camps. Barry and I would endlessly amuse ourselves with dartboards made from corrugated cardboard, constructing a miniature funfair. We played games of Cowboys and Indians with the tiny Swappit figures or, even better, we'd be the Cowboys attacking the Indians (Linda and Christine), always assured of victory.

I was very into flowers – even then. I'd pick them, name them, dry them and put them into a wild flower book. I wasn't interested in the frogspawn or any other stream life but I'd always look out for the first primrose or the wild orchids. The allotments were next to the terrace and we used to help the gardeners there. I remember the dark red peonies, garish snapdragons, lupins and dahlias along with the Michaelmas daisies and asters. I longed for a garden of my own and made one in tubs and pots until eventually Uncle Bill Lambert gave me a patch where I could grow all the flowers I wanted.

We went to Dean Bank Junior School, a 36 bus ride down the A1 to Ferryhill. The school was an imposing (to us, at least) one-storey red-brick Victorian building with the boys and girls segregated, girls on the left and the boys behind a wall on the right. We were kept apart even at playtimes when the usual rough and tumble ensued. Ferryhill was, as its name suggests, built on a hill and the school perched precariously on the edge of the 'Cut', so called because when the A1 was built, its route was dug straight through the town, cutting it in two. This ravine with its ten-feet-high wire mesh fence allowed us boys the fun of car-spotting or 'bagsying' who could spot the latest Triumph Herald, Zephyr, Austin Princess or Jaguar. It was a mindless game but one that kept us amused until the whistle blew to signal the end of break.

We must have been streamed by age, certainly not by ability (perhaps another reason why George seemed absent from so much of what Barry and I did together). I can see us clearly sitting on the polished parquet floor in the school hall, radiators hissing in the background. The overheating was a luxury that most of us children wouldn't be used to at home, despite the copious amounts of poor-grade coal that we'd scavenge from the tip heaps of the neighbouring collieries. We're listening to a piece by Haydn. It must have been something on *BBC for Schools*. Music has always been an important part of my life and it probably dates back in part to those days. We were also taught to dance in a courtly eighteenth-century manner. I loved that and the poetry we heard on the wireless then. People with posh accents read poems such as Coleridge's 'Ancient Mariner' and Masefield's 'Sea Cargoes', both favourites of mine. Classroom reading was Ballantyne's *Coral Island*, Robert Lewis Stevenson's *Treasure Island* and *Kidnapped* – good laddish fare. I've no idea what the girls got. At home, we'd read E.E. Compton's *Jennings* and Enid Blyton's *Famous Five* stories and I have to admit to secretly reading *Bunty*, a girls' comic, which was passed from Christine across the road to Linda (who was too young to read) and deftly intercepted by me.

In my memory, the school windows were set peculiarly high on the walls but perhaps it seemed that way because we were short. Nonetheless, I've always entertained the idea that it was so our attention couldn't wander to what was going on outside or so that we couldn't daydream. They stretched right up to the ceilings and class monitors had the job of opening the top sections by rope and ratchet. You became monitor by excelling in spelling games (which I was particularly good at) or memory tests (which I wasn't). In English, I was good at working out how many words you could make out of one, at anagrams and at spelling in general. We were constantly being made to learn things by rote as the teachers made a concentrated effort to drum things into us. I liked Geography and remember to this day a collage we made in class all to do with the West Country and its produce, with brightly coloured pictures of spring flowers, tomatoes and vegetables and arrows pointing to Weston-super-Mare and with lobsters, crabs and fish originating in St Mawes.

I was quiet in class. I have never particularly liked the sound of my own voice, but more importantly then I had a bad stammer. You lose your nerve when you stutter and I was only too aware of wasting time when we had to learn and say, for example, the Beatitudes out loud or when we did reading round the class. I would be so busy working out which section I was going to have to read and be practising the start of it that I never listened to what anybody else was saying. I was always too busy being four pages ahead.

Another nightmare was asking for the bus fare to school. 'Fffffferryhill' wasn't easy. But Barry and George would step in and say it for me, so there was always a way round it. As part of the church choir, Barry, George and I used to get paid 3d for singing at weddings at church. I entertained the idea that one day I was going to marry Christine and I remember sitting there thinking, I am never going to get married because I won't be able to say, 'I do.' I wouldn't even be able to say my own name.

Oddly my stammer only came to the attention of DBH after a reported incident that I don't remember at all.

> Has developed a stammer since some boys beat him up on the way home from school. Foster mother has seen doctor who said it was a form of nerves and he would quickly get over it. I'm becoming concerned because he stutters very badly now.

Exactly a year later, the stammer is reported as having gone. I can only think that it didn't appear when I was in the relaxed atmosphere at home when the welfare officer called because in fact it continued to trouble me years afterwards, resurfacing whenever I had to speak to an audience of more than about ten.

I found it hard to make firm friends. I don't think that's ever been my thing. But Barry and I stuck together both in the class and the playground. We didn't need anyone else, although when we had to, Barry was always much better than I at making friends. By then I was getting quite big for my age. I was self-conscious about that and I hated sport. I'm not a team player, wasn't then, am not now. I did enjoy personal bests though and one of my red-letter days was a school sports day in 1957 when I did astonishingly well for me. There's a photo of me grinning with gappy teeth at my completely unexpected success in the egg-and-spoon and the general sprint.

The whole education system seemed to be tied in with the agricultural calendar. When the harvesting took place in the summer holidays, piles and piles of mice used to get slaughtered in the field as the machinery chugged round. When the bales went into the barns, they used to smoke the mice out. It was quite barbaric. Linda would spend ages trying to rescue the babies. Around the beginning of the new term, Mum would take us blackberrying along the hedgerows armed with Tate and Lyle Golden Syrup tins. I was so scared of the spiders, big ones in the bushes, and they would always win, making me back off from picking the best berries. Autumn half-term would coincide with potato-picking week. Whole families would turn up with their buckets and get hired on the spot. We'd get a shilling a day but it was filthy, back-breaking work, scrabbling through the mud a row at a time. The worst thing was unexpectedly sinking your fingers into the rotten ones. We hated it but everybody did it. We'd take our thermos and sandwiches and made sure we tipped enough potatoes into the sacks at the end of each row. If you didn't, you weren't asked back the next day.

The church festivals summed up all the things that I liked – the best dahlias and chrysanthemums and all the other local produce – and are a strong part of my nostalgia for the first ten years of my upbringing. The Harvest Festival was great because it genuinely meant something to the farmers and we were made to feel part of it too as we carried the baskets of shining fresh vegetables up to the altar. I loved Easter too and the Easter hymns, with Croxdale church decorated with primroses and cowslips and the model of the Hill of Calvary with its three crosses and the Garden of Gethsemane. Because we went to church so much, I enjoyed singing in the choir and being out of the house. I can remember not being able to resist the coloured ribbons on the withering wreaths in the graveyard. They were too pretty to leave behind so I'd collect them and take them to Linda and a bemused Mum who couldn't imagine where I'd got them.

At Christmas, our special trip was to Durham indoor market where we always laughed at the sign proclaiming LADIES TO LET where some wag had remover the 'I' – not that we understood its real significance. The market was full of promise, individual stalls selling toys, food, books and comics. This is where we'd give Mum an idea of what Santa Claus might be kind enough to provide that year. I remember taking the initiative to get her to give us an idea of what she might like beyond the usual floral scented bath sets.

It always seemed to snow heavily and on Christmas Eve we would hang our stockings on the mantelpiece before leaving out something for Santa's reindeer. Mum would sit Linda on her knee, look out towards the slag heaps where the skyline was lit by the orange glow of the bin men burning rubbish, and tell us it was Father Christmas camping out waiting for us to go to bed. Christmas Day was always cheerful, the house was warm and filled with the smell of roasting chicken. We always had Christmas pudding and custard and Mum would make sure we each got a lucky silver sixpence without our ever guessing she'd stage-managed the whole affair. This was the only time of year that we were allowed to use the front room, where presents would be arranged in piles on the three-piece suite and the Christmas tree perched on top of the sewing-machine cabinet. There was one memorable year when Barry and I were given the Hornby train set, George got a black-and-white spotted record player and his first record, Tommy Steele's 'Little White Bull' and Linda got a toy Silver Cross pram. Notwithstanding the fact that they obviously came from Santa, I don't know where those presents originated. Mum must have bought some but the rest must have come through Barnardo's.

One year, Barry discovered a huge stash of wrapped presents in the front room days before Christmas and there was a lot of whispering. That must have been the year that we all realised the truth but kept up the pretence for Linda. It was always a happy occasion with everyone on their best behaviour and full of excitement. I think even Mum observed a moratorium for those few days and was especially kind to us.

There was always lots to eat, not only the stocking fillers of nuts, oranges, foil-wrapped chocolate coins, sugar pigs and mice but also sausage rolls, mince pies, butterfly sponge cakes, jam or lemon-curd tarts often smothered in icing sugar. The Christmas cake had almond paste and icing covered with coloured balls and the rather dodgy-looking plaster Santas and reindeer with their bases stuck about with last year's icing sugar – they were never washed in case they might self-destruct. The rooms were festooned with paper chains, lanterns and stars with the odd sprig of berried holly adorning the mirror. The walls would be strung with twine, supporting all the Christmas cards showing ersatz nativity scenes, robins in snowdrifts or corny Victorian seasonal activities. It all lent an air of warmth, security and conspicuous consumption and it didn't matter that it was merely a moment of suspension from reality, which by 27 December would be over for another year. Then at New Year I always used to go first footing to get a bob or two. I'd be the dark stranger first over the threshold with a lump of coal bringing luck for the New Year in return for money and ginger wine.

In the summer holidays, we were sometimes packed off to Barnardo's camps on the north-east coast in places like Redcar or Tynemouth. Again the files are full of letters making suitable arrangements for us, working out the transport and who would stump up for it. I remember the church hall and camp beds at Tynemouth. There was a record player there and the staff played Tab Hunter's 'Red Sails in the Sunset' throughout the holiday. It must have been the hit of the time. There'd be about twenty of us and we'd be taken off on expeditions to the seaside. As far as I can remember, Barry, George and I always stuck together.

A happier memory is of our holidays with Mum, Auntie

Marie and Christine at Crimdon Dene on the Durham coast. We'd pile into the Lamberts' Morris Minor shooting brake, registration YUP 555, and set off to the caravan site. Each time, we'd be kitted out with new pants, vests, socks and awful woollen swimming trunks from the Marshall Ward's catalogue. Water-logged, the trunks would sag almost to our knees as we came out of the sea. Every year we'd have a different coloured caravan surrounded by a picket fence and as soon as we arrived, we'd go to the campsite shop for supplies. This shop was the scene of Barry's and my epic shop-lifting expeditions where we would steal comic after comic. I cannot believe that this has gone unremarked in the files. We had a huge stash of *Superman* comics and never got caught. Then there was the fairground – an exciting world of Tizer and sugary pink candyfloss where we'd go on the waltzers to hunt for the money forced out of people's pockets by the centrifugal force. We'd always find a coin or two when it stopped.

The beach was a little way from the site, down some steep wooden steps to the sand and the cold grey sea where the seaweed lapped around your legs. But we didn't mind. We'd huddle behind a stripy windbreak trying to take off our sodden woolly trunks without anyone seeing. I still can't stay in wet clothes any longer than I have to. There were rocks to climb, rock pools sheltering crabs that we would scoop out with our nets, and plenty of space to play with our tin buckets and spades. Up on the cliffs, we'd fly our bright box kites in the gusting wind. One year, Mum was given a tinker's caravan, brightly painted and in an idyllic spot somewhere near Darlington. It was damp and falling apart, with mice running in and out of it and three of us squeezed up in a bed for one. But it was fun.

We were encouraged to belong to the Croxdale church choir, the St John's Ambulance Brigade and the Cubs in the church hall at Neville's Cross. These may have been ruses by Mum to get us out from under her feet but I imagine Barnardo's suggested the initiatives in the first place as ways of getting us to mix with other boys. Mum didn't like us playing with some of the local kids she thought were 'dirty' so we kept pretty much to ourselves, with the exception of Christine who was effectively brought up with us. There weren't any other local boys our age so this was Barnardo's attempt to make things as normal as possible for us. Of course the biggest abnormality was the fact that we didn't have a father so all of these outside activities provided men who were supposed to help fill that gap of the missing male role model. Years later, reading through my files, I was appalled to find that, like the doctor and our headmaster, they were all reporting back to DBH on my progress (and presumably that of the others), often far from favourably.

The only other man I remember was a travelling salesman. He was short, round and slightly sweaty and, when he visited Mum, he'd invite me over for tea. He lived in Ferryhill and took me home with him. I was only about seven or eight and didn't see anything untoward in it. He liked me to do exercises in front of him and once he lay on top of me. I hadn't a clue what I thought he might be doing but told Mum as soon as I got home. That was the end for him. He was told never to darken our door again.

The other significant outside adult influences in our lives were our foster 'aunts' and 'uncles'. These were professional people that we boarded-out kids visited at weekends to give our foster parents a break. I don't know who George had but Barry had Auntie Eileen and Uncle Neville Pierce and I had Auntie Carol and Uncle Noel Nesbitt.

Auntie Carol and Uncle Noel had retired in their fifties and lived in Salutation Road, Darlington. I would visit them about once a month. She looked like Virginia McKenna and they had a son, Jeremy, who was about ten years older than me. They lived in a quite different style from us. It was only too noticeable that they had an indoor loo, sheets that were very clean and crisp and there I had my own bedroom. They also had a pianola. I would spent hours happily pressing the treddle and pretending to play as it churned out Wagner's 'Pilgrims' Chorus'. We used to go on different outings, some centred round the church but sometimes we'd go on treasure trails in the car or follow the local hunt, always stopping for tea on the way home. On one occasion they took George, Barry and me to Whitby. There's a photo of us sucking lollipops, with me squinting rather archly into the sun. When I had my tonsils out, I convalesced with them. She used to make raspberry blancmange and gooseberry fool – both unheard of back in Barmoor.

There was an unfortunate incident when I was about ten, when I found a brooch of Auntie Carol's in my pocket. I have no idea how it got there but I was so worried they'd think I'd stolen it. It wasn't an expensive piece – a shiny marcasite starburst like a stylised flower, real magpie material. I may have thought I'd take it to give to Mum but I can't believe I would have been that stupid. I had a good relationship with the Nesbitts, I did know right from wrong and I did know it would not be nice to steal from Auntie Carol. Things went from bad to worse when they discovered it was missing and I invented an elaborate lie about finding it to cover my tracks. I was accused of stealing it but I was sure I hadn't. It became a huge problem in my mind and I still think about it to this day. After that, as far as I was concerned, they cooled off towards to me. I don't like it when people think badly of me and I didn't then.

To my astonishment I read in my files that in fact Mum was so upset that I didn't appear sufficiently 'contrite' that she asked for Auntie Carol and Uncle Noel not to have me again until after they returned from a three-month European tour. Then, when they didn't immediately get in touch on their return, she was said to be pleased and the file notes she obviously had 'some resentment at his friendship with Mr and Mrs Nesbitt'. I was oblivious to this at the time but it does support the idea that I was her favourite and she was jealous of anyone coming between us. She certainly made it clear to DBH that she thought they were a bad influence on me but fortunately DBH thought the contrary so I was able to continue visiting them.

The Nesbitts weren't the only ones singled out for her antagonism. Once we went to visit Barry's Auntie Eileen and Uncle Neville in Teesdale. We were all playing in the shallow water on the river's edge when I decided to go a bit further out, only to discover that we had been standing on a man-made ledge which dropped abruptly away. I remember a lot of bubbles, seeing the light of the sky above, flailing about in a panic, then nothing until I woke up in bed, amid much fluster-ing. I had been rescued by an angler who had jumped in and fished me out. It must have been terrifying for the Pierces almost to lose a child in their care but I suspect it gave Mum a great deal of satisfaction to witness their discomfort. There was another distinctly watery aspect to that visit – three in a bed, George, Barry and Bruce, but who was the one with the weak bladder? It wasn't me but I've always suspected . . .

These weren't the only incidents in which water played a part in my early life. Much earlier, when I was six, we had gone to visit one of Mum's sisters in Hythe. We were warned to stay clear of the waterway that formed part of the sea defences along the low-lying areas of the south coast. Needless to stay we ignored the warnings completely and I fell in the canal. This time Barry came to the rescue, earning Brownie points from Mum and reinforcing the bond between the two of us.

During all these years, I remained almost blissfully unaware of the fact that my skin colour made me different, and that speaks volumes for the people of Hett and its neighbouring villages. When I was seven, my report reads: 'Does not accept that he himself is coloured and makes many rather hurtful remarks to his foster brothers and sister. George, his foster brother, often fights him for this.' The following year it says: 'Does not realise he is coloured.' As four young black children with a middle-aged white single mother, we must have stuck out like a sore thumb in '50s County Durham, but I really don't remember any racist incidents at all. It wasn't a negative thing being black there. Rather, it put us in the limelight. There were a couple of local newspaper articles about us, one in which we claimed to be the happiest family in Croxdale, and the other quoting Mum who couldn't understand the prejudice of some foster parents who shunned children who weren't white.

> 'They are God's children. No matter what their colour, someone's got to bring them up . . . I've been a foster mother to white and coloured children and they are no different,' says Miss Masters who will not even choose her children at the Home. 'It's not right to select a child, as you would an article. Children are just born into a house.'

I must have been about six or seven when a mad woman who talked to herself all the time came up to Mum at a Durham miners' Gala, whacked her across the backside with her umbrella and said, 'God told me in a dream that we have to send these children back to where they came from.' It didn't seem significant because there were a lot of people around who just dismissed her as crazy so we decided that it was quite funny. Another time, on holiday at Crimdon Dene, the little girl in the next-door caravan once said, 'My mummy and daddy said that you children have been kissed by the sun.' But it was said in such innocence, that we couldn't take offence. One of the things that irritated us was that we were considered to be cute. It was rather like puppies: when they get older people think of them differently. Up until about the age of nine we were little piccaninnies in matching tweed suits and stripy shirts. But as we got older, people's attitudes to us changed.

In school entertainments, the casting was clumsy but I hurled myself into the parts with gusto. I remember having to black up to play the Turkish Knight in the Mummer's Play – it was quite a breakthrough for me to able to stand up and speak in public. We also did a Black and White Minstrel Show, a popular television show at the time, and had to wear balaclavas and black our hands. In those pre-politically correct days nobody thought twice about it.

There was sustained emphasis on race in my files, where a lot was made of us being 'half-caste', and there was no doubt whatsoever in some of their minds that I would turn into an 'unattractive' 'negroid' grown-up. Their racism was so heavily ingrained that they didn't think twice about it. But, to be fair to them, I think it was of its time. No more, no less.

As the years go by the tone of the welfare reports change. That cute coloured piccaninny gives way to 'an attractive boy whom people notice and all this attention has made him conceited'. The boy with a 'dominant nature' becomes 'unruly and aggressive', sometimes a bully who 'will have the last word'. There are, however, plenty of references to my sunny smile, my loyalty and affection for Mum, my apparent maturity, my evident affection for Linda and Barry and my enduring enthusiasm for my hobbies.

In 1961, I passed the eleven-plus – another big red-letter day for me. There were just two Barnardo's children in the whole country who made it that year. It changed my future. I was to go to Spennymoor Grammar Technical School. That summer we bought my new uniform and the new blazer became my proudest possession. But the school was a disappointment. I hated it. Barry wasn't with me any more and I think I became even more of a loner. I wanted to be the same as everyone else but I couldn't be. My schoolwork went downhill with my behaviour, and I was soon threatened with removal to a lower form.

One incident that has stuck in my mind over the years occurred when a boy whose father was a vicar in Durham had invited me to his birthday party and then, in class, sent a note disinviting me. When I told her, Mum was livid and wrote to his father straight away. The next day, they were both down at our gate with the son forced to apologise and reinvite me. But Mum had her pride and resolutely refused to let me go. It didn't do me much good at school, but hey . . . It did however increase my strong attachment to Mum because it was such a maternal thing to do.

On the whole though my relationship with Mum was becoming more and more difficult. There were many rows and crises, with her continually threatening to send me away. Her moods fluctuated violently and she would often send off letters requesting my removal, then change her mind when things blew over in a matter of days or even hours. The watershed finally came over an incident at school when she was summoned to the head master because I had written a 'filthy and obscene' letter. When she saw him, I now know that she poured out tales of my bad behaviour at home. The welfare officer was called in and shown the offending letter, in which I'd used the word 'bastard' a number of times. A boy had been taunting me about my colour and my illegitimacy. On talking to me, Mum realised I didn't know what 'bastard' meant but it was what I'd been called from across the street. I couldn't catch him to hit him so I'd felt my letter was a case of 'tit for tat'. I may have been sensitive about my illegitimacy then but I really don't remember. As far as I am aware, it has never been a key issue in my life.

I don't remember the incident itself but, sure enough, it is faithfully documented by the welfare officer. What I do remember is the beating I got as a result. Things were getting very fraught between us and that same month, I am reported as having shouted at Mum, 'Shut your b . . . mouth or I'll flatten you.' That was it. She wrote to DBH immediately.

It is necessary [to write to the welfare officer] as I am (and have been for some time) having a lot of trouble with the boys, especially Bruce, and to tell the truth I am afraid of him he is such a big boy. I just cannot control him.

So will you please make arrangements to get the boys away as soon as possible, as I feel they need a man to control them.

I am very sorry about this, but I have tried very hard, and cannot get any results.

By then, Mum was over sixty, with way too little energy to be looking after three young teenage boys, eight-year-old Linda and baby Janet, Linda's half-sister, who had just joined us. DBH saw sense. Even before this crisis, plans were being made behind the scenes to move me. In those days, it was the Barnardo convention to shift a troublesome boy to a residential home. You were not invited to be part of the discussion about your future. You just did what you were told. Once it had been decided I had outgrown my foster home, things progressed quickly. A lot of paperwork was done behind the scenes and within two months I was removed from Mum's care. In the month before I left, my welfare officer reports that I wasn't making a fuss but that I was very upset: '. . . although he tried, he could not keep his tears back when I saw him yesterday.'

On 7 October, 1963, I was moved from Barmoor to West Mount, a DBH Branch Home in Ripon. Looking back, it must have been shattering to leave the only home and family I'd known. But thank God I did. Without that decision taken for me, I fear my life would have turned out very differently.

CHAPTER FOUR

Leaving Mum and the others had occupied so much of my mind that, beyond a stirring of excitement, I hadn't thought too hard about where I was going to be living. Except that it wasn't home.

My welfare officer, Mrs Bowers, came to collect me in her black Austin Cambridge. Once all my things had been stowed in the boot, I said my goodbyes to Mum, Barry, Linda and Janet between tears and then I climbed in. The car obviously doubled as an office where she wrote some of her welfare reports between visits – a terrible mess of papers and letters littered the back seat, giving it a funny working atmosphere. She smoked like a chimney so the ashtray was overflowing. The air quickly fugged up but I hardly noticed and besides there was a good supply of boiled sweets in the glove compartment in front of me. The beige leather all-in-one bench seats were plump and slidey so that every time we took a right-hand bend I was in danger of shooting across into Mrs Bowers' lap, unless I grabbed at the door. Green fields rolled past the window as we approached Ripon but I hardly noticed. I was too preoccupied thinking about where we were going and what I had left behind.

Ripon was like nowhere I knew. We drove through the historic market square along Westgate and Blossomgate towards the smartest residential part of town. It was a gentrified spot, a

Georgian and Regency enclave of wealthy homes within spitting distance of Ripon Grammar School and Ripon College. It was very middle class and characterised by generously built five- or six-bedroom houses with professional folk living there whose children went to Ripon Grammar. But already the larger houses were becoming too big for families now they no longer had servants to help fill them and some were finding better use as nursing or children's homes. West Mount was one of these. It was a well-proportioned four-square rectory house that over-looked Kirkby Road. Set in two or three acres of garden, it was a handsome building with high ceilings, sash windows and good strong detail – the sort of house I'd like to own today.

But it was the back view of this bleak but elegant Georgian building that greeted us as we swept off College Road, through a five-bar gate and into the drive. I had never seen a house like it. Various red-brick extensions had been added to the rear of the original building, giving it an angular and forbidding look with black drainpipes snaking up the walls and an iron fire escape zigzagging down from the second floor. Thin curtains hung at the upper windows that were so dark they gave no clue to what might be waiting inside. An imposing shed, about the size of a triple garage, dominated the back yard. I later discovered it had been built for the boys' hobbies (shades of the Den) but was more frequently used to house the super-intendent's sailing boat. The quid pro quo was sailing trips on Coniston Water for those who were interested – not something I could ever be doing with. But no doubt it was a fair exchange for those who could.

Mrs Bowers got out of the car, encouraging me to follow her. Apprehensive but curious, I did. We went in through the cloakrooms, me trailing behind her, taking everything in. At first it was just like being back at Spennymoor Grammar as we made our way past rows of coats hanging above shoe lockers.

Then we turned left into a corridor with hand basins on the right and a couple of bathrooms and toilets on the left, then through a door past a large, clean but quite inviting kitchen on the left with huge Agas and large black-and-white chequered floor tiles and into the main hall. For the first time I became aware of the awful pall of cabbage and carbolic that hung over everything, a particularly clinging smell that still characterises the place in my memory. It was only over-ridden on Fridays by the competitively intrusive smell of boiled haddock. The large L-shaped hall stretched from the little used front door back to the grand wooden staircase and turned right behind the front room. There was a TV against one wall. Things were looking up.

I was taken to meet the superintendent and his wife, Mr and Mrs McPhail, in his office just off the main hall. An avuncular pipe-smoking Scotsman, Mr McPhail was slightly built and quite tweedy – not in a middle-class huntin', shootin' and fishin' way but in a comfortable checked shirt, green anorak country way. He always reminded me a bit of the actor John Mills. He had a nice way with him but in the end he used to get exasperated with me and then made the mistake of letting me see it. Not so Mrs McPhail. She was far more intimidating, larger, more imposing, and her clompy high-heeled shoes made her even taller. She was a plaid skirt and toning twin-set sort of woman – a winter person to her husband's autumnal one. Looking back, I think it's fair to say that they were among a dying breed of Barnardo's superintendents who, in the fifties and sixties, tended to regard teenage boys simply as trouble. Control was maintained with strict discipline. New, more enlightened views on childcare were beginning to establish themselves and with them the large institutions began to die out. Barnardo's efforts would be re-directed towards looking after children in their own homes and communities and taking account of their views. But this was not the way of the world back then.

Eventually on that first day Mrs Bowers left me and I was alone in what was to be my home for the next four years. Deliberately, it seemed, the 'family' ties I had made were to be broken. Only three days after my arrival Mrs Bowers wrote to Mum telling her that I wouldn't be going home for Christmas but I would be allowed to visit for a week at Easter and ten days during the summer of the following year 'in order that you can have a happy time together and he is not there long enough to cause a problem'.

Four days later, on 14 October, following her visit to Mum, Mrs Bowers wrote to Edith Blair, head of the northern branch of DBH: '. . . she [Mum] seemed quite hurt that he had settled, and talked a lot about the little sacrifices that she had made for the children, and now they were throwing her aside, and would forget about her.'

Settled I may have seemed but I certainly hadn't forgotten any of them. I was expecting to return for Christmas to Mum's who by now had moved house to 8 Tweed Road in Spennymoor. I was looking forward to seeing everyone again. Presumably the powers that be thought it was better not to mention their decision to incarcerate me over the holidays until nearer the time, to minimise the upset. I see in the files that Mr McPhail intercepted a letter sent by Mum on 29 October and, probably rightly, never showed it to me. In it, she writes to tell me that I wouldn't be going home for Christmas and adds the PS: 'Do not get anythink [*sic*] for Xmas as I have not got the money & have to take in work.'

In retrospect I can see that DBH were acting in what they believed were my best interests. Most of the boys would have probably stayed there, having no homes to go to, so perhaps they felt it was a good opportunity for me settle in. Going home after such a short time might only have caused unnecessary disruption. However, I was devastated not to be with Mum,

George, Barry, Linda and Janet, and spent most of the Christmas holiday curled up in bed, refusing to come downstairs. It was the lowest point of my teenage life.

In January I was visited by Miss Blair who reported back to Mrs Bowers, saying, '[Bruce] spent most of the time talking about home and Mum and his brothers and sisters, and if it is any comfort to Miss Masters she can be assured that she and the children mean an awful lot to Bruce, and I certainly got the impression that he thinks of nowhere else as being "home".'

However homesick I may have been, school was a different matter. By this time I had been at my new school for a month or so and had taken to it like a duck to water. I had eventually been given a place at Ripon Grammar School after I'd spent several weeks just mooching about West Mount, waiting for decisions to be made. God knows how I got through the days or what I did to fill the time apart from helping the cook. No doubt I was given tasks to occupy me but all I remember is an overwhelming sense of gloom and aimlessness.

When I eventually visited the school to be interviewed by the headmaster, Mr Atkinson, it immediately felt right. It was a world away from Spennymoor Grammar. It felt more solid, more comfortable and intimate. Spennymoor had looked like a typical modern comprehensive (although it wasn't) with its characterless building, housing long corridors with classrooms off it and segregated playgrounds, whereas Ripon is a school with a long history, a school having been on the site since 1555. It presented a solid Victorian red-brick façade to the world, although there were an enormous amount of 1950s' additions round the back, with playing fields at the front and tennis courts behind. It was more compact, richer and more middle-class than Spennymoor plus it was more academic than technical, more rugby than football – all that. So it more than fed the aspirations to become a middle-class boy that had already been set in train by my visits to Auntie Carol and Uncle Noel.

Mr Atkinson, known to us pupils as RA (pronounced 'rah'), was owl-like in shape, with warm eyes that contradicted his not so warm mouth. Quite an intimidating figure, he was always very well dressed in a blue or grey suit underneath his academic gown. He was particularly enthusiastic about the Air Force Cadets. That's what I took away from my first interview, feeling slightly mystified by it all. The school had its own glider that was his pride and joy. Many of the pupils had parents who were in the armed forces, since the area was dotted with Army and RAF bases at Catterick, Dishforth, Leeming and so on. And there was a uniform. Navy blue blazer, grey flannels, navy tie with red and yellow diagonal stripes and a cap until the fourth year. This time I had all the right things, unlike my Spennymoor Grammar days where my uniform was always a bit make-do and mend. True, I did have the treasured blazer but there was always something that wasn't quite right or didn't fit properly because Mum didn't have enough money for the real thing. Of course it didn't help that I was growing like a monster.

Back at West Mount, I was thrown on the mercy of Miss Irwin, one of the two house mothers. Compared to the milder-mannered alternative, Miss Cossy, she was a harridan. In my mind's eye, she's wearing a grey pleated skirt and one of an array of Fair Isle cardigans in blue and grey. The boys were divided into two groups of twelve or fourteen that were allo-cated separate parts of the upper-floor bedrooms, Miss Cossy's at the front of the house and Miss Irwin's at the rear. Mine was right at the back above the downstairs cloakroom. At first I shared with three others of my age and three toddlers in a room right by one of the upstairs loos. All the bed-wetters were woken every night at 2 a.m. and taken for a pee, so the rest of us were kept awake by the sound of running water as the taps were turned on to encourage them to speed up.

We all felt that Miss Cossy's group had an easier time of it than us. Miss Irwin was short with greying hair carefully coiffed like the Queen's. It was no secret that she religiously wore a hairnet in bed to maintain that tortured look. She was a plain, shrewish woman with a sharp tongue that she often used in her efforts to lash us into shape. It didn't take long for me to realise that there was no love lost between us. Each group had its own room downstairs that was used for meals. Ours was at the back of the ground floor beside Mr McPhail's office. It was larger than Miss Cossy's room and had two sash windows (one more than hers), anaglypta below the dado and patterned wallpaper above. At meal times we were segregated and ate in our groups but otherwise, in theory, we could use either room but I don't remember there being too much cross-fertilisation, although I do remember I liked playing the piano in Miss Cossy's. Apart from chopsticks my repertoire was limited to more of an indulgent untrained impressionistic cacophony. There's a photo of a chubby-looking me in Miss Irwin's showing off the stamp collection that Auntie Carol and Uncle Noel had encouraged me to make.

The McPhails ran the house on a tight rein, making absolutely sure their charges never got out of hand. Routine and rules were everything. Each morning we were woken at 7.15 by the clanging of a hand bell rung by whichever one of us was on kitchen duty that week. Then we'd make our beds properly with tightly folded hospital corners – they were very strict about that. So strict that to this day, I still automatically do them whenever the rare occasion demands it. Then we'd troop downstairs to the basins to wash and brush our teeth, just in time for 7.30 prayers in the hall led by Mr McPhail. Breakfast was quite major: cereal, full English always with shrivelled bacon, leathery eggs, fried bread or French toast and toast with jam or marmalade. Lovely! The whole idea was to set you up for the day – you could see them thinking that way. But like anything without much variety, it got tedious – and I got fat.

Then the real fun began. Before we left for school we had to do our allocated chores. There can't have been regular cleaners because we seemed to do most of the donkey work, dusting under the beds, cleaning the floors and tidying and dusting the rooms. The floors were never that bad thanks to the indoor shoe rule that meant we had to change our outdoor shoes for plimsolls so mud didn't get trailed through the house. Although one job was to clean the scuff marks off the floor that had been made by any overenthusiastic shoe-polishing. Then there was kitchen duty, helping with the breakfast then washing up. Particularly tiresome was the huge scrambled-egg pan that was impossible to get clean. But worst of all was cleaning the toilets. For some reason they were designed with a copper rim that turned green when peed on. It was one of our jobs to return the rims and the porcelain insides to their former glory. It was a nightmare job. In the end, I refused to touch them.

When we got back from school, it was out of uniform immediately. I always wore a shell suit with an elasticated waistband – the only one who did because I was so large. After tea, we could watch TV or play – unless you were made to stand in disgrace in the corner of the hall for some offence or other. In the summer months, weather permitting, we would be allowed out into the grounds but *not* beyond the gate. There was a cargo net slung between two of the tall spruce trees in the garden that people used to scramble up and over. There was enough space for football or cricket. After school in the winter, the shed at the back came to life (assuming the boat had been moved) to be used for snooker and table tennis – yet more boys' entertainment. But I was never in the slightest bit interested in being active. I was always indoors, sometimes embroidering tablecloths (I particularly remember one with lilacs on it) for Mum, working on my stamp collection, reading or doing homework. None of the other boys seemed to think my choice of hobbies was remotely odd – perhaps because I was the biggest and they didn't dare say anything, to me at least. In the welfare reports, one of the officers mysteriously worries about my 'effeminacy'. Another says, 'Strong reliable honest lad. Strong willed. Markedly effeminate. Quite a "snob". Good qualities outweigh the bad ones. He's beginning to question the world.' I can only think it was this aspect of my character she was concerned with: my lack of interest in traditional boys' pursuits.

> They agreed that there are tendencies in this [effeminate] direction but I gather they have never seen Bruce behave in a manner that would give cause for grave concern. Mr McPhail thinks that this could be due to Bruce's fatness. He is much too fat and overweight and I asked him to discuss this with the doctor when he visits . . .

Why they didn't consider our diet, God knows. Looking back, the food was generally horrible but I quite liked it. The low point was unquestionably Sunday lunch. We'd have a cooked meat meal on Saturday because the cook didn't come in on Sunday so then we'd have salad (lettuce, tomatoes and Heinz Salad Cream) with Cornish pasty and baked beans coming into the loop somewhere. Barnardo's were given lots of charity in kind by supermarkets – basically the stuff that wasn't selling. Sandwich spread was a favourite donation. We were practically force-fed the stuff and I loathed it.

In the four years I was at West Mount, I learned how to manipulate the system by playing Miss Irwin off against the McPhails.

'But, Mr McPhail, Miss Irwin said I didn't have to go to bed until nine-thirty.'

'But, Miss Irwin, Mr McPhail said that I could go into Ripon on my own.'

It must have been frustrating for them that they couldn't really exert very much authority over us. They could bully us but if you were of a mind not to be bullied – and I quite quickly got the idea – they grew more and more mad because they weren't getting the reaction they desired. Right from the word go, I had felt that I shouldn't be living there. It just wasn't for me. It obviously showed in my attitude – frequently a provocatively raised eyebrow – because there was the constant refrain, 'Who do you think you are?' I didn't know the answer. All I knew was that I didn't want to be the person they wanted me to be. I wasn't going to be a charity case for the rest of my life so I refused to accept that low level of expectation they tried to instil in us. The ethos in those days did not encourage us to be outspoken or stand up for ourselves but I refused to put my life on hold for four years. I was aware that I only had one shot at it. I baulked at the mentality that smacked of army training: don't make waves; don't argue; do exactly as you're told and you'll be OK. Be the same as everyone else. I couldn't do it then any more than I can do it now. One of the things Mum had successfully done was instil in us a sense of self-esteem. She was ambitious for us and, as far as she was concerned, we could achieve anything we set our sights on. And I believed it to be true.

When straightforward browbeating didn't work, they would resort to their standard threats: adding to your chores, stopping your pocket money or withholding privileges. Mum had always had the ultimate sanction of sending us back into a Barnardo's home. But that had happened now and I had survived. At West Mount the worst they could do was threaten,

'If you don't behave, you'll be made a ward of court.' But that just provoked the rebel in me. 'OK. Go on then. Do it.' I wanted to push them as far as I could, almost daring them to take it further. You don't get threats like that in a normal home, I reasoned. Parents have to put up with it or, if they can afford it, send their kids to boarding-school. It was the inconsistencies I saw in grown-up thinking that baffled me. I felt much happier once I got out of the home and into school. There it was more the way I felt things should be, more logically fair. At the beginning I did try to persuade them to let me board at Ripon Grammar but the answer was no. So I was stuck with them and they with me.

In fact, over those four years, I was never beaten at West Mount although beatings were doled out for the usual mis-demeanours: cheek, lying, stealing, bullying and so on. I used to see tear-stained boys emerging from McPhail's study. I liked to think I was exempt because I was the one and only grammar school boy and they had to be careful not to mark me with welts that would be revealed in the school changing rooms or showers. Though why I thought such things would be accept-able in the Secondary Modern, I can't imagine.

Nonetheless I relished flouting the rules whenever it suited me. I had an evening paper-round when I was about fifteen after one of the art teachers gave me a bike. It was so easy to pinch sweets and drop them into the paper-round bag when no one was looking. I enjoyed that until one shopkeeper faced me down. I refused to admit my guilt but his threatening 'I know you . . .' was enough to put me off trying it again. Every year, after Easter, Barnardo's Homes all over the country were inundated with unsold chocolate eggs. When the time came round again, I regularly crept downstairs at night, quietly lifting the key from just inside the staff-room door, unlocking the door to the kitchen, and tiptoeing down to the cache of cream eggs. I would eat them until I was sick. Then they'd have to get the doctor in because they couldn't work out what was wrong with me. And I wondered why I was fat.

Once I was once accused of stealing £5 from the gym changing rooms at school. Years later, I discovered from a memo in my file written by the AEO (Assistant Executive Officer) that this was the one time that Miss Irwin came through for me.

> Miss Irwin telephoned on Friday, 16 June, to say that there was trouble at the Grammar School over a £5 note which had been stolen and Bruce was among those suspected. The headmaster had telephoned Miss Irwin about this and asked her to go through Bruce's belongings to see if any money was in the house. Miss Irwin said she would not do this but would be willing to have a superficial look around his room, any more detailed search would have to be done in his presence.
>
> When Bruce returned home he was very upset but Miss Irwin felt sure that he was innocent but said he was in the changing rooms at the time the money was supposed to have been taken from there. The headmaster said he would call in the police for finger prints to be taken.
>
> On Saturday, 17 June, I telephoned Miss Irwin for further information and she said the headmaster now feels Bruce is not guilty of this theft but further action may still be taken as the money has not been recovered. Miss Irwin said she is more convinced Bruce is not involved and a number of small indications were mentioned.
>
> Unfortunately Bruce has adopted a rather high and mighty attitude and it may take some time for this to settle down.

*

I never would have dreamed she'd behave like that. If I hadn't so often made life difficult for her perhaps I would have seen more of this unexpected side of her character. But that was never on the cards as far as I was concerned.

The greatest bone of contention for me was to be the McPhails' son, Douglas. He was roughly three years older than me and went to the Secondary Modern. I simply could not see why he was allowed to do things that I wasn't. If we were made to change out of our school uniform when we got back from school, why wasn't he? Why could he go out at night and not us? Why could he go to bed later? If it was for my own good that I wasn't allowed these extra privileges – and that was always the reason they gave – then why was he allowed them? Of course I was jealous but I was stuck at West Mount and didn't like it. He was a nice guy, quiet and unassuming, who hardly mixed with us but lived in his parents' quarters at the top of the house. He was sporty rather than academic and often had friends round. Although he wouldn't have been someone I'd naturally gravitate towards, I felt left out, especially when I became the oldest Barnardo's Boy in the house. I did however have a fling with one of his girlfriends who worked at West Mount – probably just to spite him. I stuffed socks down my Y-fronts in an attempt to appear more developed. We kissed. Once I used her first name in Mrs McPhail's hearing and I can still hear that angry voice tearing through the kitchen hatch to where I was on malt patrol to correct my over-familiarity. If only she'd known what we were up to . . .

Of all the boys in the home, the one that sticks in my mind is Terry. We were together in the same bedroom from the off. He was in the bed next to me, the same age as me and together we were the best fighters in the house – we were the top boys. I thought he was the bee's knees, skinny with great hair (my uncontrollable frizz was awful), rather like the Fonz from *Happy Days*. He was the ring-leader of our group and sported winkle-pickers, light blue stovepipe jeans and a leather jacket. Miss Frances, our house mother, shared my admiration for Terry and his obvious charms. He could do little wrong. But most of the boys left when they got to fifteen or sixteen, and Terry was no exception, so I was soon on my own. By the time I was doing O levels I had my own room. I had my little Dansette player for my EPs – I think the first I bought was that fabulous Temptations EP with 'My Girl' and 'Girl Why You Wanna Make Me Blue'. Every night I'd listen to *Round the Horne, The Navy Lark* or to Radio Caroline under the covers and read with a torch or I'd sneak out on to the top of the fire escape outside Miss Frances's room for a quick smoke.

Getting out of West Mount was my prime objective. If I wasn't at school, I was the McPhails' responsibility and not allowed to leave the house without their permission. One of the reasons I joined the local church choir was simply because it was a change of scene one evening a week and twice on Sunday. Although I wasn't religious, I did like the music. I liked singing in the choir at Ripon as much as I had at Croxdale.

Confirmation classes were another way out as were trips to the local swimming pool, where we escaped every Saturday morning – but always under supervision. I may have loathed competitive or team sports but fooling about in the water and dive-bombing unsuspecting friends was another matter. When I was about fifteen, the great draw in town was the Underworld, a coffee bar tucked away in a basement on a hill leading off the main market square. It was considered to be a little bit dangerous but I can't think why. It was very dark inside with Formica-topped tables pushed against the wall so that we could dance. The only light filtered in through two windows at the front of the building. The further you got from them, the more exciting it became. There was a toilet upstairs where I would hide my school trousers so that I could change into the purple pin-stripes and flowered shirts that Mum made me. I'd have to engineer excuses so that I could sneak away there on Saturday afternoons. I'd usually go there on my own and mix with the local lads who were considered tearaways. We drank Coke that came from a machine rather than from bottles. They often got the syrup mix wrong so it was either overly gassy and very thin or horribly thick and syrupy. The room smelled unforgettably of coffee and cigarettes while the Temptations' 'Ain't Too Proud to Beg', the Four Tops' 'Reach Out' and anything by the Supremes or the Miracles belted out from the jukebox. We'd spend as long as we could there, talking typically teenage pseudy rubbish about the meaning of the lyrics and life. I remember one of the girls from school was often there. Babs Cockerham was a day girl, very tall with a wide-eyed, slightly bored expression. She was very fashionable, with her perfect Mary Quant haircut and extra freckles applied when not in uniform. She clearly only tolerated school until she could legally leave so had an attractively insolent air about her. She'd come down to the Underworld with her friends, Sandra Dickinson and Jackie Carling.

Before I left West Mount, the girls introduced me to the heady pleasures of the Cheltenham Club in Harrogate. Babs and I would hitch there together, with me often borrowing her navy-blue knee-length leather coat. It didn't worry me that it buttoned right to left nor that the sleeves on my long arms were only three-quarter length. The basement club was owned by a strange couple who ran a slightly dodgy establishment upstairs. The local gangsters would congregate up there and we knew that all sorts of things went on but the police rarely touched them. We didn't engage with any of that but danced away to our hearts content downstairs. Steps led down from the ground floor to a heavy wooden door that opened into a large, dark room. Going in, you were hit by a wall of smoke and sound. The Supremes, the Four Tops, the Platters, James and Bobby Purify, Wilson Pickett, the Isley Brothers – you name them, we danced to them. The DJ, Rick Hossak, had a source somewhere in Manchester's Piccadilly where he bought American imports. The music was stuff that wasn't being played anywhere else so I guess we felt we were getting something quite special. The place was pretty shabby, the brick walls stuck with posters of bands and upcoming concerts. Rick, handsome as hell and unable to do wrong in our eyes, would be on his corner dais and we would dance and dance. Part of the attraction was when he would deign to dance a solo – Mr Cool. Recently there was a reunion of the Club and I discovered I was remembered because I always seemed to be dancing on my own wearing a knee-length brown suede coat. I was easily seduced by the music, the people, the atmosphere. I would feign headaches almost every Saturday night as a ploy to get there. Usually at about 7.30 p.m. I'd go upstairs, get changed and just walk out of the house past them all watching TV. Then I'd hitchhike to Harrogate and back, returning at about midnight to climb the fire escape to my room.

School holidays were another opportunity to get away. House holidays were organised in the summer when we usually went to the coast. Once we went to Fleetwood, near Blackpool, where we hung around the front in gangs, ours led by the ever-cool Terry. God knows where we stayed but I remember the café we went to for a treat. I somehow made friends with the owners and went there every day to wash up for extra cash – ever the entrepreneur. Then, at the end of the week, they refused to pay me. They casually said, 'Oh, but we thought we gave you food and that was enough.' Not for me it wasn't. I'd counted on that money and spent it over and over again. I never went back.

After that first bleak Christmas at West Mount, Mum and DBH relented. I began to go on regular 'home-visits' during the school holidays. But I never got used to the new house in Tweed Road. It was a flat-roofed, red-brick council house in a very ordinary estate on the edge of town. I wanted to be living higher up the hill in the houses with proper pitched roofs. They were built in the fifties when they probably started at the top, running out of money and materials as they descended the slope. I hated it. Unlike West Mount, there was no central heating so the place suffered from damp and terrible condensation problems. The windows steamed up constantly. The curtains were unlined and so thin you could shoot peas through them. We had a pantry and an old butler's sink, a small table and a calor-gas cooker fitted into the small kitchen. Aunt Marie would turn up in her car every Saturday to take away the used gas canisters to exchange them for new ones. The rooms were tiny and we had no luxuries of any kind. The living room had a rudimentary three-piece suite squatting round the fireplace. The mantelpiece was filled with things I'd made and brought home from school. There were never any sheets without holes. Mum had a hard time eking out what she had to support us kids and it was tough. All through these years my Barnardo's file continued to be filled with her requests for more money to support me while I'm visiting.

Though Mum did her best, 8 Tweed Road was extremely basic. Drilled by the McPhails into tidiness and cleanliness, I would arrive home and set about scrubbing the floors and generally cleaning the place up so it would conform to their exacting standards – or mine perhaps. Mum of course was delighted. When I wasn't doing that she might help me make the clothes I wanted. As I got older I was becoming very aware of what was in and what was not and I wanted to look right. Linda remembers Mum and I having endless discussions about clothes and which fabric I should choose or how something I already had could be adapted to make it look better. Mum loved advising me and would patiently show me how to unpick and remake any disasters. We'd go to the market in Ferryhill to hunt out fabric so the front room would be covered with it. In 1966, the welfare officer reports that I'd spent all my pocket money on 'suede material that foster mother has made into a suit'. I was particularly proud of a flowery shirt that Mr McPhail took one look at and immediately damned with faint praise.

'It'd be great for the beach, laddie.'

Beach? I was planning to wear it down to the Underworld.

The same year, I was given money to buy myself a decent suitcase but I obviously had better ideas, as Mum's welfare officer reported:

> Miss Masters tells me that Bruce is badly in need of a suitcase to bring clothes home in. Up till now he has borrowed a case of George's which has fallen apart, and he has also split Miss Master's only hold-all when using that. He bought a lot of clothes with the money he earned, but did not think of buying a suitcase before the money ran out.

Coming back to Spennymoor was the pits after the sophistication of Ripon. Yet I kept on returning. Mrs Bowers probably had it right when she reported in 1966: 'Bruce feels very responsible for Miss Masters but on the other hand he is obviously able to do exactly what he likes when he is at home and this is probably what pleases him.'

I hated the Sundayness of it all, hanging out in the streets with nothing to do. There was the Roma Café where Julia and

Claudia Valenti worked with their incredibly glamorous mother. Barry and I used to spend hours there, hanging out, chatting over a cup of coffee that we would make last for as long as possible. When we got home we'd imitate the Valentis by whipping instant coffee and sugar really fast then pouring on hot water from a great height. It was never quite the same but it was good enough. By the time I was sixteen, the main attraction of the place was Linda Burt, my first steady girlfriend. We'd spend time round at her parents' place, listening to music, snogging – the usual teenage stuff. And on Monday nights there might be dances in Spennymoor Town Hall. About then, a variety club opened where travelling bands and singers would perform. Very occasionally soul bands would make it there, to my and Barry's delight. We'd always have music on at home and be practising dance steps ready to impress.

All my efforts to escape the regulation-bound confines of West Mount were of course only temporary. Every outing led back there in the end. But it was school that was to give me my real escape route.

CHAPTER FIVE

Every morning, as everyone else trailed through the streets to the Secondary Modern, I'd take the cinder track through the allotments that brought me out at the back of the Ripon Grammar playing fields. I had to get there for the daily nine o'clock assembly. The Sixth Form sat on the steps at the back of the hall, the rest of the school sat on the floor in front of them facing the dais, girls on one side, boys on the other. Every now and then, the Headmistress, Constance Gilbey, would tell the girls to stay behind after assembly, making them kneel to check their skirts were long enough to touch the floor. If not, they were sent home. On the dais sat the Head, the Deputy Head and the Headmistress on imposing wooden seats carved by Robert Thompson – the celebrated 'Mouseman', whose oak chairs and tables are identified by a carved wooden mouse. Sitting behind them and down the side on a mezzanine level were the staff.

At Ripon I did feel that I was always under the watchful though not obtrusive eye of Constance Gilbey who taught me Latin and French, the former a serious chore and the latter greatly enjoyed. I can't think why I was so attracted to French. It can't have been the wild histrionics of Racine's *Mithridate* – made no less incomprehensible or laughable by a visit to see it at the Comédie Française when I eventually went to Paris in 1968. I still remember, '*Prince, n'abusez point de l'état où je suis . . .*' Mmmm. It was probably more to do with the sound of the language and the look of the French. Think Françoise Hardy, Brigitte Bardot, Inspector Maigret and Le Beat. Yes, it was a cultural thing and I've been partial to it ever since.

Miss Gilbey was petite, with spectacles and a billowing black gown, formidable when checking the girls' skirt lengths but kind and thoughtful to her charges in the boarding-house. I do not know whether her interest in me was arranged or encouraged by Barnardo's or whether it was a natural Christian response. What I ended up with was another surrogate aunt who was to be influential in my life for some time.

My happy recollections at Ripon are inextricably linked to the teachers whose subjects I enjoyed, and enjoyment usually produced good results. French was also taught by the glamorous Miss Howstan, perfectly coiffed, svelte in her elegant suits with perfectly matched handbags and shoes. I recall that either she had hundreds of pairs of spectacles or she used interchangeable trims because she always seemed co-ordinated from top to toe. To me, this was the embodiment of Gallic chic, quite the opposite of her counterpart, Miss Craig, who would arrive in class, draw herself up to her full height and rest her substantial bosom on the record player, clearly carefully positioned for the task. She would not move until the end of the lesson when the performance would be repeated in reverse and off she'd go to find support elsewhere.

Mr Smith, the art teacher, had a very relaxed though not undisciplined approach to his charges and it wasn't long before my interest in fashion began to manifest itself. No matter what the subject of my drawings, they inevitably revolved around depictions of girls in short skirts and stilettos in coffee bars. This preoccupation was soon to be side-lined by the arrival of Miss Hurd to teach pottery and three-dimensional art, which immediately struck a chord with me. I was not so good at throwing pots on the wheel — I've never forgotten that monotonously hypnotic pot-throwing sequence which filled the gaps between TV programmes or transmission failures – but I was good at forming coil and slab pots and making the typical sixties' bowls and platters of indiscernible purpose and dubious artistic merit. I liked to produce something three-dimensional and I think I learned to see things in the round at this point – an ability that would stand me in good stead in my chosen career.

Looking back, I don't think that I made anything at all unusual at this time and probably just aped the work of Miss Hurd. I particularly remember making two three-sided slab pots which we turned into lamp bases, one of which I gave to Constance and the other to Mum. She was beginning to build up quite a collection of my artworks, including a ghostly white-glazed ceramic head and shoulders of a nun, which owed more to Ingrid Bergman in *The Bells of St Mary's* than a sudden turning towards Catholicism. There was also a terracotta bas relief which was a pretty good likeness of Janet mounted on a distressed wooden plinth, courtesy of the woodwork department. One of the reasons I spent so much time on my pottery was that I had quite a crush on Miss Hurd. She was relatively new to teaching and hadn't quite grasped the proprieties of the teacher/pupil relationship. Letting her guard slip every now and then, she called me Bruce rather than Oldfield. I'm quite sure I took advantage of this breakdown of the barriers in much the same way we did with a very new arrival in the English department, Paul Binding. He seemed not to be all that much older than the Sixth Formers and I can visualise him now wearing odd socks, or one on and one off, or with his face only half shaven. His unconventional appearance rather endeared him to us as did his teaching of classics such as *Sons and Lovers*, *Portrait of the Artist as a Young Man* and Wordsworth. He wrote in my final school report: 'His work connected with the books that interest him is very promising but he must try to apply himself with equal energy to all his work.'

He was right. I've always been best at applying myself to what I enjoy to the exclusion of everything else if possible.

Perhaps the teacher who had the most profound effect on me was Edith Allison who also taught English Literature to the Sixth Form, particularly Gerard Manley Hopkins. A passionate woman, she invested her subject with a sensuality and directness. She seemed to be totally immersed in the work of the writers she taught and this made quite an impact on me. When I eventually left Barnardo's, I asked for an anthology of Hopkins' work instead of the usual Bible and I still read his poetry to this day.

One teacher who provoked a turning point for me when I was about seventeen was Mr 'Chippy' Chambers, the Woodwork teacher. He was taking us for games and I, unenthusiastic as usual, had 'forgotten' my kit again. He angrily ordered me to cut all the grass round the tennis courts as punishment. Fine, I thought. Until he presented me with a pair of shears.

'I'm not cutting it with those,' I protested and threw them to the ground before walking out of school without looking back.

It was a hot Friday afternoon and by the time I got back to West Mount I had to account for myself to Mr McPhail. Instead of offering his support, agreeing that Mr Chambers had been petty and unreasonable, he shrugged his shoulders. 'I really don't care, you know. You've made your bed. You can lie on it.' I was left to sweat it out over the weekend until summoned to RA's office straight after Monday-morning assembly. Fearing the worst, I pushed open the door, but instead of the tirade I was expecting, I was treated quite reasonably.

'Look,' said RA, 'I know Mr Chambers can be difficult but we really can't have students throwing shears at the staff now, can we?'

I agreed he had a point.

'But the main thing that worries me about what happened on Friday,' he went on, 'is that you left school without our permission. You must understand that you are under our care until four p.m. when the whistle blows. Don't do it again.'

That seemed to me so infinitely reasonable. It showed me that there was a way in which it was possible to relate to the people in charge of me – with mutual respect. I saw Mr McPhail's lack of support as a major betrayal. I knew I wasn't entirely blameless but felt strongly that he should have taken my part. This almost certainly marked the beginning of the end of our relationship.

I was not a high flyer academically but I was good at the things I liked and managed to get four O levels after those first four years and two more in the Sixth Form. I liked the atmosphere of the school so much better than the atmosphere of West Mount and responded to it correspondingly. After living in a family, West Mount was too regulated – too many dumb rules that were there to make their life easy rather than to make yours comfortable. You didn't have a personality but were there to toe the line according either to Head Office or to the whims and caprices of Mr McPhail. I think they probably would have preferred me to have gone to the Secondary Modern because then I'd have had to be treated like everyone else. As it was they had to make allowances for me. When I was approaching my O levels, the Quiet Room at the front of the house virtually became my private study. It was intended for reading and other quiet pursuits so not surprisingly it went pretty much unused by the rest of the house.

But things were going from bad to worse. Reading my reports I can see what a pain I must have been to the McPhails. There are constant complaints about my behaviour and by 1967 there are reports of my 'arrogance', 'language' and 'insolence', particularly towards Miss Irwin and Miss Craven (one of the junior house mothers). After school hours I didn't socialise out of West Mount until I was at last in the Sixth Form when I was friendly with a couple of boys in College Road, in particular Roger Kent. I visited Tim Jones occasionally too. His father was a vicar so, as far as DBH were concerned, that was all right then. They loved professional people; in their eyes they could do no wrong. But by this stage I had become quite brazen about going out in the evening and flouting the rules. I would just walk out the front door, silently challenging anyone to stop me. But I don't think they ever did. At night I would sneak back in up the fire escape. If stopped at two a.m. I'd just say I'd been having a fag. In January a note is entered in my file recording Mr McPhail's suggestion that boarding-school might be 'the answer to the problem of Bruce Oldfield'. It goes on to say:

> . . . they [the McPhails] are apprehensive about the thought of Bruce going into private lodgings as they do not feel he is nearly ready for this, and would need a lot of holding. In boarding-school he would have equal status with his peers and would not be so resentful over the restrictions as he is at West Mount . . . He has a very superior attitude and does not take kindly to the sort of control imposed by Miss Irwin.

However, Miss Blair had other thoughts and believed I should stay put. Spurred by the doctor's diagnosis of my fatness being down to 'delayed puberty', she wrote: '. . . for this reason I think it's important he stays on at West Mount.'

I remember one episode when I had been to Harrogate and missed the last bus back so I hitched. Miss Irwin had locked up early so I stayed with Jackie Carling and her boyfriend, Eric Leggo, more ex-Riponians. I thought I'd behaved rather sensibly but the whole incident created a great flurry of excitement because Miss Irwin reported it after I'd strolled back in the next morning with no explanation. What seemed to me a great injustice was the fact that Mr McPhail disregarded the fact that she had locked the door early, took it as more of my so-called waywardness and wrote complaining to the AEO of the northern area for DBH. As far as I was concerned this was yet another example of the lack of logic in adult behaviour.

What I have managed to block from my memory entirely are the instances that provoked his catalogue of other complaints. In one letter Mr McPhail expresses his concern that I had 'begged' lifts to Durham where I had stayed over night and about my smoking in my room. In fact, I was getting pretty successful at hitching (as most people would call it), particularly since I'd made an imitation university scarf that instantly secured many more lifts. Then in February, one of the welfare officers visiting Mum reports that I had hitched home to Spennymoor. Although I had had my meals in Tweed Road, I'd made it clear I was only there so I could visit Linda Burt. Mum's welfare officer wrote to the AEO:

> Miss Masters told me that two weekends ago Bruce arrived home unexpectedly at Spennymoor, one Saturday, having hitch-hiked all the way. She did not quite know what to do, so when Bruce asked could he stay until Sunday, she said yes, but she said it upset the household quite a bit, as she had to get in extra food for the weekend, and Bruce had to sleep in her bed, while she slept on the sofa downstairs, as the beds would have had to be moved round otherwise . . .
>
> I think she feels that he's rather putting upon her at the moment, and making a convenience of Spennymoor, in order to come back and see this girlfriend of his, apparently she had to pay his bus fare back, and also the telephone call to Mr McPhail, to tell him that he was

staying the night, and all this cost her about £1, which she could ill-afford that weekend.

By this time, I was about three years older than the next boy down. Some boys did stay until they took their CSEs but most left earlier than that to go back to their families or out to work. I had been moved round the bedrooms, sharing with Terry, then with a toddler and at last I had my own. So by this stage I was living somewhere where I had no friends in a system I despised. I did not want to be a Barnardo's Boy. Even my sister Linda thought I was away at boarding-school. Again, it's my files that remind me how much of a stigma I felt it was at the time. Edith Blair wrote an internal memo:

> He is embarrassed at being in a Dr Barnardo's Home and we talked this matter over at great length. He admitted that he lies about this and gets tired of explaining to people in Spennymoor about foster mother and the other children in the foster home. I suggested he should try now, at all times, to be honest in his replies.

Those boys that left were given a suitcase, a Bible and a birth certificate if it was relevant. I'd seen this happen time and again and this must have been what triggered a renewed interest in both my parents and in my future. As O levels approached all these uncertainties inevitably preoccupied me and to some extent must have coloured my behaviour. What was I going to do with the rest of my life?

In November 1967 a note in my report reads:

> [Bruce is] an exceedingly well-made lad and continues at the Grammar School where next year he is taking A levels. It has been assumed that Bruce will probably

become a teacher, but only on the day of my visit he gave Mrs McPhail a letter and booklet he had received in response to his enquiry for training as a radiographer.

It goes on to speculate whether I'm feeling responsible for Mum and seeing the possibility of going home after O levels to get a job to help support her while studying science subjects at night school. Then when I got to eighteen I would be eligible to train as a radiographer. Mr McPhail was to talk to me about it. I've no idea what was in my mind at the time. There is certainly plenty of correspondence between Mum and DBH in which she repeatedly asks for extra money to cover the costs of supporting me on home visits. I must have been aware of how hard up she was but it never stopped me from going. However her response to the idea of my leaving school was not what I wanted to hear.

Now Miss Blair, if this is right, it's not very nice for me as he thinks it's me as I know I always told him that he can come home, when he has finished school,
So what does that make me?
And the other two boys said it's not right
And ask me to find out. Our little Janet cried when he told her – as she loves him very much. Now Miss Blair, it will not make any more work for me as I can do the same for five as for four, so please let me know what it's all about, he was very upset this time about it all. I am still hoping he will go on at school. But he said that he don't think he will get what he wants for GCE. Now about Barry . . .

And she goes on to ask for more money.

Miss Blair came in to talk to me with the McPhails and I agreed to stay on at West Mount, despite the restrictions, to take French, History and English at A level.

It was at this point that Miss Blair chose to talk to me about my past.

> I then talked to Bruce about his history. I told him that his mother suffered from epilepsy and explained in very detailed terms what epilepsy is. He wanted to know if she was clever and I told him that this was not the case but pointed out that very often epileptics tended to be of a slightly lower mentality. He already knew that his father had trained to be a boxer and asked me if I thought he was clever. I told him that in my opinion, if he was doing this training, he probably was. Bruce said he'd like to get in touch with his family and I explained that we did not know where his mother and father were but I would see if there was any possibility of contacting members of his family.

She went on to record 'a very important section of the interviews with Bruce on 3/5/66'.

> Bruce: Was my mother married when I was born?
> Miss Blair: Yes.
> Bruce: Then my birth certificate is alright. [*sic*]
> Miss Blair: Yes, your birth certificate is absolutely in order.
>   Further relief expressed by Bruce. I felt it was important to tell Bruce the whole story regarding his birth at this moment as he had already communicated several problems which he is experiencing at this present time but he must be told at a later stage that although his mother was married at the time of his birth she was not married to his father and I hope to be able to take him this step further in his history myself in order that I can

explain the reason for dealing with his questions in this way.

In March 1967 McPhail sent a letter that was to trigger off the next big change in my circumstances. Apparently he had to reprimand me for bad language and my arrogant and insolent behaviour towards Miss Irwin (no surprises there) and Miss Craven; threatening and striking very young children (I have no memory of this at all); and being rude to Miss Cartridge. He concludes: 'All the staff here are now in a state of *extreme* anxiety about the situation.'

Things finally came to a head when the AEO Mr Kjeldsen was summoned to the house and I was brought before the court. First of all I was seen alone by Mr Kjeldsen, then I was brought before judge and jury – the McPhails. Needless to say, it is all faithfully reported in my file. The meeting covered three areas of complaint and I seem to have been allowed my say.

I accused the McPhails of being inconsistent in their treatment of Douglas and me. Then I refused to continue doing the kitchen duties and cleaning the toilets while conceding to washing up and sweeping my own bedroom. Although it was apparently 'impossible to reach agreement over certain episodes' (God knows which ones) it was concluded that I would care for my own clothes in the future and be freed from household responsibilities. Hallelujah.

My next objection was to do with all the church-going. I told them I was agnostic and so no longer wanted to attend the services, take communion, attend morning assembly, say grace or join in prayers. Kjeldsen reports that he advised me to visit other churches to broaden my experience of Christian worship. Some chance. Otherwise they agreed to everything except my wish not to attend assembly because they thought I should be setting an example to the other boys. The one thing

Mr McPhail suggested that has stuck in my mind was to continue going to church, if only for the music that he knew I enjoyed. That was the one sound piece of advice I remember.

Lastly they agreed to a ten p.m. curfew with agreed exceptions.

Trying to get to the root of my unco-operative behaviour, Mr Kjeldsen wondered:

> ... why the situation with Bruce is so highly charged. I have come to the conclusion that Bruce may be deeply jealous of Douglas McPhail and this is something that touches Mr McPhail closely. I wonder if the whole thing has become an emotional conflict between Bruce and Mr McPhail. It may be that the whole thing has grown even worse now that there is an obvious association between Douglas and Miss Cartridge. Bruce has had as good a relationship with Miss Cartridge as with anyone else at West Mount and his irrational behaviour could well stem from the fact that he cannot have the place with Mr and Mrs McPhail that he would wish – or now with Miss Cartridge.

What sort of relationship did he think I wanted? I wonder. Did he think I felt Douglas usurped my place as their surrogate son? It's certainly not how I remember it.

According to Mr Kjeldsen the meeting was satisfactorily concluded by making it clear that the McPhails could impose sanctions by imposing chores, stopping pocket money or withholding privileges, and ultimately had the power to bring me before the Juvenile Court.

> I explained this not as a threat in any way, but that I wished him to know that we're in control of the situation

and that, while he is under age, we have a responsibility to see that he is satisfactorily cared for.

But the matter was not closed there. In all other areas of my life I was doing well, according to DBH's notes. Earlier that same year, Edith Blair had written that any earlier worries about my 'effeminacy' were unfounded.

> I was able to observe Bruce at the party on Saturday night and was interested to see that his partner was Mrs Brown's daughter, a very attractive and well-groomed girl who danced superbly. Bruce is a better dancer than I anticipated in view of his flabbiness though he is lacking in rhythm . . . Bruce was very proud to introduce her to me and, in fact, behaved like a perfect gentleman.

No worries there, then.

As for my progress at school, there were no complaints there either. Mr Kjeldsen accompanied my current welfare officer, Mr Taylor, and Mr McPhail to an open day at the Grammar School on 8 March where they met Constance Gilbey, Miss Allison and my history and art teachers.

> The consensus from the school seems to be that Bruce has the ability to succeed in his 'A' level studies to the point of obtaining 2 or 3 'A' level passes. This may be hard work and he is unlikely to go beyond this level . . . I am now convinced that it is the West Mount environment that is creating his difficulties . . . Particular interest was directed towards Bruce's efforts in ceramics and dress design. He has expressed an interest in teaching . . .

1. My Mother,
Betty Eileen Oldfield

2. A very white looking me –
on the Strays in Harrogate, 1951

3. Me, George and 2 foster brothers
in the back yard at 18 West Street,
Hett village, 1952

4. Violet – with obligatory fag washing dog
at Hett, *c.*1950

5. Violet, Marie Lambert and chums,
late 1940s

6. Group of local kids in Hett
village (I'm third from right)

7. Victorious at sports day, 1957

8. (Left to right) Linda, George, me, Christine
at Crimdon Dene, *c.*1958

9. Summer hols – Linda (centre front),
me, George, Barry

10. Janet on tricycle, Christine,
Mum and me, *c.*1962

11. The Lally sisters: Christine, Joan, Betty and Enid, *c*.1940s

12. Holiday snap. Christine, George, Barry and me with Linda in the front row with offensive smelling seaweed or am I just squinting into the sun?

13. Auntie Carol, Barry, me, and George in Whitby, 1959

14. George, me and Barry

15. Family picture taken in Spennymoor, 1965.
Me, Barry, George, Linda. Front row: Janet and Mum

16. Me and fellow inmate at West Mount, 1964

17. Alistair and Ann Lambert, *c.*1957 – my first wedding dress!

18. Janet and Mum outside Number 8, Tweed Road, *c.*1964

19. Me with afro in cemetery in Sheffield, 1969

20. My Student Union ID card

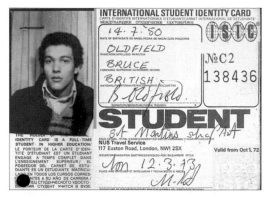

21. Carina Fitzalan-Howard, now Lady Carina Frost at the Revlon Fashion Show to launch the fragrance Charlie, 1973. My tutors, Lydia Kemeny and Bobbie Hilson in the front row

22. One of the models in my St Martin's leaving show

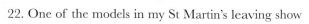

23. Charlotte Rampling, wearing a smocked jersey dress and cape for Jackpot, 1974

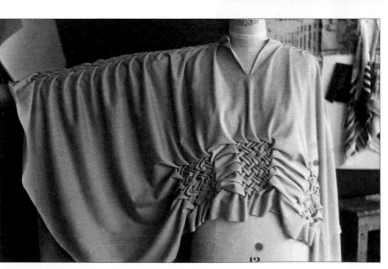

24. Work in progress on a piece of smocked jersey, Ravensbourne, 1972

In June I was about to go home to Spennymoor for the holidays but I'd had enough. I leapfrogged the system and wrote directly to Miss Blair, asking her to arrange an advertisement for lodgings so that I could be boarded out from the following term. The last straw was yet another argument with the McPhails, who had told me off for being out when Miss Irwin had given me permission. I had no idea that Miss Blair was already liaising with DBH about the possibility of finding me lodgings in Harrogate.

> Dear Miss Blair
> About the arrangement that we talked over at Christmas i.e., boarding me out. Well, I think that it is now time that I should board out. I have had just about all I can take in this house. I'll go round the bend. I was given permission by Miss Irwin while the Macs were away, to stay out until 11.15, on the last bus from Harrogate. This morning I got into trouble off the Macs for this, they said that I was overstepping the mark – I had permission to stay out & so I hardly think I was in the wrong.
> Anyway could you please get an advert in the paper or something? This is not written after a heated argument, it is something which I have thought about for ages.
> Yours faithfully
> Bruce Oldfield

This is followed in the files by another letter to her within the week, this time complaining that Barry has been completely rigged out in clothes while at a Leeds hostel whereas I had only had one pair of trousers and a jumper bought for me in four years. I felt this grave injustice could be partially rectified by reimbursing me £3 for a pair of shoes. Miss Blair saw her way to letting me have 15/-.

That summer, while I was in Spennymoor, I had another holiday job in a pop factory, helping with the van deliveries – very hard work. It wasn't long before the welfare officer had reported that out of my magnificent £6 per week pay I had only offered Mum 10/- towards my keep. And more importantly I was 'reluctant' to repay her the £1 she had loaned me that time I had gone home unexpectedly to see Linda Burt. In September Mum spoke to her:

> Miss Masters told me today that she does not want to have Bruce home for any more holidays. She says that he is not at all co-operative, and during this holiday he very grudgingly washed up a dish. She says that she has had enough with the three boys and that she really can't cope with Bruce coming and making a convenience out of her house, as she has to do quite a lot of re-organization when he comes home.

Typically, Mum blew with the wind. Only a month had gone by before I was welcomed back to Spennymoor again for a weekend and, to the astonishment of the DBH memo writers, she invited both George and me back for Christmas. I remember the tearful moment when Mum broke down saying that she'd always done her best for us kids. She must have been close to sixty-seven and looked very frail. I comforted her, telling her that we all loved her and that it was our turn to look after her now.

But before the holidays came, my pleas for release had not fallen on deaf ears. At last, Barnardo's advertised and found lodgings for me in Harrogate. The welfare officer in Harrogate thought that Mr and Mrs Watson might offer suitable accommodation. Both were in their fifties, he was a gardener at the National Children's Homes, she was a housewife. They had a grown-up son and a 'male gentleman' lodger thought to be a stringer for the London *Times* though highly unlikely. The accommodation and support they offered were deemed ideal. So on 23 October 1967, I walked out of West Mount for the last time.

CHAPTER SIX

With one bound, I was free.

At least that's what I thought. The reality was a little different.

167 King's Road, Harrogate, turned out to be a three-storey Victorian terraced house at the Skipton Road end of King's Road right opposite where Jackie Carling and Eric Leggo lived. It was a busy road but reasonably central and within walking distance of the bus station so I could easily travel to and from Ripon. My accommodation consisted of a large top-floor bedroom with a big bed and a spare single bed in the corner, where friends could stay, a wardrobe, a chest of drawers, two easy chairs and an electric fire. I was to share the bathroom with the other lodger and was able to use the Watsons' lounge. For a weekly charge of £4, they provided bed & breakfast during the week, full-board at weekends and carried out my laundry. DBH paid the rent direct to the Watsons, at the same time sending me a weekly allowance of £1.12.6d to cover my pocket money, clothes, fares and 'incidental expenses'. So for the first time, I was in control of my own finances.

I suppose the Watsons welcomed the extra money that I would bring in. Despite Barnardo's positive view of her, I thought Mrs Watson was unpredictable, with more than a dash of vinegar in her soul. She had wild greying hair and suffered from a gum disease that meant her teeth were eternally loose and causing problems. She'd guffaw loudly, then have to check none of them had been accidentally dislodged. She wore a pinny high on her large stomach and as she shuffled about the house, ash would drop from the cigarette permanently in her mouth. Mr Watson was deaf, virtually senile, it seemed to me, and barely tolerated by his wife. As far as I could see, he spent most of his time watching TV and saying very little. That brings me inevitably to their son. Just when I thought I was free of Douglas McPhail in stepped Adrian Watson. About twenty-two, he had an eerie similarity to Victor Buono who played Bette Davis's shifty suitor in *Whatever Happened to Baby Jane?* He was large and round with Brylcremed hair. His principle interest in life appeared to be getting me in trouble. Otherwise there was an elderly lodger, think Alec Guinness in *The Lady Killers*, who slurped his soup, as evidenced by the stains on his lapels, but ate everything else like a rodent, masticating endlessly with his front teeth. He was the sort of man who probably wasn't very well behaved in public libraries. Not the most edifying of company.

More important to me though was the fact that at last I had escaped the confines of West Mount. As far as I was concerned, I was only expected to turn up at school and otherwise my time was my own. However the Watsons had somewhat different ideas. At last I was free (or so I thought) to put posters on my walls, something I hadn't been allowed to do at West Mount, not caring or even thinking that drawing pins leave holes. Not something that would concern most seventeen-year-olds, I guess. Adrian had given me the posters so what else was I meant to do with them? But they'd only been up a matter of minutes before Mrs Watson poked her head round the door to see what I was up to. She was appalled and immediately wrote to my new welfare officer complaining. My entire time at Kings Road was full of similarly petty incidents. The real problem was that I resented any interference with the way I wanted to lead my life and the Watsons were toothless. They never once said, 'You're in our home and these are the rules.' Instead they just complained when I went out, when I came in late, when I stayed away, when I smoked, drank and so on. But would it really have been different if they had said anything? If I'm honest, I doubt it. And perhaps they recognised that.

That Christmas I returned to Spennymoor for four days as arranged. Mum had written to DBH explaining she was finding it hard to make ends meet so it was agreed that Mrs Watson would contribute £2 from the rent and that I would take a parcel made up of surplus gift food from the Branch Homes. There's a note in my file, listing the festive supplies that went with me:

> I Large family Smith crisps [*sic*]
> 1 tin Salmon
> 4 tins fruit juice
> 1 Spam
> 1 tin strawberries
> 1 tin cream
> 1 tin raspberries
> box nuts
> packet dates
> Moorhouse Christmas pudding
> Jar of Mincemeat
> Also pair of gloves given to Bruce for Christmas

But while I was away, my new welfare officer called on Mrs Watson and was making plans. He wrote:

> I feel that when Bruce returns that he and I must have quite a talk about various things. E.g. I know that his money was late coming through, but even before it was

due he was borrowing from Mrs Watson, and then of course if and when he repays, he is immediately short for the ensuing month . . . I feel if Bruce is quite sure that he may not borrow, he will have more incentive to accept and keep a job which I know is available to him. Unfortunately he lost his last one, owing to the fact that he did not bother to go one Saturday as he 'did not feel like it', since when he has been disinclined to make an effort to obtain another, although I know he enjoys the extra money . . . I also think I could include that while sometimes we change our mind about things, that we all have to be careful about suddenly telling those with whom we live that we are staying away another week, and should give ample time if we do, for in some cases these good people return for the specific purpose from their own holiday in order to attend to the needs of our youngsters for whom they care . . . I am not saying this happened in this case, but it might well have done . . .

Battle lines were being drawn. It did not help that I wrote to Mrs Watson telling her I was going to be staying on for a few extra days and would she send me the appropriate money for Mum. Mum's welfare officer reported back:

> She [Mum] was not aware that Bruce had written until after he had posted the letter when he had told her and she was extremely annoyed with him and had a very frank talk with him. She said . . . she did not want his landlady to think she had been demanding money because this was certainly not the case . . .

Trouble began to simmer when I stayed out all night late in January without calling Mrs Watson to let her know what I was doing. She complained angrily to my welfare officer who supported her. Then for the first time, we seriously locked horns when one of Adrian's library books, an expensive one worth 63/- was discovered with four pictures of Hollywood heartthrob Robert Stack cut out of it with a razor blade. He phoned my welfare officer to complain, claiming I had borrowed the book without asking and taken it to my room. When he asked me where it was, I fetched it and the crime was discovered. More incriminating still was the bulky letter I had sent to Spennymoor that week. I had told him Robert Stack was Linda's pin-up so he deduced I must have sent the missing pages to her. There was a huge fuss as I protested my innocence. I'd been brought up to respect books and the last thing I would ever do, then or now, is deface one or rip a page out. For once my welfare officer was on my side:

> Although things looked suspicious against Bruce . . . I would be really surprised if he had done it. Mrs Watson also accepts Bruce's statement, and I find that her son now says that the book MIGHT have been like it when he got it, it is rather old. My own impression is that it is possible, that as Adrian makes no secret of rather picking on Bruce, at times, though it never gets out of proportion, has made the most of this, and has now agreed to return the library book . . .

But our relationship was turning from bad to worse. When Mrs Watson berated me for not cleaning the bath properly, I 'replied airily', 'That's what you are there for.' She was hurt enough to write to DBH to ask for my removal but deliberately left the letter unsealed on the mantelpiece while she thought things over.

. . . She could tell that Bruce had read it, by the complete change in his manner of wanting to be helpful and useful quite suddenly. This melted her heart, for as she agrees with what I feel that Bruce is fundamentally a nice enough young man who hides his lack of confidence in himself behind an outward shell of arrogance and bostfulness [*sic*]. . .

However she was adamant that I must leave when I left school because she wasn't prepared to shoulder that responsibility.

She says that although underage, he is quite a beer drinker, and when old enough will most likely be a great deal worse in this respect.

Money – or the lack of it – continues to dominate the files throughout my teenage life. 1968 is no exception. Mum is always writing, agitating for more financial contributions to help her cope with my visits. I imagine if I were to see the files of George, Barry, Linda and Janet they would be full of similar requests. Mum was forced to exist on the breadline while doing her best to bring us up at the same time. If I went home to Spennymoor I was meant to take the cost of my keep for the days I was away from Mrs Watson and give it to Mum. But, always on the look out for ways to get my hands on spare cash, I was never entirely, shall we say, 'reliable'. DBH decided that it was better to give me rail warrants for travelling to Spennymoor in the holidays knowing that otherwise my game was to spend the money and hitch up there. Barred from that source of income, I got myself a job doing 'general duties' at the Granby Hotel. I was working in the kitchens – endlessly chopping. With hindsight, if I was earning money, I should have given Mum some. I accept that. But at seventeen, you don't see the world in that way. To me, she was just someone else trying to take it from me. As the months went by, there were endless examples of how badly, at least in the eyes of the authorities, I handled money. As a result, it was decided that my allowance should be paid to Mrs Watson who would help me budget. Fat chance.

Then in June it was discovered, by Adrian naturally, that I'd been hoodwinking Mrs Watson. I'd asked for, and got, a month's school dinner money in advance. Ever suspicious, Adrian apparently phoned the school to check and to ask if it could be sent with me weekly only to discover that there was no arrangement for pre-paying in place. Of course my welfare officer reported it all.

> Much to his surprise the secretary told him that no such arrangement existed, and that it must just be another of Oldfield's devious ways of obtaining money for his ever-lasting cigarettes.

When I wasn't off following my own pursuits, I was at school. Up till now I had been a bit of a loner, never quite fitting in with the group I was supposed to be with, but in the Sixth Form I began to find a place. Every day, I joined the other pupils who lived in Harrogate and sat bunched up at the back of the 36 bus. I spent most of my journeys with Monica Scott being 'intellectual' on the back seat. She was about two years younger than me, lived in Harrogate with her family, was good at hockey and very intelligent. She remained a good friend for many years. I introduced her to the Cheltenham Club while she intro-duced me to her cosy, very middle-class life. The Scotts lived in a large comfortable detached Victorian house in a nice part of town. I often stayed over. This had even been permitted in my last days at West Mount – Monica's father was a doctor, so that was all right. I liked the set-up and they seemed to like me but it wasn't till later that I discovered they were far from happy on the race card. That was never more obvious than when Barry arrived on the scene and he replaced the platonic brotherly attention I gave to Monica with something slightly more carnal. It was through Monica's younger sister, Fifi, that I met Tina Shingler. Like me, she was a black Barnardo's child who had been fostered with her sister by a family in Ripon. She was much younger than me and apparently I completely ignored her as you do the kids who are three years below you. But then we met on a more social level later and formed a friendship that has carried on over the years.

Somehow I had got through my GCEs and was taking English and French A level with Art as an extra O level. My plans for my future wavered and I considered the idea that I would leave school before A levels and go to do fashion at Jacob Kramer College in Leeds but I was persuaded to stay on, setting my sights on a more academic future. I applied to Leicester Teachers Training College and Eltham Teachers Training College but didn't get a place. However hope was not lost and I was offered a conditional place at Leeds University to study English and Social Studies and one at Newcastle. I knew that the chances of my getting the required grades were slender although I was pretty sure I'd at least pass.

I should think the idea of visiting Paris to improve my French originated with Miss Gilbey. I welcomed it and wrote to DBH: 'It's imperative that I should go so I should get a good grade at A level French.' To my delight, they agreed.

I went with Ann Gilbey, Miss Gilbey's niece, and the head girl, Jane Ridley, at Easter just before the exams. One of them had an aunt who loaned them a flat somewhere in the suburbs. Of course I wasn't allowed to stay there although I did once or twice. Otherwise I stayed in a large youth hostel in Pigalle that was pretty awful in itself but it was so exciting to be living in such louche neon-lit surroundings crammed with night clubs, strip joints, bars – a million miles from anything I'd seen before. If Barnardo's had been able to see the hostel they would have had a fit. It was a series of tall rooms spread across a couple of floors in a very dilapidated building with no fire escapes, very basic washing facilities and of course the stand-up lavatory. The beds were metal bunk beds, three tiers high. I suspect they were ex-military – why else would they be built like that? I remember the daunting task of climbing into bed and the constant worry that if you turned over quickly, it was quite a drop to the floor.

The most memorable thing about Paris was its scale. The tallest buildings that I had seen so far in my life were the elegant nineteenth-century terraces of central Newcastle that we'd passed on the odd occasion that Mum took us to deliver the piece goods she produced as an outworker for a garment manufacturer in the city. But here it seemed that the whole city was made up of five- or six-storey buildings, sweeping leafy boulevards and familiar picture-postcard scenes that I was experiencing first-hand. The streets were always crowded with people going about their business so I was continually struck by the noise, the bustle, the accents, the waft of Gauloises. I had never seen food displayed in such an appetising way. In fact, I'd never realised that there were so many different cuts of meat or varieties of fruits and vegetables. I'd been to the weekly markets of Durham, Darlington, Ripon and Harrogate but in Paris, this was the norm every day.

Exploring the streets around St Michel, I came across shop after shop offering delicacies from the Middle East aimed at the indigenous North African population. I was amazed by the variety, the colours, the shapes and the way everything was laid out in Moorish patterns on huge salvers, the air pungent with spices. On practically every corner, you were assailed by the sickly smell of crêpes and their sugary fillings. The exuberance of the display was unlike anything I was used to. In my experience, food was simply there to be eaten, not looked at or enjoyed visually.

The people were more stylish than any I'd seen before. There seemed to be a look about them that I'd never encountered – perhaps it was to do with the size of the city after Ripon. I spent a good deal of my time on the left bank, surrounded by students. Pony-tailed girls wearing slim skirts, tight sweaters over artfully pushed-up brassières concealed under a shapeless duffel coat seemed to be the norm. What's more, I never had any inkling of student unrest. I regarded the heavy police presence on the Boulevards St Michel and St Germain as standard. How I spent my days has faded into the mists of time but I can still visualise that trip to the Comédie Française to see Racine's *Mithridate*. Apart from odd visits to rowdy pantomimes in Sunderland, I had never been to a theatre so I was impressed by the respectful hush and resigned awe that I found there. But the declaiming and the gilt-and-red plushness of it all didn't help me understand what on earth was happening on stage. It was far clearer in room 4 of the annexe where Miss Gilbey would talk us through it explaining the nuances that were hidden somewhere in the text.

I must have run out of money by the last day so decided to spend the night in the waiting room at the Gare du Nord. Half-awake, keeping an eye on my luggage, I spotted a man who seemed to be moving from seat to seat. Eventually he found his way next to me and invited me to spend the night in his apartment rather than stay at the station. I didn't see any reason not to – after all, I was seventeen and capable of taking care of myself. I was quite attracted to the sense of danger without knowing why. He lived close by in a pretty basic set of rooms where he asked me to sit down so he could show me some photographs of a recent trip to Africa. As I flicked through them, they were interspersed with pictures of a naked white youth. I passed over them without comment, frustratingly for him, destroying what must have been his opening gambit. Anyway I spent the night and recall a little unreciprocated fumbling on his part but I left in the morning, extremely tired but with my innocence more or less intact. I felt a mixture of alarm, nervousness and intrigue. The whole experience certainly opened my eyes to a new world out there. As for my language skills? Forget about it.

When I got back I was caught out scamming again. Like an idiot I gave myself away when my welfare officer mentioned that it was hardly fair to hitch to and from London when I'd been given the fare.

> . . . had Bruce been entirely innocent he would have replied 'Don't be like that' and giggled, but he was completely taken aback, and said, 'Good heavens, how did you find out?' I may say I was as surprised as he was, and had a job to wriggle out of that one, but nevertheless it was obvious he had done so, how much more fiddling went on may be left to conjecture, no doubt.

Taking up art O level was really just another excuse to draw clothes. I used to doodle all the time but I particularly remember doing a night-club scene that was basically just girls – another opportunity to draw women in short skirts and fishnet tights with the right hair. It was no different to dressing Linda's Cindy. I was definitely on track although as yet I had no focused idea of what I wanted to do with my life. One of my favourite art teachers, Tony Smith, almost hit the nail on the head in my 1968 report:

'His interest in art has always been towards pottery or fashion designing. This last interest may give a pointer to a career – some kind of design work in textiles . . . He expresses interest in this but I fear he hankers after a more intellectual life.

I managed to bring my interests into school by organising dances in the school gym at lunch time. But I didn't socialise much with the other Sixth Formers apart from those who travelled back to Harrogate with me on the 36 bus. Despite everyone's efforts to prevent it, I discovered a completely different life in Harrogate to the one I'd been leading before. If there wasn't any pressure to sit down and do homework for two hours then why do it? I ended up doing so little work that it was a miracle I got any A levels at all. It was only a matter of months before Mum began to complain. When I went home that first Christmas, I must have been showing off about my new life to Barry and Linda, because in January Mum's welfare officer wrote to Mr Kjeldsen after a home visit. Mum was concerned that my latest school report was 'not particularly good' and she knew why.

She [Mum] was also very worried about the way Bruce was behaving at school. She says that he told her that often he misses the bus on a morning, and arrives there late and also she said that he does not do his homework in a separate room, but in the room where the TV is, and, therefore is not putting his full attention to it . . . She feels that Bruce is more or less on his own and not under strict supervision. His landlady may not realise just how much pushing he really needs and possibly this should be mentioned to her. She always kept the boys up to the mark as far as homework went and never allowed them much latitude . . . and she never stood any nonsense about them staying out late etc.

Living in Harrogate felt to me like the next step on my way somewhere, though I had yet to formulate where exactly it was that I wanted to go. Spennymoor was isolated; Ripon was kind of isolated and had nothing much going on but Harrogate was a much bigger town with a buzz and access to a lot more places: Leeds and Manchester beckoned. The biggest attraction was still the Cheltenham Club. It was right on my doorstep and I could go as often as I liked. I was looking for a place to belong and I had found it at last. This was the first time I met people with whom I really had something in common and I could identify. The one thing that bound us together was a love of soul music. More than that, we all wore the same sorts of clothes – neat suits, shiny mohair three-button, high-revere Ben Sherman shirts with button-down collars and knee-length leather or suede coats or the fur-lined parkas that went with the ultimate Mod symbol, the Vespa. In my 1968 DBH review, they comment on my immaculate appearance qualifying it with 'A little exotic with clothing at times'. But the people at the club were like-minded. Many travelled in from the nearby towns and went on the circuit of northern soul clubs – the Twisted Wheel in Manchester, The Spinning Disc in Leeds and The Mojo (owned by a young Peter Stringfellow) in Sheffield. Suddenly I'd become part of a much bigger picture.

I made plenty of friends there, particularly among the women. I have always been more comfortable in the company of women. Judy and Gail Pyrah were great friends. Their father owned a garage on the Skipton Road and was less than keen on men hanging round his daughters, particularly black men, but their mother took to me.

There was no doubt that the parents of the girls I showed any interest in were distinctly unkeen on me because of my colour. For the first time I began to experience racial prejudice first hand. In those days, whites and blacks were far more uneasily integrated than they are today and as far as those white middle-class parents were concerned, I was the last thing they wanted as a boyfriend for their daughters. What did I do? I didn't have to see them so I ignored them and the girls did too. But I couldn't help but be aware of the situation.

By then I knew I would have to confront prejudice in other areas of my life too. I was finding far more was made of my colour than I was prepared to accept. I was already planning my next step – perhaps a flat with Barry in Leeds – but my welfare officer thought my age and colour might make one hard to find. Later that year, Edith Blair records in the file that 'Bruce's real problem is one of colour' and quotes me as saying, 'I do think a lot about it and I have been told at school I should not do this as it seems to be becoming an obsessional problem with me.' When I discussed racial integration with my friends they jokingly called me 'wog' which didn't help. I knew full well that this prejudice didn't help in finding a job so I affected an off-handedness about the subject. I knew too that I was in a unique position. As someone of mixed race, I was also shunned by black people for not being one of their own. Edith Blair wrote, 'He knows he is much more rejected by fully coloured people.' It's a thing about belonging. I wanted to belong but I found I had a foot in both camps at a time when racial prejudice was rife. Was being half-white better than being wholly black? It seemed not. These days it couldn't matter less and when I was in my twenties it didn't matter either because I was considered exotic. I was wanted because of it. But not at this stage in my life. I think I compensated by building a protective wall round me.

While still living at the Watsons, I stayed at a flat where every-body went when they missed the last bus or needed somewhere to crash. 101 Valley Gardens. Lis Mcleod and her two flat mates were only too happy to share it with all us waifs and strays. Men friends used to come over from Manchester to stay. Some of them were gay. They were among the first gay men I'd met and I was very 'tut tut' about them – still heavily in denial. People ask me why I didn't come out when I was sixteen but it never occurred to me – homosexuality was illegal. It may have been different in the big cities but it certainly wasn't 'done' in the small towns where I lived. I had discovered I wasn't interested in girls sexually but I just put it down to being a late developer. I remember Mr McPhail talking to the older boys. 'In my time there was a thing called pulling your wire. Now then. It's one thing to pull your own but pulling someone else's . . .' Where you have an all-boy community, there's inevitably a certain amount of messing about but nothing serious as far as I was concerned.

These men would bring over 'black bombers' a type of amphetamine. You'd have to time when you took them as there was a delay before the full effect kicked in so it was important to get it right to guarantee a good night out. All I know is that I managed to get the timing hopelessly wrong and it took me a day to come down. The other experience that sticks in my mind is seeing a mouse in the bedroom. When the mouse made its appearance, I was on the nearest chair faster than anyone. Liz had the job of trapping it behind a wardrobe and squashing it. We just left the corpse there because we didn't know what to do next. After that we bought mousetraps but we couldn't bear to empty them so we would throw them out of the window. There's probably still a pile of trapped dead mice above one of the bay windows lower down the building.

At the beginning of the summer I tried to make more definite plans to get a flat with Barry in Leeds and spend the summer working on the buses. But Barry, who was living in a residential hostel for the over-sixteens in Leeds, had other ideas. The hostel superintendent had also become my welfare officer. He had a very low opinion of me, writing,

> I am sure Bruce does feel that he doesn't much want to be supervised after he is 18, his kind never do, and I wonder very much if he thinks anyone is looking forward happily to this duty. I was however flattered to hear that he appeared disappointed that I was his welfare officer. I didn't think he cared!

While waiting for my results, I carried on living at the Watsons' and worked as a porter at Harrogate General. My abiding memory is of great pots of kidneys bubbling away in the kitchen so the place used to smell like a vast toilet. When the results came, they were disappointing – a C for English and O level passes in the rest. My lack of work over the final year meant that I had blown my chances of university. Behind the scenes the welfare officers had been agitating about my future, concerned by my behaviour. Mrs Watson had told them, 'He lives to the limit now, he smokes and drinks very heavily.' My principal interests were recorded as 'pop music, coffee bars, GIRLS' and my school leaver's report damned me with faint praise:

> Although basically honest and truthful, has a tendency to get as much for nothing as he can, from any available source. Inclined to be overpowering and plausible but has some very likeable ways.

At this stage, with no real idea of what I wanted to do with my life, I agreed to carry on portering, which I liked, with the idea of taking night classes so I could resit the A levels. The Watsons felt that now I was independent, my behaviour had improved so much that they were happy for me to stay. But I was determined to move on. The Barnardo's leaving ceremony had been fixed when, inevitably, the question of my parents had arisen again. Edith Blair came to see me in July as she had said she would.

> I reminded Bruce of the discussion we had had in May 1966 when I told him that his mother was married at the time of his birth. I reminded him that I had seen how relieved he was to have this information. I then said that I had something further to tell him concerning his birth and then stated that although his mother was married at the time of his birth, her husband was not his father. I then discussed the whole question of extra-marital relationships which he took extremely well. At first he threw his head back and sighed, then settled back in the chair and was prepared to think a bit about this. I thought it came as a shock but I am not very sure whether he had not been expecting this. He then said, 'I don't mind. . .'

She went on to tell me about my father, a Jamaican training to be a boxer.

> We then talked at great length about boxers and the strength of character and skills which are required to be a successful boxer and I left him to think that his father was a successful boxer. He then asked if he had any brothers and I told him there was a half-brother, a child of his mother's marriage who was called David. Bruce then said, 'Is it David Oldfield?' and I told him that it was and he would now be 23. I did not tell him of the other illegit-imate child, William, who was legally adopted. Bruce wrote down his father's name, his mother's Christian names and the name of his half-brother in a little book.

*

Looking back at her memo, it's touching to see how concerned Miss Blair was for my future and how willing she was to put herself forward as someone who was prepared to go on seeing me, if I got into trouble. I had no idea at the time how much she was doing for me. I'm glad that later, having read all the evidence, I was able to thank her.

However, it was Constance Gilbey who came to my rescue. She had left Ripon Grammar when I was in the Sixth Form and gone on to be Senior Tutor at Sheffield Teachers Training College. None the less she had kept in touch with me and, on hearing my dismal results, took the trouble to explain about the Clearing system. I hadn't known much about it so it was entirely thanks to her that I secretly applied and as a result was given a place on a three-year residential course studying Art/Craft and English at Sheffield Teachers Training College. My future might be brighter than DBH was expecting after all.

Edith Blair had the last word in that chapter of my life:

> I know you will be delighted that you have been accepted for Teacher Training and I feel sure also that you will realise the importance of applying yourself to the training as it is only through sheer hard work that one can be truly successful in life.
>
> Don't forget, Bruce, that I am always interested to hear about you and, indeed if you are ever in the York area, do come and see me.
>
> With kind thoughts – God bless you.

CHAPTER SEVEN

Because it was so close, leaving Harrogate for Sheffield didn't feel like that big a wrench. I was sad to leave the friends I'd made but equally I was glad to try pastures new. I'm one of those people who, once they've decided on something or when something's in motion, just go with it effortlessly. I can turn on a pin and go in a completely different direction.

However my heart did sink slightly the moment I realised I'd be living with ten men in a small hall of residence in Broomgrove Road, Sheffield. Yet another institution. The whole range of masculine hierarchy was there from the jocks – Nick Berry look-alikes with awful bravura – to the fairly intelligent ones and the misfits, like me. I was almost certainly the only one doing Art and had little in common with the rest, although the camaraderie that ensues from proving one's ability to light farts with a match did bond us to a degree. The only other thing we shared was a love of playing cards. But the real disadvantage of staying there, as far as I was concerned, was that I would have to go back to Mum's every holiday where I knew I'd be bored and it would be tough to find holiday jobs. There wasn't much going for me socially there any more and I thought I'd fare better on both fronts if I could stay in Sheffield. So the first plan I made was to get out of the hall.

It was not too difficult to orchestrate even though in theory I was obliged to stay for a full academic year.

'I've got nowhere to go in the holidays,' I pointed out. 'What am I supposed to do?'

I think Constance Gilbey must have been giving a helping hand behind the scenes. As Senior Tutor she lived in Marshall Hall, a women's hall of residence right in the centre of the college – a big multi-storey purpose-built accommodation block. I used to visit her often. We never had meals together or anything formal like that but I visited her as I would an aunt. The girls I knew who lived there thought it was hilarious that I was so chummy with her because she was considered to be a bit of a dragon. However she was always welcoming to me and we would often listen to classical music together. I have her to thank for introducing me to all the major composers. I loved what we listened to and was encouraged to take my new interest further by going to concerts at the Sheffield City Hall.

By Easter the following year I was in a top-floor flat in Cemetery Road and Barry had moved in with me. It was a rather ramshackle corner house in a residential area overlooking Sheffield General Cemetery, a vast Victorian cemetery opened in 1836 that stretched down the hill towards the College. It had been built with a dual purpose – as a burial ground but also as a place where the living could meet and walk through inspiring architecture and uplifting surroundings. By the time we discovered it, it had become extremely run down and hardly the Elysian green space that the designers had originally envisaged. However it provided us with a superb if creepy short cut to College past the Egyptian gate and the dissenting wall, in front of the non-conformist chapel and past catacombs and crumbling tombstones. Occasionally foxes and brown rats would scuttle back into the undergrowth and after nightfall we imagined bats wheeling over our heads as we rushed up the hill on our way back home.

The flat was small but as far as I was concerned it was

everything I had ever wanted. It was mine. And once the key had turned in the lock, no one could disturb us, spy on us or report us. At last I could live the way I wanted. We had a room each, a small kitchen and a filthy bathroom downstairs shared with a university student who was on the ground floor and a very strange guy who lived on the middle floor. Fortunately there were more hygienic showers at college that we could use. Barry's room was tidy and painted white. He was much more fastidious than I was in those days. He made a collage on one of the walls in my room, cutting pictures from fashion magazines and sticking them straight on to the wallpaper. I'd be constantly patching it with new additions and laqueuring them down. God knows what the landlord thought. But I don't think we ever saw him over the three years we were there so it can't have mattered. My room was the largest with a divan, table and chairs so it doubled as a sitting room. The whole place was in pretty ropey condition. But for £4 a week what could we expect? We shared it with mice and I don't think the common parts were cleaned at all. I certainly don't remember cleaning them. I don't remember cleaning the flat very often either.

We soon had a social life worked out. We were considered pretty cool having our own flat when most of our contemporaries were still in halls. Our lives were very pub-oriented and we ate well courtesy of the college canteen (I'd sneak Barry in as often as possible) supplemented by fish and chips on the way home after the pub. I must have cooked at some point but I didn't have a clue how to cook a proper meal, just beans on toast, that sort of easy student thing.

We'd throw great parties that spread through both our rooms. They were always incredibly loud with music blasting into the night. People came and went in a general free-for-all – drinking, dancing, heavy petting and smoking dope. Not a lot of that though. At least not for me because I'd just fall over in a heap. We had a big heavy record player that I'd 'borrowed' from the college. I was still into soul then, Nina Simone, Joni Mitchell and Richie Havens being favourites but my tastes were broadening to include Leonard Cohen and Fairport Convention while Barry, who had a huge record collection, was more Black Sabbath and Pink Floyd. I know we had to be incredibly nice to the neighbours before and afterwards simply because we didn't want to invite them. And we didn't want the police turning up when they complained either.

Our welfare officer – yes, Barnardo's were still keeping a watchful eye – reports that I was jealous of Barry. But that was never the case. I looked up to him, admiring his self-confidence. Our relationship was incredibly important to me. He was always much more socially adept than I was. He makes friends quickly whereas I'll make acquaintances. I'm much more stand-offish. I've always felt that people don't really like me so I have to work harder. I guess in part it goes all the way back to that rescinded invitation in Spennymoor Grammar days though I'm surprised it should have had such a long-lasting effect. Barry and I got on very well indeed and we were both popular with the girls. I used to hang around with a group of them from Marshall Hall to begin with. Alison Anderson was one of them and I used to fancy her like mad but it all went wrong – I've still got the letter to prove it – and Barry ended up going out with her.

I had reached a point where I wanted to show DBH how mature I'd become by living up to and, even more importantly, exceeding their limited expectations.

In October 1969 I wrote to DBH:

> My social life is quite good. I have got a steady girlfriend called Irene and we are getting along fine – NO plans yet!! I am standing in the coming yearly elections for the

position of Chairman of the Social Committee. This is quite a coveted position as it deals with all the college entertainments.

I surprised myself at the hustings by being able to get on my feet in front of other students and sell myself, telling them why I was standing (to have a good time) what made me different from my rivals and why they should vote for me (because I would do the job better than any of the other candidates). Until then, I hadn't felt confident enough about myself to be able to get up and speak publicly. Fear of my old stammer had always held me back but when I stood up, I found it had mysteriously disappeared. And I won. I've always looked back on that as one of the defining moments of my life.

The social committee was made up of a gregarious Brummie and me. I'm sure there must have been others but I don't remember them being very active – probably because I took over and did it all the way I wanted to anyway. I used to have to organise the College dances, the dates and venues. The last wasn't hard because they were always in the dining hall of Marshall Hall. We'd have one every other week. I'd book the bands, get Barry to do the posters for a small fee (I was in charge of the finances as well), and organise the sound, lighting and entrance charges. The bands came from all over the country, the most important criterion being that they had to make the right amount of noise. Lots of rock 'n' roll. I was quite successful because I managed to get the music that everyone liked dancing to. I have a dim memory of organising the taped music in the junior common room at college until I 'borrowed' the Hi Fi. I must have done it at home after that. They had better bands up at the University but equally they were better funded and had much bigger audiences. Theirs were more head-banging happenings than dances. My other venture into the music world was organising outside discotheques at the Fiesta Club, a purpose-built disco near the College, where we used to have nearly all soul music. Of course I was typically autocratic about that too.

Every Friday or Saturday night, or both, Barry and I used to go to the late-night showing of Hammer Horror at the local cinema. We saw the whole blood-curdling catalogue from *Dracula Prince of Darkness, The Mummy* and *The Curse of Frankenstein* to *The Devil Rides Out*. We went to every one, loving their staginess, so corny and camp, and the way the nineteenth-century vampiresses came back from the grave in the most fashionable of twentieth-century peek-a-boo nightdresses. We'd leave the cinema sated with gore and the satisfaction that Peter Cushing, Vincent Price, Boris Karloff, Christopher Lee and the rest got their just desserts. My interest in cinema was developing and I remember when the Andy Warhol films came out, they caused a huge furore. I went to see *Flesh* at the arts cinema. That was a very gay moment. I saw it several times – more to see a naked Joe D'Allesandro than anything else. Unexpectedly meeting Warhol a few years later at Studio 54 was one of those pinch-me moments.

Then, in August 1969, Woodstock happened and Woodstock the movie was all the rage. It put Tamla Motown in the back row for me. Richie Havens, Joan Baez, The Who, Joe Cocker, Country Joe and the Fish, Crosby-Stills-Nash and Young, Ten Years After, Sly and the Family Stone, Santana and Jimi Hendrix – to name some of the stars who blew me away. OK, at College discos and dances we were still using the Isley Brothers' 'This Old Heart of Mine', but however much we might have loved 'Big Yellow Taxi' or 'We Shall Overcome', you could hardly call them dance tracks.

The longer I was at Sheffield, the less I mixed with other students at the College. What happened was typical of me. In the same way I got fed up with the hall of residence and wanted to change the rules and have my own flat, so Barry and I started socialising more at the University and Art School. I think we simply found more like-minded people there. There was a much bigger social life to be had and I soon hooked up with Paul Gutteridge and Mick Murfitt, who shared a flat near us, and Dean Pepall, a local guy, who had his own flat. They were considered to be 'the lads' and perhaps their reputation rubbed off a bit on me. By the time I'd got to the second year at Sheffield, I was considered quite a catch. Looking back, I can see that being found desirable was a much-needed part of my growing up. Unthinkingly, I encouraged it like mad. I enjoyed flirting.

I was considered a bit of lad but it couldn't have been farther from the truth. It was a convenient view for me though. Most of the sex I engaged in only went *so* far. Most of the girls I went with were probably virgins, definitely curious and keen but unskilled in making it easy for their partner. It wasn't until a voracious blonde came along who knew exactly what she was doing that I finally succumbed. I can't say that I enjoyed it particularly, nor that it set in motion a desire to repeat the experience, but I suppose I had come of age – finally! I'd say Sheffield almost flushed girls out of my system.

On the other hand, I wasn't particularly aware of any gay scene at that time in Sheffield. I do remember whiling away one hot Sunday afternoon – I've always hated them since Spennymoor days – in an art gallery and being picked up by a guy. We did go back to his flat but it was all very unsatisfactory. There were a few men around that I did have crushes on but no more than that. The gay thing wasn't part of our culture in those days, especially up North. There was a huge stigma attached to being homosexual and at that stage it wasn't within my scope to imagine what people did and certainly not what I would do. I was beginning to be more aware of being attracted to men but I carried on going out with girls. That's just what you did. Not that I was much of a date. I was so busy organising the College events, they just had to sit around and wait or go and dance with their girl friends. It was accepted that they were with me but that I was busy putting on records, organising the band and making sure that the whole show ran smoothly.

The question of money raised its head time and time again. Like most students, we were constantly struggling to make ends meet. However, thanks to Mum, we were very handicraft-oriented so my great entrepreneurial moment had arrived. Barry was already good at graphics so together we set up a small business custom-making T-shirts. We'd buy them for 1/9d at Tesco, dye them at College, then print them in the flat. We used all those popular Disney images of Mickey Mouse and his mates. Infringement of copyright? We didn't give it a thought. We'd hang them out to dry like brightly coloured pennants on the fire escape outside. I'd sell them to shops for 3/6d and they'd retail at 7/-. Everyone was happy, though had I really thought it through, there was certainly more than 1/9d in labour cost per T-shirt so in reality we made NO profit at all. We also made belts with leather that we got from a tannery in Leeds. Barry was better at that than I was and created intricate plaited, linked and cut-out belts that sold successfully. We were both creative and I was particularly tuned into what was going on in fashion. I could sell ideas but lacked the capital to turn any into a decent business.

I got involved with one of the shops I used to sell to in the centre of town. We were all slightly hippy then and the owner stocked the designer clothes that I liked such as Ossie Clark and Janice Wainwright. It was a million miles from the chic boutiques you find today. A small square room with a fitting room shielded by a curtain. It wasn't at all posh but neither did it stock the ubiquitous studenty afghan coats and floaty Indian scarves. This was definitely smart London kit. I'd spend ages hanging around in there checking it out, working out how I could afford to buy stuff. Selling them our T-shirts and belts helped.

That first summer Barry and I took jobs in a gloomy scissor factory huddled among all those steel works on the east side of Sheffield. We had to stamp out the shape of the scissors, then put them into pebble drums to smooth off the rough edges. It was really dreary. The owner took us aback by saying, 'Look, guys, you shouldn't really be doing a job like this. It's OK for the summer I guess . . .' He needn't have worried, neither of us had any intention of staying there a moment longer than necessary.

Apart from the rent, I spent my money on clothes. I was getting very into them then and I remember people remarking on how many I had. I'd hitch down to London, make my way to Chelsea and do the King's Road, picking my way through the different boutiques, including Bazaar, Ossie Clark and Granny Takes a Trip, then up to Kensington High Street with Biba, Crowthers, Bus Stop and Kensington Market where I'd buy clothes that I couldn't afford. I got a huge buzz even from being on the fringes of it all. After all, I was only a student down from the North for the weekend, usually staying with a friend's parents in Blackheath. I was very keen to see what the girls were wearing and watched them parading up and down the King's Road in their mini skirts. As for me? My hair stuck out in a wild Afro and I did have a long Biba mac, like a trench coat, and calf-length boots. Although I'd never lived in the South, London was definitely establishing itself in my consciousness as my next stop.

It wasn't long before I discovered for sure that I was not cut out to be a teacher. My first month of teaching practice was enough. Two or three of us were drafted out to a secondary school in Rotherham. It was a nightmare right from the start. I had visions of the staff room based on the one I'd imagined at Ripon with teachers sitting around in fading upholstered chairs, smoking pipes, discussing intellectual issues. The one I found was dismally mumsy. The staff sat about reading the newly relaunched *Daily Mail*, doing the easy crossword, eating Rich Tea biscuits, smoking and knitting. Nothing wrong with any of that but it wasn't terribly challenging. It was ordinary. And I didn't want ordinary any more.

Then there was the teaching. That was certainly challenging but it was terrifying too. To go straight from school as an eighteen-year-old and have to stand up in front of a class of fifteen-year-olds, some of whom were bigger and certainly tougher than you, was no joke. Mr Stockdale, our tutor, had delivered some fairly useless advice: 'If you stand up straight and talk to students rather than talking down at them, you'll get a better reaction from them.'

Stand up straight and you might get respect if you are big . . . I was big all right but I wasn't at all confident that I could do what I was supposed to and it must have showed. I got very little respect. Perhaps more importantly I wasn't that interested in the subject.

I was fine with Art but the English was way over my head. I had to struggle to teach it at all competently. My other dis-advantage was, having been taught in the old-fashioned grammar school way by rote, I assumed that the kids would be interested in the subject and all I'd have to do would be to lead them through it. In fact, what I discovered was that, as a teacher, you have to be madly enthusiastic and want to get more out of your students than they seem prepared to give. You have both to inspire and to nurture. I just wasn't the nurturing type. What's more, I thought the artwork they produced was crap. I didn't have the sophistication, the knowledge or the understanding to see potential. Although I never did it to their faces, I'd just dismiss their creations out of hand. All I could think was that if someone were to produce some fabulous work, I would be excited by it, even feel confident and pleased to be part of it. But it wasn't like that at all. I was soon disillusioned. Mark you, I do have a photograph of me with some of the pupils in the art class. We all look as if we're enjoying ourselves so perhaps I was better than I thought.

I knew I could do better than to pursue teaching as a career. My experience in the classroom confirmed it. I felt I was treading water while looking for a new direction. I decided not to leave but to get an education out of it. I dropped English and changed to studying Art and Craft exclusively.

I'd been moving towards fashion since I was thirteen without really articulating it to myself. True, I'd flirted with the idea of a career in it when, in the fifth form, I had considered applying for Jacob Kramer College in Leeds but I was easily dissuaded. I spent my second two years at College doing what a lot of students do, i.e., not working very hard and seeing what would happen. For me it was a means to an end. I got a higher education but it also meant not having to make a decision about work, about my life or about a career. I don't see how anyone can at eighteen.

My interest in photography gave me the perfect opportunity to indulge in what could loosely be called fashion photography. Alison Anderson, my muse, would loiter elegantly in a birch grove looking mysterious in a velvet hood or lounge in wet T-shirts (not that old chestnut) coyly accusing me of page three-ism – as if . . . Another friend, a stunning dental nurse from the Uni, modelled in a dress that I actually made from cloth that I had printed – so I was almost there. These pictures formed the main part of my portfolio when applying to Art School and they stood me in good stead.

When I went to Mum's for Christmas in 1970 I took a folio of drawings which, to her delight, I worked on over the holidays before going back early to Sheffield to do more. My goal was to get into fashion school and I was determined to pass my final exams. In spring 1971, I was offered a place at Ravensbourne College of Art and Design for a First Year Diploma in Art and Design. As a result my DBH file for that year is full of letters and internal memos about how I'm going to be funded. It's true that until then I had put them out of my mind until I needed them. The senior child care officer noted that 'Bruce was striving towards personal independence and is slightly anti-Barnardo'.

It was my guardian angel, Edith Blair, who stepped in once again to help. On 18 May she wrote to me explaining that a Barnardo's Trust Fund could be tapped to provide me with £30 a term but that if I wanted more I should detail my needs. But I had already been applying everywhere I could think of for grants and replied to her:

> I have been applying to the West Riding County Council, the Borough Councils of Sheffield and Bromley and also various trust funds that I have discovered in the Charities Digest . . . I will give a brief outline of the amount I shall need per annum.
>   1. standard full independent grant for residents in the provinces £420 p.a.
>   for residents in London and districts £420 + £50 = £470 p.a.
>   2. fees payable to the college for the actual course £45.00 p.a.
>   Total £515 p.a. × 3 = £1,545
> As you can see this is a great deal of money . . .

*

Edith Blair went into battle, memoing the DBH Administrative Office to ask for more than £30 and explaining why they should cough up:

> Bruce came to us as a small child so that in fact he has been brought up within the Organisation and, as happened so often in those days, we were not working with the family, so that now he tends to be a rootless boy. He and I have discussed this situation over the last 5 or 6 years and he has come to terms with it, be it he has very real problems over his colour because when he was wanting part-time holiday work before leaving school he knew that he was being turned down by employers because of his colour . . . Bruce presented many problems at West Mount, partly because he was more intelligent than the main group and partly because he adopted 'snob' attitudes . . . He once told me that he was so ashamed at being at West Mount that he had difficulty passing on his address to friends.

The problem was not that I was so ashamed of being a Barnardo's child, it was the 'pity' that this revelation usually evoked. I didn't want or feel my circumstances justified the reaction.

Within a month Miss Blair had secured the promise from the Trust department of £1,545 over the next three years.

By September I was in London, living temporarily with Barry, who had got himself a job as a printer with Zandra Rhodes. By this time, I had told him I was gay but he just shrugged it off. It didn't matter to him. I wrote back to Miss Blair, thanking her for the money and explaining that I had had no luck with my other applications for grants.

> I really am totally indebted to you and the organisation and I am going to commit myself to a well-thought-out

promise that is when I get famous or perhaps before, I shall give the money back.

By the time I left Sheffield, I'd gained enormously in confidence and I had acquired more of a talent for socialising. It has been something that has been incredibly valuable to me ever since. It was the first time in my life that I had felt liked. And with self-esteem came ambition. Somehow I was going to be famous.

CHAPTER EIGHT

In those days, Ravensbourne College of Art was in a modern purpose-built block that occupied part of a site belonging to a technical college on the outskirts of Bromley in Kent. Graphics occupied the second floor, Fine Art the fourth with us, Fashion and Textiles, sandwiched between them on the third. There were only about fifteen to twenty people on the course, mostly girls. The first few days were spent mostly getting to know one another and finding somewhere to stay. Fortunately I was spotted and grabbed by Kate Best, one of the third-year students. Within days I had moved into a flat with her in Widmore Road, Bromley. It was a perfectly nice top-floor flat but it was too far from the action – I'd set my sights on being in the centre of London. But I stayed there for two terms until I moved on.

The whole experience of Ravensbourne was unexpectedly unsettling. Everyone on my course was younger than I was. They were almost all straight out of school and many had just left home for the first time. For me, independent and already armed with my teaching certificate, it was like going back three years to my first year at Sheffield, so kind of strange. I think if I had moved on from Sheffield to study for a Master's with people my own age, going back into class would probably have been easier to take. As it was, my attitude to the whole course was slightly different from the others' because, inevitably, I had travelled somewhere further down the line in thinking through my design approach and what I wanted from the course. Because I'd already done three years I was in a bit of a hurry and was clearly focused on what the end result should be: leaving college with the expertise and knowledge to be a designer. It didn't take long for me to be convinced that Ravensbourne wasn't going to supply that. At Sheffield, I had already studied textiles. I'd made garments out of the textiles I had printed so I had seen the natural progression of things. But at this particular art school, that was not how they wanted you to see things. With them it was always one academic, laboured step at a time.

'Today, we'll do a patch pocket.'

'Today we'll do a welt pocket.'

'Today we'll do a sleeve.'

Eventually, in exasperation I'd say, 'Look, tell you what, why don't I go away and make a jacket? I'll do a patch pocket on one side, a welt pocket on the other . . .' And I'd do just that, coming back in the next week with it all done. I disliked the patronising attitude of many of the teachers who treated the students like kids. I felt that I was beyond that by then. I wanted to learn how to design, not to sew samplers as if I was going to be a dressmaker. I was looking for the whole picture. In December of the first year, the head of the textile department, Anna Watson, wrote to Edith Blair:

> I am happy to tell you that Bruce Oldfield at this stage of his course has approached his work intelligently and enthusiastically. He has found difficulties coping with the lack of strict disciplinary teaching . . .

Strange how her report doesn't quite tally with my memory of it all.

I wrote to Miss Blair early in 1972, explaining to her in the most uncompromising terms the positive advantage of being older than the rest.

> I have already experienced the indecision and frustration that my fellow students are experiencing now. They are unsure of what they want, but I know exactly what I want and what I need to know or do to get there. Perhaps my single-mindedness is not a terribly good thing as it would lead to an even more selfish attitude towards life – anyway I won't know until I reach my goal what effect the 'way-up' will have had on my personality.

Anna Watson was the one who put me touch with Dave Hobday, a friend of hers who had bought and converted a Victorian terraced house in Santley Street, Brixton. Dave had the ground floor and mezzanine and the upper floors were to let. It was an opportunity too good to miss. I advertised in the Junior Common Room to find two people to share the flat and I moved in with two graphics students. I appropriated the biggest room at the front of the house. That was partly finder's perks but I needed the extra space to accommodate my dressmaking. We were the first occupants and it was very pleasant. Dave gave me a free hand to do whatever I wanted in the way of decoration over the two years that I lived there. It was the seventies so, in line with contemporary trends, I kept it very white, very Habitat and very very clean – a far cry from Cemetery Road. A far cry from Harrogate too as I put up some remnants of hippydom – several pre-Raphaelite prints and a Chinese kite. On one wall were pinned my design sheets and fabric swatches. I made it into a studio bedsit with a big bed against one wall with shelves behind that were stuffed with magazines, files and portfolios. There was a Charles Eames chair (courtesy of Dave) and a big table painted white and a stool where I did my pattern cutting and dressmaking. In one corner stood my dressmaker's dummy with various bolts of fabric and bags of fashion paraphernalia. The table butted against one of the two windows overlooking the road. It was lit by one of those big white paper globe shades that gathered a lot of dust and, not to be forgotten, the music was supplied by the record player I'd 'borrowed' from Sheffield. It was the cleanest most comfortable place I'd lived in yet and at last out of the orbit of Ravensbourne and Bromley.

I wrote to Edith Blair:

> The apartment in Brixton is a really smart place unlike the one in Bromley and as I had full rein over how this place was decorated and furnished, I feel I can make this place like home.

Every day I'd commute to the College. Sometimes I'd get a bus to Tulse Hill and wait opposite the flats and children's play park for Anna Watson, to roar up in her red Alfa Romeo at 8.50 a.m. on her way from Clapham and give me a lift.

Looking back, I realise that the atmosphere of the College was pretty suburban. It was certainly entirely different to Sheffield and I had problems dealing with that. Dolly Foster was the head of the department though we never saw her. She was a harmless old thing but was very sombre and officious – a law unto herself. I later found out that when I'd made my initial application to the College, Anna had championed me, fighting my corner to get me in when Dolly Foster hadn't wanted to admit me. History doesn't relate why. Perhaps it was because she didn't believe my time at Teachers Training College, with only two years studying Art, justified my skipping the Foundation Course and going straight into the first year.

The senior tutor was the blue-rinsed Honourable Teresa

Ritchie. She was a very elegant woman, sixty-five if a day, tall and commanding, rather like Penelope Keith, though like Dolly, we didn't see her from one week to the next. But there were teachers there who were inspirational and who were to have a profound influence over my life.

Victor Herbert taught the second year every Thursday. As usual I was never content to stick with my own but had to be up with the person who taught the year above. He had come out of the Royal College of Art with a first-class honours and had worked at Stirling Cooper. Wiry and energetic, he was incredibly busy designing and making clothes for private clients and asked me to help him in the evenings. He lived in a two-floor flat in Grove Mansions, Clapham, with his wife and child. We'd work together in a downstairs room with a balcony overlooking the Common and a big table for cutting patterns. The room itself was strikingly simple with white walls and black woodwork. Victor was keen on photography and we'd sit on high stools under the blown-up photographs he'd taken from the TV of the 1969 moon landing. It was less of a workroom for me and more a place of refuge where I could concentrate uninterrupted on what I was discovering I loved best: designing and making clothes.

Victor took time to help me and I learned more from him, developing my own techniques under his guidance, than I ever learned from the course work at Ravensbourne. He also gave me the key to drawing. I couldn't capture any dynamism in my drawing style until Victor said, 'Draw what's in your mind, fast and furious. Don't think so hard about it.' That was enough. It freed me to a point where I could churn out as many as thirty or forty sketches while we'd be having a cup of tea, of which 10 per cent would be of any relevance. Victor was a manic perfectionist, making toiles (garment mock-ups in calico) for everything he designed. He cut everything to be a second skin so the fit had to be absolutely perfect. That's how I work to this day.

In that first year, besides helping him with his commissions, I made a couple of leather coats, a denim suit, a grey suit for Barry, a big black swing coat with a white lining for myself and a red leather bomber jacket with hand-smocked blistered hearts on the waist band. I don't think I wore it much – too racy for my conservative taste. I've got boxes of drawings from that time that show I was designing fashionable clothes. I particularly remember a series of animal prints, platform shoes and high-heeled boots – all very contemporary and cutting edge at that time. A lot of structured things. Victor never once let me feel something I designed couldn't be made. If necessary we would work all evening until we got it right.

Anna Watson not only got me into the College but, like Victor, became another close friend. She was gamine, with a Julie Driscoll haircut and a tiny scar on her lip that she was self-conscious about and tended to hide with her hand. She was a T-shirt, jeans and amber necklace type of gal. She and her partner Ivor used to ask me round to their place a lot. She was important in my socialising because she was very liberal and wanted to break down the barrier between students and staff. They'd often invite other students over as well as their friends, we'd sit for hours round their big pine table, eating, drinking, talking and listening to music. I'd often spend time fiddling around in the kitchen, picking up the basics of cooking and entertaining, watching and helping her cook. I know I learned how to make a vinaigrette and some simple meals – soups, bread, salads, roast meat. I also picked up a lot about wine – red wine in particular.

Anna's speciality was knitted textiles. She would design a pattern and then make the graph for the knitting machines, which involved filling all the dots on graph paper representing the separate stitches of the design. She used to pay me to make up the graphs. It was painstaking work which required absolute concentration. Once that was done, it could be translated into a punch card that went into the machine. (I'm sure these days there are programs that will take an image, put into repeat and, at the flick of a switch, knit a hundred metres!) I was always much more focused on clothing, clothing construction and design and wasn't that interested in textiles, so it was mechanical work but at least I earned some much-needed cash.

I was the least political person I know, and political unrest was very much the mood in the wake of the Hornsey student riots and the various lock-ins round the country. The textiles department run by Anna was much smaller than the fashion side of things but there was a huge fight between the two about the allocation of funds. Anna wanted the course to become more textile-oriented. She was full time and had a very political and bolshy staff while the fashion people didn't have a strong leader as the majority of them were freelancers. Art schools rely on people who are working in the business to come in and teach for a day. They can be especially valuable because they have knowledge of what's going on in the commercial fashion world whereas a lot of full-time staff may have little or no experience of that world.

It should have been an easy victory for Anna but it remained an ongoing battle, not resolved until after my time – and not to Anna's advantage, I think. So the background to my time at Ravensbourne was fraught with students being lobbied to concentrate either on fashion or on textiles. I don't believe we should have been drawn into the feud or expected to take sides, because it inevitably affected our attitudes to the teachers and the courses.

The other part-time teacher, apart from Victor, who was an inspiration and long-term friend to me was Colin Barnes. He was a successful fashion artist and what you might call an old-school homosexual, more in the mould of Jules and Sandy, those outrageously camp comic creations of Kenneth Williams and Hugh Paddick in *Round the Horne*. Sixteen years my senior, brought up in the Far East and returning to England at the outbreak of war, Colin had childhood memories of luxury travel on liners, something that remained his passion in life. I believe he approached Hartnell for a job and, although he didn't get it, was given encouragement. He went to RADA (hence the voice and the stately bearing, all 6 foot 4 inches of it), but didn't have much luck in the acting game. Eventually he decided to enrol at St Martin's to learn fashion illustration. There he met Elizabeth 'Su' Suter, the Senior Tutor, who remained a lifelong friend, and his career took off.

Colin taught us to develop our skills in fashion illustration. Apart from his knowledge of drawing in the academic sense, he knew how to make a drawing come alive. He could feel the essence of the garment he was drawing and could imbue it with a sense of style and context. He was greatly inspired by the great masters of the art, names such as Bouchée, Bérard, Pagès Gruau and latterly Antonio Lopez, all of whom worked for the fashion houses and magazines from the twenties to the seventies, earlier decades when their skills were more appreciated and commercially pertinent. During those periods, the couturiers and designers did their own drawings to explain to their workshops what was to be made. These drawings were working drawings and not necessarily for publication though Yves St Laurent's Cocteauesque drawings were excellent. It was when the collections were finished that the illustrators who often worked for the houses were then employed to illustrate the collections much in the same way as the clothes are photographed today for the publicity campaign. The drawings were shown to the clients or sent to interested grandees who would make their purchases in absentia. Now, as then, designers are not trained to make finished illustrations unless they specifically opt for it as a discipline over design. It's a unique skill and a dying one because the public understand a photograph more easily than a drawing. At Ravensbourne I might have discovered a passion and skill for fashion illustration which could have been my career route but I was never that good. I look at the illustrations I did then and shudder.

I'd sometimes catch the train back home with Colin and Michael Fay who worked for Wallis but taught part time at Ravensbourne. They were hilarious travelling companions, revelling in fashion gossip and in the struggles between the earthy textile staff and the flamboyant fashion lot. It was a real piece of theatre. This was a completely new thing for me as well as finding myself a student confided in by staff. This was one of the major differences between Ravensbourne and Sheffield. I learned a lot from them about life. I was so greedy to know how things worked that I'd bombard them with questions: How do you do that? How do you get from here to there? What's the best way to succeed there? Colin had a sharp tongue and a whole wardrobe of withering looks. If he liked you, fine. If not, watch out.

My sketchbooks began to fill up as I became more adept at visualising a garment, then representing that idea two-dimensionally on paper. At one point, I was criticised for not restricting one idea to a page, but I found it difficult to do that as I could never find a place to stop and say, 'This is it.' I found one idea tended to move on to another on a sort of conveyor belt of lateral thought. I suspect that what my critics meant was that I could perhaps edit a bit more, abandoning the non-starters as I went along.

The other discipline that I came to enjoy was draping ideas directly on to the dressmaker's dummy or stand. This gave direct control over how the finished garment would look as you created it, sculpted it almost, in 3-D. It was a way of creating and developing shapes and forms and working them out 'in the round' as you considered not only the front of the garment but also the sides and the back and how they flowed from one into the other. It was considered to be a real discipline, traditionally used in the great Paris couture houses where the 'toiliste' would be a key player, someone who straddled the grey areas between the creation and the enablement of a design or idea.

The skill was to create a pattern at the same time as evolving the form, so many rules and 'givens' were employed from the outset. You always started by finding the straight grain of the material, usually an unbleached calico or fine muslin, a vertical line that notionally ran absolutely parallel to the selvedge or outside edge of the cloth. The easiest way to envisage this is to see it as one of the threads in a loom that make up the warp. This was your plumb-line and you would almost invariably begin by pinning this to the centre front of your stand and start working outwards from this point. You would then continue, deciding where you wanted to put your seams to enable the shape to develop, and the design to emerge – a little dart here to suppress some excess cloth in a concave area, some fullness there, perhaps to accommodate a convex shape such as the bust, a bit of flare at the hem to give lightness. All of these additions and adjustments for contours and style lines were 'drawn' on to the toile, not in pencil, but in rows of equally spaced pins.

You would only make up a half garment in this manner, then remove it, intact from the stand, a shell of muslin or calico, held together simply by a grid of pins – a work of art really – which would then be painstakingly dismantled. With the aid of a spiked wheel, the 3-D muslin would be traced on to paper or card and you then had your 2-D representation of the 3-D form, or in other words, your paper pattern.

Another way of arriving at a paper pattern, equally skilled

though perhaps more relevant to commercial manufacturing techniques than couture, is cutting on the flat. This involves arriving at your flat pattern by manipulating what every fashion house would call its basic block or house shape-and-fit template. This would be developed over many years of trading and would typify the fit you would come to expect from that manufacturer. Hence if you can only wear Nicole Farhi's pants, it's because their house block is suited and should remain suited to your particular body shape. The basic block says a lot about the way a designer sees the woman he wants to dress and quite often the body shape of the designer him/herself magically finds itself transposed into the house psyche, for example you would expect Yves St Laurent's clothes to be best suited to tall willowy women and that Kenzo favoured a more petite body. The Bruce Oldfield basic block is tall but curvaceous and I think that this has been my ideal shape to work with from day one.

Flat pattern making was never my forte. I preferred to see the shape evolving on the stand. I realised quite early on that I was never going to be a pattern cutter so, although it was important to learn my 'grammar', I didn't need to get a Master's degree in it. I needed to be able to discuss things intelligently with a pattern cutter. I find in my business now that the pattern makers employ both flat and stand work to achieve the shapes I want and as in College, I still spend time creating on the stand myself but take it to a point where the pattern makers can take over and make it happen.

Just as I had been at Ripon, at Ravensbourne I was attracted and intrigued by the middle-classness of my new friends. Their comfortable lifestyle, their values and the apparent ease with which things came to them appealed to me, as did the ease with which they negotiated their way through life. One of my girl-friends there was Sarah Reed, a good-looking blonde a year older than me who was teaching the pre-diploma foundation course. Of course students and staff weren't meant to fraternise closely but we ignored all that. I remember going to the supremely trendy Hard Rock Café with her. I really felt I'd arrived. She was extremely smart and sociable and I recall she once made a chequerboard of caviare and smoked salmon for a party – it was quite the most sophisticated thing I'd ever seen. I made some kitschy dresses for her in the Mr Freedom, Anthony Price vein – very retro and a bit pop art – a lot of brightly-coloured satin with big spots. We got permission to photograph them in the Rainbow Room at the top of Biba's – the height of London chic at the time. It was a great addition to my portfolio and that enterprising streak got me ahead and put me aside from the others. It wasn't that I was much of a money-maker, more a go-getter. My money-making ventures were pretty few and far between at this stage simply because any spare time I had I spent working with Victor.

But by the summer term, I'd had enough of Ravensbourne. Round about Easter I was already thinking I should be doing something else. I remember talking to Victor about the Royal College of Art and him bolstering my confidence by saying that I had got what it would take to succeed as a designer. He certainly encouraged me to think about leaving but in the end it was Colin Barnes who pushed me towards St Martin's School of Art where he had been teaching. By this time I was fully focused on what I wanted. What my time at Ravensbourne had done was sort out in my mind that I did like fashion designing and that I'd found something that I was actually good at. I wanted to pursue it. I knew then that I wanted to be a top designer and I also knew the way to break into that world depended on arriving from somewhere with a good profile. At that time Ravensbourne just didn't have it. It was time to move on again and nothing was going to stop me.

CHAPTER NINE

I sat for a long time in that long empty corridor on a sticky plastic chair, feeling like Gene Kelly in *An American in Paris:* that bit when he's walking up and down Broadway with a suitcase knocking on all the agents' doors singing 'Gotta Dance'. Here I was at St Martin's School of Art with my portfolio, waiting to see the head, Miss Pemberton. *Gotta be a fashion designer. You've gotta let me in. I'm in St Martin's. I'm in Central London.* I was not going to be turned away.

In fact, I already had been. I was told that Miss Pemberton was busy, that she couldn't see me, that there was absolutely no possibility of my joining St Martin's halfway through a course, that I had to complete my stint at Ravensbourne. My life so far had taught me never to take no for an answer. As a result I had gone back to Santley Street, collected my portfolio and returned to wait until Miss Pemberton would agree to see me. I sat there for two days until she relented and grudgingly agreed to take a look at my work. *You've gotta let me in.* And she did.

There were a few technicalities that had to be observed but Dolly Foster was probably pleased to see the back of me so any difficulties were swiftly smoothed over. I hadn't been the most co-operative of students and had virtually been running my own course. In my defence, all I had been doing was what I think a student should be able to do – using the staff and facilities to customise a course that most benefited the *individual's* needs – although they may need a bit of guidance. After Sheffield, I wasn't prepared to submit to the nursery slopes again. My sights were set on the black runs.

The leading designers of the moment were Bill Gibb, Zandra Rhodes, John Bates, Gina Fratini, Jean Muir and Ossie Clark but, although aware of their designs, I never tried to model myself on any of them. The bubblegum fashion of Mr Freedom and the rest was never for me. A greater influence on me by far were those films of Fred Astaire and Ginger Rogers that I'd started watching all those years ago in Barmoor.

I'm not sure that I particularly stood out at Ravensbourne but when I arrived at St Martin's and carried on working in the same way, things changed. I went to very few classes and carried on doing stuff with Victor but the people I met . . . I was so right to have gone. I was only there from October 1972 to June the following year but a lot happened in that short time.

I once came across a man looking through all my stuff in the second year's room.

'Hello. Excuse me.'

'It's rather good, don't you know,' he said and turned on his heel.

He was none other than Bernard Neville, now a professor at the Royal College, then a graduate from St Martin's, who was majorly important as the resident designer for Liberty fabrics. Liberty's was very influential then. He had taught Victor at the RCA. Subsequently he got me to make him a tweed coat lined in Liberty fabric. When I went round to his house in Glebe Place for a fitting, I spotted David Bradley, the boy who starred in *Kes*, leaving. A film star. The first I'd seen. This was the start of what St Martin's could give you, connections with the world I aspired to belong to. And I knew it.

On another occasion Judy Brittain, fashion editor of *Vogue*, came to talk to the third years. Guess who had skipped his own classes and was in there with them? Afterwards I went up to her and asked loads of questions, including whether she would take a look at my work. The third years were really miffed. I was like a great big cuckoo in their nest. But I refused to take any prisoners and just grabbed every opportunity that offered itself, so intent was I on pursuing my dream. I wrote to my DBH contact, Mr Hall:

> Last term Judy Brittain, one of the *Vogue* people, gave a talk to St Martin's. I dashed home and got my work, took it to college and managed to see her on my own and show her my own work. She was very interested and wants to promote me. She is looking for a financial sponsor to set up a business.

In the spring Judy took me to a Bill Gibb fashion show and afterwards introduced me to Barney Wan, the art director of *Vogue*. 'This is Bruce Oldfield. Oh, he's very Eve Harrington.'

'That's a bit much,' Barney protested.

She laughed. I hadn't seen *All About Eve* so I hadn't a clue what they were talking about. I don't suppose I'd have minded if I had but their exchange stuck in my mind. It became clear some time later when I saw Anne Baxter playing the unscrupulously ambitious starlet Eve Harrington who ruthlessly uses Margo Channing, an arrogant Broadway star played by Bette Davis, as a stepping-stone to stardom. All Judy had spotted was that, like Eve, I knew what I wanted and was determined to do almost anything to get it. And for me, it was flattering to be dragged around by one of *Vogue*'s heavy hitters.

It was all part of my introduction to the fashion world, helped along by DBH who contributed £50 towards the cost of my joining a second-year trip to the Paris collections. In his letter of application, the St Martin's student advisor wrote:

Bruce, incidentally, is a very good student indeed; he is considered to be very talented and certainly makes use to the full of the course he is following. His attendance is excellent and his enthusiasm and energy very infectious.

Even within a few months, things were starting to go in my favour. I summed it up in my letter to Mr Hall.

I have come into a fantastically lucky patch and everything points to great success (touch wood). My first success was designing costumes and making them for a small modern dance company . . . the dance was shown at the International Dance Competition in Paris (the same week as the couture collections). We won the prize as the most professional company with a special mention of my costumes. The company has been invited to dance at the Avignon Festival in August and at the Edinburgh Festival. I will design for both.

I don't remember the details of the designs I made now but I do remember João. He was a great-looking dancer with the company but I met him because he was a life model at St Martin's. He also introduced me to a friend of his, a black girl, who I drew a lot and who, for a brief moment, became my muse. I was becoming more undecided about my sexuality then, uncertain what I wanted, and had started seeing one or two men but I was extremely secretive about them. João and I had an intense but short-lived fling while publicly I still went after the best-looking women in the college – the school catches. At one point while I was there, I clearly remember going out with Sonia Tester, the most beautiful girl at St Martin's. Trophy woman – typical me. It wasn't that I felt any pressure to appear heterosexual – it was a given that all male fashion students were probably gay – it was more that I preferred the company of women but disliked the pressure of having to perform sexually. I enjoyed that side of things more with men, although I didn't want to be tied down into a relationship with one. I simply couldn't figure out how such a permanent commitment would work – so it was all rather confusing.

At that time, I was far too busy working to have all that much of a social life anyway. I was completely focused on my career. I never thought, not even for a moment, that I wouldn't make it. I was 100 per cent driven by ambition, even making pacts with myself to push me on. If I was not going to become a family man (at least I'd worked that out for myself by then) the pay-off was to be that I would be successful. If I wasn't successful as a name designer, then I would use my entrepreneurial streak and become successful on the commercial side. Failure was not a consideration.

I spent a lot of my spare time with Colin Barnes who had become a good friend by this stage and worked in a conveniently close (Brewer Street) fourth-floor walk-up studio high in the rooftops of Piccadilly. He taught me a lot about the simpler pleasures in life. Although he aspired to a more expansive and luxurious existence, he was the master of the small gesture: less is more; don't over-egg the pudding. This showed in the way he dressed, nothing flamboyant there, the way he entertained and the way he lived. He had two rooms, no more than 600 square feet in total with stripped floorboards, low ceilings and white walls. One of them was the living room, with white roller blinds at the sash windows, a ticking-covered two-seater sofa and a single bed. An ornate white-painted, floor-to-ceiling mirror reflected his drawing board, a plan chest full of his drawings and a trolley full of artist's materials. His clothes were kept in one of the chimneybreast recesses, hidden by another white roller blind. The other room was the kitchen-cum-dining room where we'd spend evenings eating and drinking at a small pine table, looking towards a tiny terrace brightened by vivid geraniums.

I existed in a bubble where what was going on outside my world didn't bother me. Being black and gay in the early seventies weren't matters that concerned me in any political way. I suppose partly because I had been subconsciously building up my defences from an early age. Arrogant of me, perhaps, but I just chose not to let anything else apply. It still seems to me a much nicer way of going about things. OK, the bubble can be burst now and again and minor irritations dealt with, but I find that cocooning oneself is a more comfortable way to be. You're just saying, 'Talk to the hand.' None of that stuff gets to me.

Of course I was still seeing my family. Barry was doing his own thing in London and came round often. Linda visited too and by this time was working as a chambermaid in a Piccadilly hotel. Mum was still in Spennymoor with Janet who was only about thirteen. I had very little spare time so only visited occasionally and returned to London as soon as I could. I had travelled a long way from Spennymoor and recognised there was nothing there for me any longer. All my energies were concentrated on building my career and I had little room for anything else.

Back at St Martin's, my next test was entering the Saga Mink Competition. It was open to second and third year students from every fashion college in the country and offered awards in various different design categories. Everybody eligible at St Martin's entered. In those days my drawings always looked inexplicably like drag queens with great big lips and hands and these were no exception. I thought they were dreadful but Bobby Hilson, one of the tutors, said she thought they were good and encouraged me to send them in. To my astonishment, my design was short-listed and I was asked to produce a toile of the garment. It was a 1940s-style swing coat that came just above the knee with a stand collar made up in a black-and-white window-pane check – very graphic and slightly vulgar. Subtle it absolutely wasn't. The final judging was held in what is now the Kensington Tara Hotel. About twenty students showed their designs for the overall prize of a trip to the Frankfurt Fur Fair. Extraordinarily, I won it. The second prize was £500 – thank you, I'd rather have had that. Sidney Massin made up the coat for the House of Worth in Mayfair's Grosvenor Street and there was a page in *Vogue* – my first mention. As a result, the big American chain store Neiman Marcus asked me to design a mink collection for them and to fly to the States in the autumn to discuss it. But by then things were moving so quickly I wasn't able to take them up on the offer.

The next defining moment was a request from Shirley Giovetti, Revlon's press officer, to produce a range of six outfits for the promotion of their new perfume, Charlie. I've no idea how I was chosen but, with a third-year student Paulina Mucha, I was. We could design whatever we wanted.

Some months earlier I had begun drawing various long draped garments that were very Romanesque but that hadn't quite come to life. Then the match was put to my powder when Victor and I were walking down Lavender Hill one day. He spotted a second-hand book on dressmaking techniques in the window of Tony Davies' junk shop. While I was collecting some pictures from the framer's on the other side of the road, he nipped in and bought it for me. (I wish I could find it today, there were plenty of ideas I could usefully recycle.) As I leafed through, I saw a page on lattice smocking. That was it.

In order to realise these dresses, I needed a paper pattern. The only way to achieve this was to mock up the whole thing in a fabric similar to the one I'd use in the finished garment. This would also mean I needed to do all the smocking, drape the fabric on to the stand, manipulate it to remove all the excess cloth, folding it into pleats or gathering it into swags, arriving at a shape and silhouette that pleased me. Then I'd have to mark all the seams on to the toile, remove it from the stand, unpick all the smocking to arrive again at a flat piece of cloth that hopefully bore all the necessary marks and information to enable me to reconstruct it. A true labour of love!

Smocking was the predominant feature of the collection and, as it was to become almost a trademark feature, a detail I'd return to periodically throughout my career. The dresses were extremely labour intensive but I was shrewd enough to use the budget Revlon was putting into the production to pay other students to help me make them. I remember us working, hunched over the table in my room in Santley Street with Marvin Gaye's 'What's Going On' playing over and over again. It must have driven the neighbours mad. I loved that album so much I used a track from it in my end of college show and used it years later as one of my eight Desert Island Discs.

I had five weeks and a minuscule budget but this was my first real taste of the fashion world. We had models, fittings and a show to devise. Penny Graham and Roger Hutchins, who were the great fashion show team of the time, organised the show, putting the music and lighting together to create the right mood and making sure the models were thoroughly choreographed. I would go home or to Victor's every night and develop my ideas. I had made clothes for Bernard Neville, Su Suter, Barry and myself, but devoted myself now to the Revlon show. The toiles and the hand-smocking took hours and hours and hours. But it was worth it for the result.

I can never understand why everyone insisted that I had only produced evening wear, when the show was split equally between day and evening. I suppose that the elaborateness of the daywear probably earmarked it more as special occasion wear than everyday 'fashion' wear. I chose a fine wool crêpe for day as it was the most suitable fabric for the smocking. The high twist in the yarn meant that the smocking formed soft, rounded folds at the same time as being firm enough to tailor into shape. The jackets were intricate in their detail but simple and body hugging in their silhouette. For that reason they were highly wearable and also extremely light, being lined in jap silk. The bottoms, two skirts and a pair of pants, were bias cut and feminine. The colours, forest green trimmed with pink, chocolate brown piped with green and dove grey toned with shell pink were quite unusual for that time and marked my future interest in eccentric colour combinations.

The evening section was less themed, consisting of a bias-cut 1930s' dress in pale green satin, hand-painted with cabbage roses by top textile design sister act Susan Collier and Sarah Campbell, a bat-winged smocked dress in shell pink Hurel jersey and a 1930s' dress in pale blue sequined tulle, the bodice formed of intersecting diamond cut-out shapes and worn to stunning effect by the Hon. Carina Fitzalan-Howard, now Lady Carina Frost. I remember that the clothes were shown quite simply, not over-accessorised nor reliant on gimmicks, with the highest platform shoes from Chelsea Cobbler and a vampy fox stole for Carina. The music was of course Marvin Gaye's 'What's Going On'.

By this stage I was aware that people were working behind the scenes towards my success. But it wasn't just a matter of luck that they were there. Not an awful lot happened where I hadn't already sown the seed. It could be said I'm a control freak (me?!) but that's what helps me make my own luck. It's not something that just falls out of the sky. When I want something to happen, I almost subconsciously convince myself that it has. It can lead to devastating disappointment or a nonchalant shrug of the shoulders!

The show was a hit. I had three garments that were booked

and photographed to appear in *Vogue*. In September there was a double-page spread with the green hand-painted dress followed in October by the window-pane-check winning fur. In January 1974, I had the front cover with shoe designer Manolo Blahnik and Angelica Huston modelling one of the dresses from the collection shown subsequently at Choses in Sloane Street. It was the first ever gatefold featuring a full-length shot instead of the more traditional headshot. Inside that issue was another smocked dress worn by model turned fashion editor Grace Coddington. For a new graduate from fashion school, this was an extraordinary achievement. There was only one decision to be made. I had seen it coming and had already written to DBH:

> I shall leave college this term. I hope that the trustees will not feel let down by the decision in that I am not finishing the course. I am sure that nobody could find any real justification or necessity for me to stay on for my last year. I will not learn very much staying at college that I couldn't learn from a job.

Their response was more than encouraging. In June I received a letter with a cheque from the Trustees for £150 – 'which they hope will assist you and make it a little bit easier for you at this exciting time in your career'.

The die was cast. I had behaved at St Martin's rather as I had at Ravensbourne. I attended lessons but a lot more selectively than the other students. I'd come in with designs and toiles I'd been working on at home. They would go, 'Wow. So that's what you've been doing,' and off I'd go again. I took from the course the things I felt I needed. I was getting so much practical tuition from Victor and, through an introduction from Sarah Reed, was spending time at the Royal College of Art with a final-year student in textiles, Jenny Frean, for whom I designed and made two jackets for her final show, using her woven textiles. By this time, the emphasis in my relationship with Victor had changed. Instead of teaching me, he enabled me to do what I wanted. We would spend hours working out how to overcome the problems presented by my designs. Neither of us was hidebound by convention and as I became more confident we were game for experimenting with unconventional methods if they suited what I was trying to achieve.

However, for the time being I had done enough to secure work for the short-term future, though what I was planning to do beyond that, only God knew. I reasoned I was nearly twenty-three and I'd been a student for long enough. In the circumstances, getting work on the back of everything that was going on seemed both the positive and the right thing to do. Because I had the clothes from the Revlon promotion, I asked if, as an exiting student, I could show them as part of the third year end-of-college show. St Martin's agreed although there was no reason why they should have since I was already getting more than the average student's fair share of press attention. I opened the show with my collection and Keith Varty, the hot boy, indeed the only boy, from the third year, took top billing at the end. As usual, journalists from the fashion mags, the trade press and the daily press crowded in, anxious to be the first to spot a potential name. The first thing that was written about me was in the *Evening Standard* that trumpeted, A STAR IS BORN, followed by an interview by Prudence Glynn in *The Times*. I was approached by Liberty and Choses to design capsule collections for them.

No question about it, my star was in the ascendant. I hadn't a clue where I was going, had given little thought to any kind of planned route, but there was so much going on, I was confident I would make it. With all the attention I was getting, I must have been completely full of myself but that's what gave me the impetus to aim higher. In retrospect, I think I would probably have been better going to Paris and working in-house with someone like Dior or Givenchy. In those days though, however helpful a job there might have been, you could only ever hope to be someone else's assistant and that role wasn't on my game plan. I still had so much to learn but I was far too young and arrogant to realise that. If I had stopped at that stage and learned the tricks of the trade it would have been much easier setting up my own business later, when it was constantly like reinventing the wheel, whether in a practical aspect of dressmaking or in basic business good practice. In the end I had to teach myself.

CHAPTER TEN

Bianca Jagger reeked of Hollywood glamour. As I walked into her house in Cheyne Walk for the first time, Ryan O'Neal dashed past me and I looked up the stairs to see Bianca standing at the top, wearing an elegant silvery grey housecoat, the sort of outfit Lauren Bacall would have worn in *The Big Sleep*. This was not at all the kind of thing you'd expect to be finding on a wet afternoon in Chelsea. It was fabulously exotic.

I was shown upstairs into an elegantly decorated room facing south over the Thames. The blinds were down so it was like entering one of those gloomy 1940s' Hollywood film noir interiors and, except for the accent, Bianca was exactly like a Hollywood diva with that long wavy dark hair and glossy lips. She had bought a suit of Rita Hayworth's at a Hollywood studio wardrobe sale and, having been to the St Martin's show, thought I could make the alterations to it. It was caramel wool crêpe with padded shoulders and a nipped-in waist – very Bianca. I really wasn't competent to do the work but I kept shtum and agreed to do it. This was my first real brush with stardom and my first brush with the demands that very famous people make on not very famous people. I was probably a little daunted by the idea of who had once owned the suit and I was certainly awestruck by the idea of meeting Bianca but I instinctively knew how to handle the reality. Where that instinct came from is anybody's guess. I grasped the routine quickly – how much soft soap to apply, when to back off and certainly not to be in awe. It wasn't until I'd left Cheyne Walk and made my way back on the tube to the considerably less salubrious back streets of Brixton that a delayed reaction set in, in the form of my first panic attack.

Married to Mick in 1971, Bianca was already a celebrity icon, so working for her was a good career move for me. In the fashion business, the power of getting clothes on the back of a glamorous woman is unbeatable. It's a sure-fire way of getting your designs in the press and talked about, one of the best ways of advertising there is. As it happened, of course, I didn't get *my* clothes on the back of that particular glamorous woman, despite press reports claiming she bought all the outfits from the end-of-term show. I just helped a revamped Rita Hayworth suit get there. However I did discover the key that has been crucial in all my dealings with clients over the years: while knowing your place and showing respect, you must be able to talk to customers as an equal without becoming obsequious, tongue-tied or embarrassed. More than that, it helped me suss out the showbiz aspect to getting lots of publicity.

None the less, after that first encounter, Bianca invited me to an Ossie Clark show in Club Arethusa in the King's Road and that's where I met two lynchpins of the fashion set, journalist and illustrator Michael Roberts and shoe designer Manolo Blahnik. The whole event was impossibly glamorous but I couldn't help feeling that it was all a bit shallow as well as something that I had no right to be part of. I hadn't earned the right to be there. (I certainly wasn't in touch with my Eve Harrington side that day.) I felt people must think me some sort of usurper. I think that I'd spent so much time locked away working that I'd missed a vital part of fashion socialising and didn't fully understand the game. I realised then that fashion shows aren't meant to be business-like but I still couldn't help wondering why designers paid to put on shows? A lot of people were invited who weren't necessarily going to buy anything but their presence was enough to create a mood, a particular vibe round that designer's name. I have never had that. It doesn't appeal to me and I'm not the kind of person to attract it because I am too much of a loner and never felt the need for an entourage. The difficulty for me in this career has always been that while I like clothes, I really don't like the whole fashion thing. Every season you're expected to make obsolete what you made six months earlier. Whatever is the point of that? Surely it's preferable to develop what you've done and take it a step forward.

Meanwhile, apart from beginning to sample the dubious delights of the fashion world, I began to make clothes in my Santley Street flat, supported by various fashion editors who liked my style. I dived straight into making the two capsule collections that continued the Revlon styles, one for Liberty's and one for Choses at 6c Sloane Street. Choses was owned by a fabulous woman, Mimi O'Connell, who gave the shop her personal stamp. Upstairs there were frocks and downstairs there were still more frocks, accessories and bits and pieces for the home arranged in a fantastic lounge where customers would come down, drink champagne, eat canapés, try on dresses and listen to music. It was very civilised, very European and unique at the time. It was one of the first shops that combined fashion and lifestyle. Making these collections was my first taste of being involved in a wholesale operation – I bought the fabric, made the clothes and then handed them over for the shops to do the rest. I hated letting go like that. I remember going into Liberty's to see what the clothes looked like there, silently willing people to buy them and missing that direct contact with the person who's going to be wearing them.

Work was still paramount to me then, simply because I had so many orders to fulfil. I employed a good machinist to help (bang went the £150 sent to me by DBH) and we'd sit at opposite ends of the table in Santley Street, listening to music, me smoking like a furnace, and churning out my designs. By this time I had also been asked to prepare a collection for Tsaritsar, a shop in Pont Street run by Annette Worsley Taylor, that was showcasing young designers.

One of the people I had met at St Martin's was Joan Juliet Buck, then London correspondent of the influential American fashion bible, *Women's Wear Daily*. It was thanks to her working behind the scenes on my behalf that my next big break arrived. It purred down Santley Street in the form of a long white stretch limo. How it got round the corners, I have no idea. Out stepped Geraldine Stutz, the president of Henri Bendel, the chic New York store, and an incredibly important fashion figure in those days. Dressed all in white, an elegant trouser suit and turban, with a cigarette in a long holder – think Gloria Swanson – she cut an incredible figure in this down-at-heel South London street. The neighbours had never seen anything like it. I rushed down to meet her and got her up the stairs to the flat with a lot of, 'Can you manage?'s and 'Are you all right?'s. In she came, sank into the Charles Eames chair and breathed,' Now tell me about yourself.'

I've always thought that it was rather odd that I didn't have to sell myself harder but, thanks to Joan Juliet Buck, Ms Stutz had already made up her mind that she wanted me. Like everyone in that world, she wanted the hottest new thing and thanks to St Martin's that's how I was then seen. It was definitely my moment in the sun. She was very matter of fact, examining what I was making, then offering me a deal to come to New York to do a collection for the store.

Henri Bendel was legendary, even in the UK. Established at the turn of the twentieth century, it was considered a little jewel box, even featuring in one of Cole Porter's songs, 'I could write a sonnet about a Bendel bonnet . . .'

In the early seventies, America joined the rest of the world in realising that a slightly younger, leaner, fitter twenty-something was out there who didn't want such formal clothes, and a number of smaller stores and boutiques were addressing this new customer. Henri Bendel had the edge in so far as it looked like a miniature department store and so had a certain 'gravitas' and Geraldine Stutz had her own vision about retailing that she followed meticulously. She was probably one of the first to recognise that clothing and beauty services, hair and cosmetics could sit equally well alongside specialised household items such as cushions and throws, candles, linen and tableware, as long as the entire 'offer' was set in a coherent ambience. Bendel's had an enormously strong sense of itself unlike today's large over-branded shops that are more like shopping malls. Under her direction, it had quickly become a watchword for everyone in retail and fashion.

Walking into Bendel's was like walking into your own home, the doorman would greet you, sales staff were friendly: 'Good morning, Mrs Saperstein. How's the dawg?' The place oozed unctuous comfort and glamour and if the sales team were slightly aggressive, you hardly noticed it. The other thing that set the store apart was that it ran contrary to current retail thinking by eschewing size and declaring that small is beautiful. It wasn't until Bendel's was sold many years later that the original site was disposed of and it began to be replicated by its new owners, across the country.

Bendel's was situated at 10 West 57th Street, a very expensive junction on Fifth Avenue, within spitting distance of the jeweller Tiffany & Co. and Bergdorf Goodman, another grand department store, I suppose that the three stores all shared similar clientele, but Bendel's definitely had the reputation of being younger and trendier, which is why I was very lucky to have been singled out to 'come on board'. As manufacturer of 'Bendel's

25. Me, looking sultry for my modelling portfolio

26. Su Suter after my Berkeley Hotel show, 1975. 'Oh Bruce you've done it again!'

27. Ninivah at Campden Hill Square in front of the Colin Barnes drawing with a missing sleeve

28. Me at Campden Hill Square, Christmas, late 1970s © *Harpers & Queen*

29. Tim Lamb's original artwork for show invitation mailer, *c.*1977.
Jerry Hall photographed by Eric Boman

30. Marion

31. Redcliffe Gardens – Mock Last Supper.
Michael Roberts, Robert Forrest, Bill Reed, Rifat
Ozbek, unknown and Raymond Paynter

32. Michael Roberts photographing
Jacques Azagury at Redcliffe Gardens

33. Colin Barnes and Pauline Denyer (now Lady Smith)

34. Victor working on a sample
in Walton Street, 1977

35. Anita at home during a party
she gave for my 31st birthday

36. Another party at Redcliffe Gardens – David Reeson, Anita, and Colin Barnes

37. Romilly, Lady McAlpine

38. St. Martins. Back row: Joe Casely-Hayford, Andrea Sargeant, me, Ninivah Khomo and Alistair Blair. Front row: John Flett, Nick Coleman, John Galliano and Rifat Ozbek. Eamonn McCabe/Vogue © The Condé Nast Publications Ltd

39. Reception at the Barnardo's Gala 1985. HRH Princess of Wales, me, Joan Collins, Charlotte Rampling, Jean-Michel Jarre, Barry Humphries. Photograph by Desmond O'Neill

40. Shirley Bassey, Dame Edna Everage, Charlotte Rampling, Christopher Reeve – all in BO except Superman! Photograph by Barry Swaybe

41. Charlotte Rampling. Photograph by Eva Sereny

Studio', a small designer collection of its own, it could offer a product that was exclusive to them in New York City.

The store designer I was to replace was Stephen Burroughs, one of a handful of black designers working in the city. His speciality was matte jersey, a slithery, silky knitted fabric, producing simple modern evening wear for the woman with a body. (Not many similarities there, then.) The clothing was bold and innovative, downplaying the formal in both styling and technique. His signature was the 'lettuce' hem that he achieved by stretching the material as it went through an over-locking or marrowing machine to give a fluted affect. He applied this to greatest effect on jersey fabrics but also experimented with wovens and he had a very wayward eye for colour. Stephen had been wooed away to Seventh Avenue, the garment district, with finance to set up his own independent label.

The sheer scale of the home market allowed American designers the luxury of knowing that they could develop a large business rapidly, given the talent and the funds. They didn't have the problem of having to deal with export markets, they could become substantial on their home territory. Fashion was geared towards the older client and the top designers, Halston, Geoffrey Beene, Bill Blass, were all producing high-end dressy clothing for the big retailers such as Saks and Neiman Marcus, who had department stores all across the States. These shops understood the power of designer merchandise. The designer would show his collection to the press, sell it to his partner stores and often go on gruelling 'trunk shows' across the country to meet and sell to the client base established by the local department stores. Even today this practice remains a good way to meet your clients and increase business.

American Vogue in the 1970s was the epitome of minimalism in clothing. It wasn't since the enduringly modern designs of the greatest American designer, Claire McCardell in the 1940s and '50s, that American fashion seemed to have a voice of its own. Unless you wanted to keep a small low-key business, you had no option other than to aim high and go for big volume sales. I don't think there was a middle way in America. Because American apparel manufacturing was not particularly sophisticated or flexible, corners were cut to increase profitability and fine details and traditions in manufacturing were side-lined. Not a great environment for the burgeoning designer market to flourish in. The American designers cleverly countered this by making a virtue out of it and adjectives like 'simple' and 'pared down' became the by-words. Hard to tell whether the punters were in any way instrumental in this revolution in clothing, but American fashion writers of the time were espousing a more relaxed attitude to what should be worn so it all began to fall into place. The designer Halston was probably the best and most fêted designer of this period, his sophisticated lines where practically all non-essentials were removed were as legendary as the people in the front rows of his shows.

I was bursting to get there. I had got the collections for Liberty and Choses out of the way with Tsaritsar's in place for the end of the year and, although I'd hoped initially I might be offered more permanent work, I hadn't been. The move made perfect sense.

So in September 1973 I arrived in New York in style, sporting a Hawaian shirt, a Mr Freedom blue suit (sold to me at a very favourable price by Tommy Roberts) and dyed green sandals. Bendels had seen to it that I'd flown first class and been met at the airport by my own stretch that drove me to the Plaza, where I stayed for the first few days. What unheard-of luxury, being right on Fifth Avenue with a room overlooking Central Park – it couldn't have been more New York. I'd never been anywhere like that before but I confess to thinking, Mmmm. Just as it should be. I remember standing with a lit cigarette by the lift

waiting to go down when the attendant snapped, 'Put that out!'
Somebody standing near me said, 'Just listen to the way he talks
to that boy. For all he knows he could be a prince. Shame on
you.' I knew then I was going to like this place although my
British good manners were to be shocked by the brusqueness of
Seventh Avenue, the fashion district. The attention I received
was remarkable. Young, black and . . . the voice! They loved the
English accent. I'd telephone to order some fabric and they'd
say, 'Oh, just keep on talking. We love to hear your voice.'

After a few days of life in the fast lane of the Plaza, Bendel's
moved me into the very different atmosphere of the Algonquin
on 44th Street. Small, intimate and dark, imbued with literary
history and the shadow of Dorothy Parker and other ghosts who
stalked the tiled black-and-white floor to the Round Table. It
may not have had quite the same cachet as the Plaza but it
had the distinct advantage of having Bendel's a few blocks
further away.

My office was on the tenth floor of Bendel's, above the retail
areas and next to the production rooms, where Stephen
Burroughs' legacy was evident in the rolls upon rolls of jersey
left over from his previous collections. There were several
machinists busy producing garments from his last collection,
which would find their way down to Bendel's Fancy on 2.
Otherwise a pattern maker was awaiting instructions from me
and there was Jeff the production manager whose job it was to
see that the goods ordered were produced and shipped on time
and in perfect condition. The entire operation was run by Pat
Tennant, a very patrician American in her forties.

I looked out over 57th Street directly at number 9, the Solow
building, a huge 1960s' skyscraper, an-upended wedge
suspended on slim pillars. Its façade was constructed entirely of
black glass that faithfully reflected the weather outside, so
gloomy days were made gloomier still and when it rained,

frequently that fall, the building became a gigantic water-feature as the rain slid down the concave surface in torrents.

The whole experience was initially pretty daunting because I had no idea what was expected of me and no one made it at all clear. I had my first run-in with Ms Stutz not long after I had arrived. She came into my office and commented favourably on a dress I had on the stand. 'Yes. But will it sell?' I wondered out loud.

'Come and see me in my office at eleven a.m.' she retorted sharply and swept out.

A moment later, Pat Tennant came in and looked at the same garment. 'Mmm,' she said. 'It's very nice but will we be able to sell it?'

Anxious about the future of the design, I went along to see Geraldine Stutz at the appointed hour. She was livid. 'Don't ever let me hear you say, Will it sell? That is not the remit of the designer.'

I was very confused. Should I take notice of Pat Tennant's concerns or just leave it in the hands of Geraldine Stutz? I began to realise the considerable pressure I was under. Not only did I have to shrug off the mantle of Stephen, my predecessor, I also had to prove myself a designer who could produce a collection that the press would like and, despite Geraldine Stutz's remonstrations, that the wholesale buyers would like too. The collection was to be sold not only at Bendel's but also into other stores and boutiques. It was unveiled on 9 November in the Oak Room of the Plaza and consisted of about eighteen designs in viscose jersey, the fabric most associated with me. The feeling was definitely art deco and 1930s which, considering my surroundings and the prevailing trends, was hardly surprising. They were simple, sexy and understated, using some of the designs I'd developed for the small collection I'd done for Choses earlier that year. Smocking was everywhere and gave the clothes their edge and trademark. No one else was doing it and they were quite hard to manufacture (therein probably lay their downfall). I was taking the ideas that Geraldine Stutz had seen photographed for Revlon and developing them a stage or two. I wasn't consciously following a particular design route. She had seen my clothes and seemed to think they would fit in.

Working there was tremendously exciting. It was marvellous to be in that retail atmosphere and being able to wander around three floors of clothes that included individual rooms featuring various name designers such as Sonia Rykiel and Jean Muir. They tended to stock the slightly more classical end of the market place, steering away from more *outré* designers such as Norma Kamali and Betsy Johnson. I made friends with the people who worked in the store and with the people who came to illustrate the collection. They paid me $100 a day, which meant that, for the first time in my life, I was earning a living and not having to scrimp and save.

As a twenty-three-year-old with no experience in the business and a whole new set of surroundings and influences, it took me a while to settle down to any real work, despite the deadlines imposed. To go straight from art college to this was quite a leap. The first night, I went to Le Jardin on my own. I'd heard about this place somewhere around 45th Street, in an old warehouse, where a big industrial lift carried you up to the club. There was lots of white space and I remember white-painted trellises and purple light. My kind of music – the Philly sound – rocked the place. It was packed with people dancing and looking good. There were a lot of black people, models, cute boys and girls. I was sitting at the edge of the stage, taking the whole thing in, when someone came over and asked, 'Are you Bruce Oldfield?'

Fame! I thought.

He introduced himself as the designer Scott Barrie. He had recognised me from a picture in *Women's Wear Daily*. From that moment he took me under his wing almost as if I was the latest accessory and we became great friends. He was a few years older than me and, unlike me, was totally besotted with fashion. He loved clothes – the clothes he was designing and the clothes he was buying for himself. He lived it. If we were in a restaurant, he would notice everything everyone was wearing.

'Did you see that suit over there?'

'Did you see the way that was cut?'

'Did you see how that collar was finished?'

I'd just think, Oh, please. Can we just get on and order some food!

Scott was a small man, probably around five foot five, very dark skinned and concerned with any scarring which on black skin caused an even darker mark. He would try endless potions and creams to keep the skin from drying out, particularly in New York where winters could dry up dark skin to produce an 'ashy' surface. He had articulate hands that sported a Russian triple wedding ring and the tank watch, both from Cartier, fingernails buffed and neat. And then there was the smile that lit up his whole face, often. He was popular because he'd talk to anyone, was very aware of his inauspicious beginnings but very happy to have arrived where he was, comfortable in a position that he would find impossible to relinquish.

Everything about him was expensive, chic and branded. Anything that was in, he'd be there first. He was also totally besotted with boys to the extent that we'd be in a restaurant and his entire concentration and conversation would be focused on the waiter that he fancied. I could never understand this. I watched everything but kept my thoughts to myself unless there was a reason for sharing them with someone else – and there rarely was. He was great fun to be with and I liked him enormously. He knew everyone and was on the A list for every opening; every night we'd go to the best restaurants and clubs.

He pursued the lifestyle relentlessly. For me, it was great. Although I was a stranger in town, albeit one people had heard of and were interested to meet, Scott shared with me the kind of access to 'society and the night' that only a seasoned veteran like him could expect. Bendel's loved it too. They wanted their new designer to be seen at all the club openings and the fashionable hang-outs like Pearls, a trendy Chinese restaurant, or Elaine's where he could always get a table at short notice. I so much preferred the nightlife in New York to the one I'd found in London. It was a life of hanging around with designers, models and photographers – a life I didn't have back home. It was a lot more stylish and everything was catered for on a much larger scale. The large open spaces had yet to be used for clubs in London in the way they were in New York. There was also a sense of 'levelling' that could never work in London because of the class system. There were celebrity rooms so it wasn't totally unsegregated socially but otherwise anyone could go to these places provided they looked right. If you didn't have on the right clothes or were on the wrong person's arm, you didn't get in. Simple as that.

Scott was on everyone's list so I just went along with him. At weekends we'd go to dinner then go home, change and head off to a disco – Hurrah, Infinity, Le Jardin. Very much later, we might head down town with a few others and visit some of the less salubrious bars in Greenwich Village. The 'scene' in the Village was aeons away from the up-town gay life which was deemed too cissy. This was a place where a unique type of maleness prevailed. It was pure self-parody, where icons of masculinity such as fireman, policemen and hard-hat-toting manual labourers jockeyed for space at the bar with moustachioed cowboys and bikers. It was very cliquish and if you were wearing anything that smacked of designer labels, you wouldn't even get past the door. I was curious to see what went on in these places and they did hold a sinister fascination for me. To an extent, the anonymity of it all did appeal but my natural reserve always prevented me from totally letting myself go and throwing myself into that scene. The sexual revolution was in full fling. The lowering of social and sexual barriers and the rise of celebrity status meant that we were encouraged to behave as outrageously as possible. Scott and I did get up to some pretty adventurous things but they are best left unwritten here.

Instead imagine us spending daylight hours trawling through thrift shops looking for clothes and designs that we could knock off. He loved nothing more than rootling around thrift shops for that 1940s' frock or that fabulous 1950s' double-breasted man's coat . . . any item that had a manufacturing detail or something about the cut or the scale or the volume that he could work into a design in his forthcoming collection. He was great at finding a key piece, a combat pant or a utility jacket from Paragon at the intersection of Broadway and Fifth. Sometimes we'd go and spend hours at Kiehls on the Third Avenue, way down town around Twelfth Street, where we'd buy colognes and essences with unlikely names such as 'Morning Rain', 'Exquisite Rain' or vintage Patchouli. He had a great eye for judging the stuff we found both for himself and for his collection. But the pace of Scott's nightlife left me standing. He was always going on somewhere else until well into the small hours but I'd have to disappear home so that I could get to work the next day. I could never understand how, in the circumstances, he ran his business. But run it, he did. His clothes were young and sexy and, like myself, he was more known for his evening wear than his day clothes and though best at slithery jersey and delicate print chiffons and georgette, like me he was a tailor manqué. Like his American contemporaries, he had a very commercial ethos, although he marvelled at the shenanigans/fashion high jinks of, say, Zandra

Rhodes or Bill Gibb, in making one-off 'art' clothes. He
visualised his collections completely merchandised and hanging on racks in Bloomingdales or Saks and that is precisely what
happened.

He was fiercely proud of what he had achieved during the
sixties, being part of the vanguard of black designers to emerge
along with the civil rights movement: Willi Smith, Jon Haggins
and Stephen Burroughs. He was outwardly very confident and
relaxed, so I would be amazed when, late at night if an empty cab
passed without stopping, he'd say, 'That's because we're black.'

'Nonsense,' I'd retort. 'The guy probably didn't see us.'

But he was adamant and so often did this happen that I did
begin to doubt myself.

Scott lived on 39 and Third – not the smartest part of town
by some way but not bad – in a triplex above a dry-cleaner's. A
steepish flight of stairs led into his drawing room, high-
ceilinged with mirrored walls and long banquettes in beige
ultrasuede. Everywhere were objects he collected, 1920s' and
'30s' vases and statuettes. It was very much a 'front' room. He
was so overlooked at the back of the building that the blinds
were permanently down in his small sitting room, my favourite
room. It was painted forest green and so poorly lit that all you
could do in there was listen to fabulous NY soul and jazz
stations or to some of Scott's impressive record collection.
There was a red lacquer kitchen that was rarely used and in the
bathroom he had hung mirrors so an infinity of images
stretched out in front of you. The stylish formality of the lower
floor contrasted with the upper one, where nothing was
properly finished off. He kept his overflow of clothes in a small
box room where I used to sleep whenever I stayed there. The
only downside to the whole set-up was Scott's dog, a borzoi that
was far too big for the place. Scott was too lazy or too busy to
take it out often enough, although he did have a daily who

came in and cleaned up after it and may even have taken it out. I never felt that as a house-guest it was something I could criticise. It seemed better to keep quiet and take the poor creature for the odd walk myself.

The Coty Awards was a flamboyant fashion ceremony, the annual Oscars of the fashion world. It was hugely influential and important. That year, 1973, at the Lincoln Center, Ralph Lauren picked up the main award. He had just designed the costumes for the Robert Redford movie *The Great Gatsby*, which had heavily influenced the fashion market that year. Once again, it was a completely new experience for me. Everyone was out and about, all the good lookers and the models. It was much more than a single notch up from Bianca and the Arethusa back in sleepy old London. I was only too aware that I was moving very quickly and never had to wait long for the next 'up'. And I was loving every minute of it. Afterwards there were lots of different parties to choose from. Scott and I went to one at Joe Eula's. When New Yorkers throw those big parties, they do them with huge pizzazz and panache, and with no expense spared.

Eula was a brilliant fashion illustrator and his apartment was appropriately fabulous. It was in one of those expensive mid-town apartment buildings with impeccable parquet through-out. The place was heaving with beautiful people, from Halston to Liza Minelli. I hadn't been there long when I caught sight of Marion. I remembered seeing him modelling in *L'Uomo Vogue*. He was taller than me, perhaps 6 foot 3 and part-Indian, which gave him an extraordinary sculptured face. He was quite beautiful. I approached him with the most crass opening line, along the lines of, 'I'm an agent. Do you have a card?'

To his credit, he wasn't particularly impressed. 'Oh yeah?'

I persisted but didn't have to try too hard because he thought my clumsy overture was so funny that his interest was engaged.

I was astonished that it was so successful. After that I lost track of the party. That was the start of a close relationship that lasted till I left the States and a friendship that continued for years after that. Marion was from North Carolina and his career high to date was modelling the St Laurent fragrance Eau Libre campaign with Marie Helvin. He was also a catwalk model. Cool and stylish, he was in demand for all the best shows. He could as easily look like a toff as he could a working-class, down-country black person. Like Scott he had a knack for putting things together in very stylish ways but with Marion it was on a budget and more natural. Scott was more polished in his designer clothes but Marion had the edge in cool, able to look the business in trainers, baggy jeans and a reefer coat. As a model, he could do something sharp for Yves St Laurent or something homespun for Kenzo. His adaptability meant that he was incredibly popular and got plenty of work in Europe during the show seasons. He was the sort of model that every designer wants, one who can bring something of their own to the clothes.

He rented an apartment in Stuyvesant Street and by mid-October I had moved in with him. It was a nasty uncomfortable ground-floor flat which he shared with a friend. But because he had a peripatetic model's lifestyle, I suppose he always knew he wouldn't be there for long so it mattered less to him. As a place it was entirely unmemorable. We did make a good-looking couple though! While feeling less scrutinised for my behaviour in New York and able to see whoever I wanted, I was still not at ease with the emotional side of relationships. I tended to get bored with the physical side of things very quickly and was usually reluctant to make the necessary effort to carry on a relationship in those circumstances. However, with Marion, I shared many interests, so in a way he became more like a brother to me. The relationship was based on adoration on my side and a strong reciprocation on his – but I think it wasn't very even-handed. I didn't like the fact that I was always paying for things or lending him money – and he did expect that – and I never trusted him absolutely. I learned a lot from him though. He wasn't a sex fiend like Scott but was more reserved and sure of himself, certainly not one to go out trawling the bars. We used to walk a lot rather than take the subway or taxis simply because he liked to. I wasn't used to the closeness I had with him but missed him when he wasn't around.

I spent my first month in New York almost exclusively in Scott's company but after that I went around more with Marion, though sometimes we'd all go clubbing together. Both these guys were quite different from anybody I'd met before. I don't think it was anything to do with 'black bonding' but much more to do with the fact that we had common interests: music, fashion, style, restaurants. They introduced me to a different life, a different mood. And they were both inter-national. After New York, the next place I saw Scott was in London and Marion, in Paris.

Back at Bendel's, my hard work was monitored as the weeks went by and eventually they clearly felt confident enough to decide to show, not from the in-house showrooms, but at the Plaza Hotel where I had spent my first few nights in NY. They printed invitations:

Please come see
Bruce Oldfield's first collection
For Bendel's Studio
At breakfast, Friday, November 9th, 9.30 a.m.
The Palm Court at the Plaza

As if that weren't enough, the ad that appeared in the press read:

Bruce Oldfield
our superfind
is much too young to know so much about glamour –
the allure of bias-cut jersey
the muted colour mystique
the marvellous surprise of smocking
but never mind
if you come in and see his first collection
for Bendel's Fancy –
you'll know he knows.
From $150-$260
on 2 at 10 West 57th

I really felt I'd arrived.

I don't recall a lot about the show but I do remember choosing the models and Marion helping me by introducing me to some of the star girls of the time, Alva Chin, Pat Cleveland and Billy Blair – a recent clutch of black girls who were spearheading the black domination of the international fashion runways. The reason they were so good is that they could move so well to the music and were stylish interpreters for the designers, not walking regimentally in the old couture way but swaying and sashaying to the rhythm of the new disco sounds proliferating on the catwalk shows. Best of all they had attitude, as if to say, 'Look, honey, you may have thought that I wouldn't know how to do this 'cos I'm black but . . . watch out.'

The show was a success and I even got a standing ovation. It had good reviews from *Women's Wear Daily*, who had been watching my progress, and from the *New York Times'* fashion editor Bernadine Morris so I think we all felt confident that we had a winner on our hands. There was no reason for me to think that my future was anything but secure and I began to plan where I was to live in New York.

The bombshell came a few weeks later when I was told by Pat Tennant that there wouldn't be a job for me the following season. The reasons given were that the sales hadn't reached the projected targets and I think that there was some question as to whether or not Bendel's Studio would be continuing for much longer. Although I think I was let down gently it still came as a great shock and disappointment. Perhaps it had been a foolish idea to take a twenty-three-year-old straight from college who had never done a collection and believe he could pull it off. I felt that they hadn't been entirely honest with me and that they should have notified me of their intentions weeks earlier.

I was a given a week in which to pack up and go. I was sent to the airport on a bus with my tail between my legs to the strains of 'Midnight Train to Georgia' – mine and Marion's song. My departure was in stark contrast to my arrival – economy flight only and making my own way to and from the airports.

Manhattan had been a huge buzz from beginning to end. It's the only city that thrills in that way. What I got out of being there for those few months was wisdom. I acquired no technical experience but I learned from being lionised, then dropped like a stone. I learned not to believe my press or to assume that things would last. I adapted. Next time I would be prepared.

CHAPTER ELEVEN

November 1973. Back in London, it was time for the Tsaritsar show. In those days, Tsaritsar was a relatively unique venture. It had been set up in 1968 by Annette Worsley-Taylor and Tania Soskin, both of whom had worked for Dior before deciding to join forces to open a boutique for the smart young London set. They had high expectations, bags of energy and inspiration and their fingers were right on the pulse. When they opened, the London fashion scene was very limited with six main designers: Bill Gibb, John Bates, Yuki, Zandra Rhodes, Jean Muir and Thea Porter. Fashion was polarised between the semi-couture designer market and the thriving cheaper instant market, the new fast fashion of Mary Quant or Biba. The couture end of the market was mainly interested in evening wear or knit wear. Designer collections, as in clothes you might wear through the day and evening, were not something you found in the UK. Good young designers were emerging from fashion courses but there was absolutely no platform for their work. Annette and Tania spotted this and, apart from designing their own lines of clothes, aimed to target and promote new names in a way that hadn't previously happened. They put on fashion shows, showcasing the designers they thought would be the most successful and wholesaling the garments from the shop. When Tania broke her leg in a car accident, she and Annette decided they needed another designer to help grow the business. They talked to the PR Liz Shirley who suggested they take a look at the college end-of-year shows.

That year, after the St Martin's show, I was the name on everyone's lips. So Annette asked me to come over to the shop to discuss things. The first time she saw me, she still remembers glancing towards the front of the shop and there I was with Serena Sinclair, fashion editor of the *Daily Telegraph*, checking out the clothes. Cheek or reasonable behaviour? I thought it was quite reasonable. I wanted to know where my clothes were going and which other designers they'd be displayed alongside before agreeing to any contract.

When I returned from America, I had a number of designs ready to be made up into samples. The garments continued the soft and sexy jersey theme in two or three styles. Bendel's had allowed me to work on them while we waited to see the result of the show. Even in those days, I employed a professional pattern cutter to make the commercial flat patterns. I designed the collection and provided the workable sample patterns for a flat fee of £1,000. We weren't talking royalties. I was wise there. Another designer doing a freelance collection for them was Carlos Arias. I had met him before at shows and had always had difficulty with his incredibly quickfire Spanish accent. He would turn up in a flamboyant floor-length wolf-skin coat, his hands expressing what he was unable to articulate in English. He worked very differently to me, engendering an enormous amount of chaos. The samples were made above the shop where we could use the workroom and equipment to prepare our collections and we'd be around to oversee the fittings and so on. I remember once sitting there at one o'clock in the morning helping stitch pieces together at the last minute so Carlos's collection would be ready for the next day. In December, Tsaritsar held a press show in the shop.

During my stint at Bendel's, I had met Joan Burstein from

Browns, London's most prestigious fashion store. It's ironic that I had to go all the way to New York to make her decide that I was OK. She asked me to make some things for Browns. I made the garments myself in Brixton. Unlike those I did for Tsaritsar, those for Browns involved lots of smocking.

At this point I had a very clear attitude to life. I wanted to get things done and to move on up. Even now, once I have set my mind on something, I won't be deflected. If someone says, 'No, you can't do that,' my instinctive response is, 'Give me one good reason why not.' Of course I set myself restraints. I was realistic about what I could and couldn't become. I knew I wanted to be a famous designer so I found the right way of doing it. I recognised the value of publicity and set about finding ways to get it. Within a short time my clothes were getting a lot of press and I was being mentioned in the same breath as the established designers. Instead of shouting about my plans I just got on and carried them out. I was lucky in that I had an extraordinary ability to glide through things and slip past many obstacles.

On 1 December Linda got married. She had met Patrick, a cool young musician, through her friend Shirley and had come down to work at the Strand Palace Hotel on Piccadilly to be with him. They decided on a winter wedding at Lewisham Register Office. I didn't make the dress, which I think she may have bought up north with Mum, but did ask my friend Ivor Montlake if he would drive her in his white Mercedes. I know he and Anna came with me to the service although Linda had never met them before, but that's about all either of us can remember. It was a very small affair recorded in a fading black-and-white photo that shows us lined up as if in front of a firing squad. There was no money for a reception. The fact that they are still happily married to this day is testament to the fact that the size of the do has no bearing on the future.

Then, in January, Mum went into hospital for a routine hip operation. I had sent her flowers and was expecting to go up to visit her after she came out so it was a total shock when Aunt Marie called me to tell me that she had died, having a fatal heart attack during surgery. I called Linda who was by then living in Lewisham and we travelled up to Durham with Barry. I remember we sat on the train in silence, none of us able to express what her death meant to us. We stayed at Tweed Road. It was purgatory. The tiny house was lifeless and cold having been empty since Mum had gone into hospital. It was all very poignant because there was nothing of much personal significance in the house. She had never had enough money to treat herself to anything special. It really brought home to me that anything she had always went on us. Under the tatty old sofa in the front room we found a copy of *Vogue* featuring my clothes, kept there specially so Mum could whip it out and show off my success to visitors. On her bedroom dressing table stood the unopened bottle of cologne I had brought back from my school visit to Paris. I thought that it was so sad that she never used it, saving it for special occasions that hadn't arrived. There weren't enough beds for us so the pre-family-funeral tension exploded in a great argument – in this case about who should sleep where – so by the next morning we were all three feeling tired, scratchy and emotional.

The funeral had been organised by Aunt Marie to take place in Durham Crematorium and afterwards we went to hers for tea. I can remember how quiet it was when we first arrived, all standing round uncomfortably not knowing what to say, the only sound being the solemn tick of her grandfather clock. Eventually the ice was broken in true style with a tiff between Barry and me over my unasked-for assumption of responsibility for the proceedings with Linda stepping in to shut us up. I don't know what we were all feeling. Stunned and sad, I can only imagine now. When parents die, it brings home the fact that you are next in line. It's a chilling moment but perhaps easier to shake off when you are as young as we were. I was more pragmatic. For me, her death meant that I no longer had anyone who was concerned with what I did. Not that I wanted her approval and recently I'd been so busy that I hadn't gone home as much as perhaps she would have liked. I also had the strong feeling that I no longer had anyone who I needed to be concerned about. I was on my own.

I was in charge of clearing the house. Gradually the cupboards were emptied and we decided what to do with her few possessions. Linda kept Mum's favourite necklace of carved Whitby jet and gold while I took lots of her old photos and her bangle. The Burts stepped in to help with the furniture, getting the few bits that Linda wanted down to London and getting rid of the rest for us. They were very kind.

The worst thing that happened after her death was that Janet, still only fourteen, was put into Aycliffe Reform School. It was absolutely disgraceful. We were all very unhappy about it but there was nothing we could do in the face of Barnardo's bureaucracy. Today they would have dealt with her very differently. Her family and the local community would be directly involved in any decisions about her care and Janet's opinions on her own future would have been taken into account. Not so then.

When I got back to London, all I could think about was how I wanted to cut all ties and run. After the spring show at the Chelsea Rendez-vous where I showed alongside Carlos Arias and Tania Soskin, I signed an agreement with Tsaritsar committing me to designing two more exclusive collections of twelve to eighteen evening and cocktail dresses. The first one was due at the end of the year, so although I still had my heart set on being an English design success, I had time to do something different for a few months and the lure of Paris, the epicentre of world fashion, seemed to beckon.

In February, Charlotte Rampling was photographed for the cover of Andy Warhol's *Interview* magazine. This was an incredibly cool publication that basically celebrated people for being famous – famous for being beautiful, famous for being a good dancer, a good actress, and famous for being a good fashion designer. This was nothing like the B-list celebrity fanzines of today. You really did have to be good at what you did. It seemed to me to be a pivotal moment in magazine publishing because it was distributed worldwide and read by the international in-crowd. It was part of the demi-mondaine café society that has always been with us, now celebrated in print. I was phoned long distance.

'Hello. This is Rosemary Kent from *Interview* magazine in New York.'

'Yeah. Sure.'

'No, truly. I've got Charlotte Rampling here at a shoot and she would sure love to speak with you.'

And she did. She was contracted to star in Terence Young's *Jackpot* and wanted to meet up with me to discuss the possibility of my designing her costumes. I didn't need to be asked twice. This was potentially a huge break for me in terms of publicity although we didn't get together until August in Milan.

Around that time I was still seeing a lot of Colin Barnes. He was fantastically encouraging to me because he admired the speed at which I did things and my rapid trajectory through fashion circles. I quite often used to go round to his place in the evenings for supper – usually rack of lamb, green beans, bread and cheese, and a bottle or two of wine. When I told him of my plans to go to Paris he loaned me £100. I was able to repay him later but it was all I needed to enable me to give up the Santley Street flat and leave London in May.

For £20 a week, I rented a tiny flat in the Rue des Anglais, so-called because at the turn of the twentieth century, it was full of brothels where all the visiting Englishmen came to pleasure themselves. It is a tiny dog-leg near the Place Maubert metro at the bottom of Boulevard St Germain, just a short wiggle away from the Seine and Notre Dame. So central, I couldn't believe my luck. The narrow street was entirely residential apart from the Manhattan Club, a gay bar in the next-door building's basement. Otherwise there were just lots of tiny apartments in true Parisian style. Mine was on the fifth floor – no lift in those days – of a building that had been very well converted. All the residents were tremendously self-contained. I never knew anyone else in the building apart from exchanging the odd '*Bonjour*,' or '*Bonsoir*' in passing.

The apartment itself was a stylish white-walled studio flat with its own bathroom and a kitchen that was tucked into a cupboard. There was a mattress on the slate floor and a table and chair. I don't suppose I needed much else, although I did buy a tape recorder so I could listen to music. It was pretty dark with its one not very large window overlooking the street but it did have the benefit of being quiet apart from the distinctive omnipresent hum you get living in any city. I don't remember ever doing any cooking, although there was a market in the Place Maubert. I must have existed on baguettes with jam and coffee. Of course it's so easy in Paris to go to one of a thousand cafés or bistros and just pass the time. It was amazing how long you could eke out a *sandwiche jambon* and a *café crème*.

By night, I was a club animal. Paula Marie, a girl friend, and Marion were occasionally around and I would go to the Club Sept with one or other of them. Never together. Paula Marie would try to get me to go to the straight clubs like Castells but the music was never as good. My relationship with Marion was inevitably much more casual than when we were in New York so when we did meet he made few demands on me. Club Sept was the place to go and the place to be seen. On the ground floor was a restaurant too expensive for us, so we skirted it and went downstairs to the club. The décor was pretty hard edge with a lot of art deco style red lacquer and mirrors. The music was fevered and the best to be found in Paris. There was a great atmosphere – good dancers and lots of beautiful girls and boys. We'd bump into people who were like-minded, alike in skin colour, in absolute gorgeousness, in musical tastes and career. There'd be Kenzo and his assistants, St Laurent, Karl Lagerfeld, Jerry Hall, Stirling St Jacques and the rest so it was a great place to network and have fun. The Parisians loved blacks and exotics, seeing them as a bit different and elegant, lionising models like Marie Helvin, Tina Chow and Pat Cleveland for their ability to showcase Paris's favourite industry – La Mode. At the same time it was a bit like New York – very international and free of any class stigma. In that atmosphere, you were never sure who you'd end up in bed with or where. It didn't matter and besides, half the time you were too drunk to do anything. Sometimes Scott would be in town too. I remember laughing with him at a sign, somewhere around the Rue Richelieu, for a tailor's called 'Bruce and Scott'.

The lynchpin of the fashion set was Antonio, the most important illustrator in the business. He was the darling of the fashion editors who commissioned page after page of his illustrations in international editions of *Vogue*, *L'Officiel* and *Harpers*. This made him the obvious choice for fashion and cosmetics firms with big advertising budgets. He lived in an elegant apartment on the rue de Rennes with his partner Juan with a huge gang of people that hung out round them, its make-up depending on who was in town. There was Paloma Picasso, Jerry Hall, Grace Jones, Jessica Lange, Marion, Marie Helvin, Tina Chow – all beautiful creatures who knew how to enjoy themselves. At one party I remember Jerry showing off her Texan leg-wrestling prowess. This unusual sport involved wrapping your legs round someone else's and then bringing them down. Jerry could beat anybody.

We used to congregate around the corner from Antonio's apartment either in the drug store or in the Café Flore. Café Flore had its own distinguished past and by the sixties had become a hang-out for the fashion world as well as for artists, actors and members of the intelligentsia. If we were particularly flush, we'd take a pavement table – a bit chilly but with a great view of who was coming and going and a place where you were easily spotted if a friend was walking by. Very occasionally we'd drop into the prohibitively expensive (to us, at least) Brasserie Lipp or go to La Coupole in Boulevard Montparnasse. It was a very free time: free love, free lunch, free coffees. People would drop in and buy you a coffee and you'd sit for hours chatting.

Although I'd been to Paris before, this was a very different experience. I like the fact that because of its size, most significant places are within easy walking distance of one another. I like the elegance of the city and the way the Seine is such a part of daily life. What stands out for me about that time is wandering around the city, through the narrow streets of the Marais, along the grandiose Haussmann boulevards, through the dust-bowl of the Tuileries, along the banks of the Seine. It was so nice to walk. To get from my flat to Club Sept, I'd cross the Seine, go through the courtyard of the Louvre – pre I. M. Pei's pyramid – to the Palais Royale, up the Avenue de l'Opéra into the Rue St Anne. That triangle was our travelling zone. Nothing cheap even in those days. I remember introducing Barry to Paris one weekend. We went up the Eiffel Tower and I had such bad vertigo that I had to get out at the first floor and walk down. But that was even more terrifying because of all the fretwork on the cast-iron treads. I almost died of fright. Sadly I didn't take proper advantage of Paris in a cultural sense but you rarely do when you live in a place and certainly not at that age, although I dimly remember going to some of the galleries and I definitely went to several concerts in Notre Dame.

After a hard night clubbing, I'd get up at about eleven, work for a few hours and then get on the road. When I say 'work', by today's standards I did very little – just enough drawings to get by. Sometime I might have appointments and sometimes I just went cold-calling. I'd been lucky enough to find a surrogate Colin, one Jacques de Hornois, who was fantastically important in directing me towards certain fashion houses and making sure I knew the top people to contact. Yves St Laurent and Dior would pay 500 francs for a sketch and they were certainly in the market to buy in those days. I sold shoe designs to Yves St Laurent and Mario Valentino, furs to Maurice Kotler and Christian Dior and worked on a cheap range for Anna Marks, ex-wife of Monty Marks. At one point, I thought about going into modelling – anything to earn a crust. I put a moody portfolio together but for reasons I don't recall, it never came to anything. I was on the look-out for a job. If I'd been offered one, I'd certainly have taken it. I needed to get some of the technical expertise that by then I was admitting to myself that I lacked. In Europe, particularly in Italy and France, there were huge quality manufacturers that we didn't have in the UK. When I was starting out, the UK could do big production lines but only on basic quality, low-end and middle-of-the-road fashion. At the other end of the market, we could do couture and Savile Row tailoring but we have never been able to turn out that high-end ready-to-wear fashion that the French and Italians do so well. They not only have the market for that kind of fashion but also the manufacturing capabilities, the marketing budget and know-how.

In August, I flew to Milan where Charlotte Rampling was filming *The Night Porter*. I stayed in the Irina Hotel in a district bereft of much street lighting so it was rather like being in one of those grainy 1950s movies, with tarts and larger-than-life characters slinking past in the shadows. Charlotte was staying in a pension behind the Duomo with her husband Brian and her young son Barnaby. I remember he grizzled distractingly through our conversation and she was very attentive to him. She was fabulous, very down to earth and practical – completely the opposite to my other star client, Bianca. We hit it off from the start and she asked me to make the costumes for *Jackpot*, which was due to go into production early the following year. They ranged from evening dresses to suits which I'd never done before. I went through the script myself and worked out the areas where different outfits would be needed – twenty-three in all. Then I went through my ideas with the wardrobe mistress and whoever was in charge of the budget. Naturally I was racking up the number of garments as much as I could and they were reining me back, pointing out where the same thing could be worn twice. Charlotte had her own input, in as far as what she thought would be true to the character. Luckily for me she was playing a woman who was just my kind of client. Her life consisted of business meetings and parties so she had to look professional and gorgeous. Funnily enough, what I enjoyed most about the job was finding the accessories to go with the outfits. As a fashion designer, there's nothing more frustrating than only creating part of a look and nothing worse than seeing one of your designs teamed up with the most inappropriate shoes, hat and bag.

We didn't start making the outfits until I was back in London later in the year when Charlotte would come into Tsaritsar for fittings or I'd go on fabulous expenses-paid trips down to the South of France. She was staying on the Cap d'Antibes at la Domaine de la Garoupe, an exclusive gated estate, with three or four houses in the ground of a very palatial principal residence. The film company had rented the very pretty Le Clocher (Bell Tower) for her. I took the clothes down but I managed to make sure I had a holiday between fittings and fashion shoots. For one of them, Norman Parkinson came down and took a series of shots of Charlotte on the rocks in a pale grey chiffony job for *Vogue*. It was in January and full of cold, bright sunshine. My over-riding impressions are of mimosa, clear blue skies and crisp days. Most of my time was spent talking clothes but we went out to St Tropez for fun and to the occasional party at Lady Oonagh Oranmore & Browne's house on the estate and once we had lunch with the film stars Cappucine and Philippe Noiret. One night we went to a gala opening where I remember Charles Aznavour serenading Charlotte. It was my first experience of the red carpet and yet another part of the learning curve as I consciously held back to let Charlotte take centre stage with her husband Brian. I disliked the rudeness of the paparazzi who shouted for the stars' attention and waved the other members of the party out of the way. But I accepted it pragmatically – this was the business of stardom and Charlotte was on a different level. Afterwards we went to a gay club where we met a European royal whose boyfriend took a shine to me. For the rest of the holiday, he'd turn up at Le Clocher in a red Ferrari and we'd drive around ostentatiously and very fast before going to one of his friends' places for a tryst.

While waiting for the film to start, we tried to get the producer to pay what he already owed us. He was a complete rogue who would keep us all hanging about downstairs in the lobby of the Carlton Hotel, Cannes while he did a runner out of the back door. Perhaps understandably he couldn't face us, knowing we had no idea that the whole project was on the point of going belly up. Indeed, in the end, *Jackpot* never happened. The plug was pulled, but only after I'd made all twenty-three costume changes. We'd stake out the Carlton Hotel, trying to see if we could spot the producer creeping in or out. But either he made off with whatever money there was or, more likely, he couldn't raise what he needed. This could have been disastrous for me, despite the fact I was still working for Tsaritsar, but Charlotte stepped in and saved me by buying all the costumes I'd designed. I racked the whole thing up as part of my learning curve.

As far as I was concerned, Charlotte was the perfect client – feminine, liberated, not overdressed, sensual not overtly sexy and with an aversion to clutter or anything trendy. She wasn't at all demanding, had a very good body and liked things to fit well. Working with her made a huge difference to my ideas about what women want. Whenever the press did a story about her, there she'd be wearing Bruce Oldfield. Over the next few years we became very associated, in the way that, a decade later, I was to be with the Princess of Wales.

CHAPTER TWELVE

Arriving back from Paris with nowhere to stay of my own, I had no choice but to move in with a series of obliging friends and acquaintances. First was Johnny Gairdner, a successful model and friend of Annette's. He rented me his flat in a purpose-built block in Elystan Street, just off the King's Road at the heart of Chelsea. It couldn't have been better in terms of location though it did have a tendency to steam up with condensation, reminding me of the old days at Tweed Road.

The one memory that particularly stands out, and to an extent characterises this period of my life, has to be going with David Reeson, an illustrator that I had met at Colin's, to the Drury Lane Theatre to see Patti Labelle in concert. The show was a visual feast in itself but I had taken a half tab of something with David beforehand, which intensified the whole experience beyond my wildest imaginings. Neither of us had a clue what we'd taken – that's how stupid we were but it's what it was like then. Nobody gave a damn. My limited experience with the Black Bombers in Harrogate and with the occasional joint had suggested drugs weren't exactly my thing. A few drags and I'd just slide down the wall wherever I was standing and remain in a heap until it wore off. However this was something else altogether. Only afterwards we found out it was mescalin.

I'm normally a pretty reserved person but as the drug began to take effect, I was up dancing like a mad man in the stalls at

the front of the stage. The audience's clapping hands transformed into flapping doves' wings while every other movement
became impossibly exaggerated. It was kaleidoscopic, surreal.
In the chaos, David and I got separated. I was in a hopeless state
with no idea where I was going. Fortunately I was rescued by a
guy bearing an uncanny resemblance to Jesus – or so I thought.
He was Lebanese and knew exactly what was happening to me.
As he helped me to his place past the British Museum, I
remember the railings zinging in front of my eyes like a Bridget
Riley painting. My saviour was a university student and, of all
things, we apparently sat and read Hopkins and Wordsworth
together – a very odd couple, in all respects. The next day, he
told me that while I'd read, my hand had hovered sensitively
over each word. Me? I couldn't remember a thing. Never again.
No. Drugs definitely don't do it for me. I don't like being out
of control and mescalin especially gave me a jolt, an experience
not to be repeated.

Meanwhile I was trying to establish myself back in business in
the UK with two collections for Tsaritsar, but the economic
climate was far from favourable. The property market had
collapsed, many of the small banks were going under and the
larger banks started calling in their loans. The 1974 stock
market crash spelled disaster for many small businesses. By the
end of the year, things had become very tight and the future of
Tsaritsar stood or fell by its next collection.

By this stage, Tania was already making plans to move to
Paris while Annette and I had thought about raising funding
together for a Bruce Oldfield company. We had put an
ambitious business plan together whereby 'Bruce Oldfield'
would become a big designer label that would be properly
manufactured, properly shown and sold in a big way. I think I
rather let her do the business planning while remaining pretty
laissez-faire myself. To set something up at the level we envisaged

would need substantial backing and Annette was absolutely clear that she didn't want to be involved in running anything on a shoestring. In fact that came as something of a relief to me. At the time I was a little ambivalent about our working together. We had something of a love/hate relationship and quite often disagreed. We were alike in that we were both ambitious and knew what we wanted but sometimes our routes to getting there conflicted. I'm sure she found me frustrating to deal with but from my point of view, I liked Annette very much but I sometimes felt she was too keen to tie me down so she could run my business and I was absolutely not going to let anyone else do that.

Despite these set-backs, Annette was never one to sit twiddling her thumbs. She had something else up her sleeve. During the sixties, English fashion had received a decided shot in the arm from Mary Quant and all the other boutique designers. But since then the perception of the rest of the world was that it had become rather dated and uninspired, with few designers that could match those in France, Italy or America. The Clothing Export Council (CEC) held fashion exhibitions in the Grosvenor House Hotel or in various exhibition halls, where the problem for any small designers was that they were always presented as an intrinsic part of the great rag trade. The result was that the buyers and press looked at their garments and were simply outraged by the prices. They were used to what the British were best at: stack 'em high, sell 'em cheap. They just didn't understand the structures of our businesses and what we were doing. I might be showing twenty labour-intensive, high-quality dresses while, for example, on the next stand Wallis or Jaeger might be making two hundred at a lower price point. To understand the designer brands, it wasn't appropriate to show them in such a cheap and cheerful setting. On the other hand there wasn't an alternative platform in

Britain from which young designers could successfully market their work. The French showed young designers much better and Annette had talked to me about the idea of going to France and exhibiting in the designer section of the *Prêt à Porter* exhibition but I knew exactly what would happen. The few British designers that turned up would be totally lost in a tiny corner of a huge exhibition hall. It would be a disaster. But it struck me instead that maybe she could initiate something new back home. She needed to find a group of designers who were prepared to work together and the quality of whose work would match the marketing concept.

Once Annette had got the promised support of the Clothing Export Council in the bag, she swung straight into action and was on the telephone, starting with the established top designers. Quickly realising that she wasn't going to get anywhere with them, she moved on to the younger ones, including me. I was already getting good coverage in the fashion press but it wasn't enough on its own so of course I, just like the others, was desperate to find a way to show my work, raise my profile and make some money. That's when she began to get some more positive feedback. Gradually her plan gathered momentum.

It was vital that whatever show she put together couldn't be mistaken for a mass-market fashion exhibition so she had to find the perfect environment for marketing and selling us. The Ritz it was. She also brought in Percy Savage, a very established PR man, who knew and could attract the international buyers. He was a savvy, flamboyant Australian who had lived for years in Paris where he'd worked as a textile designer for Lanvin, Nina Ricci and Dior among others. He had put on fashion shows there and had started to do the same thing in the UK. He took up the baton Annette offered with relish.

The show had to be run on a very tight budget and organising it in principle was, of course, quite a different thing to organising it in fact. The Clothing Export Council's petty cash float ran to standard chrome shop rails for the garments and a small bunch of violets on every stand so it was all pretty basic. Invitations were sent to everyone we knew. There was no money for models, so we begged those we knew to help out. Grace Coddington, then a senior fashion editor at *Vogue* stepped in to model for me – a great coup as far as I was concerned. My collection was made up of day and evening separates in silky jersey again.

Nobody had any idea how the show would be greeted. Neither had anyone anticipated the influence of Percy Savage. The doors opened and in he came like the Pied Piper of Hamlyn. About five hundred people followed him into the tiny space reserved for the expected one hundred. The front row of chairs was already occupied by the executive of the Clothing Export Council. There was no room for this sudden influx of people and the manager of the Ritz was having a fit but more chairs were produced, more drinks laid on and somehow the whole thing happened.

And the event itself? It was a wild success. My collection was described by *The Sunday Times* as 'soft and sexy: the most distinctive feature is the intricate smocking and pin-tucking done by hand . . . He prefers to work with plain fluid fabrics which can be tucked, smocked, embroidered and hand-painted'.

Everybody was excited because grouping and showing the young designers together for the first time was viewed as a powerful statement. We – Wendy Dagworthy, Juliet Dunn, Carlos Arias, Anna Beltrao, Catherine Buckley, Sue and Helen, Ann Buck, Yuki, Jane Cattlin and me – were dubbed the New Wave. At last we had a profile and a platform for selling – all thanks to Annette.

But the show had far greater significance than that. It was the seed from which something much bigger and very important for British fashion would emerge. There was a real sense of everyone trying to get London fashion back on track, of making London Fashion Week as exciting to visit as Paris. The Clothing Export Council wanted to capitalise on the success of the show at the Ritz so a second was arranged for October that year, 1974, this time in Le Coq d'Or in Stratton Street. Mindful of the chaos engendered by the first show, the CEC steered clear of Percy Savage and hired Tony Porter to handle the PR. This time my collection was in a slightly sportier vein than before with well defined lines and colours – a lot of red and white glazed cotton with lots of tab detail – and an element of the throwaway about it. I had been thinking about it since I'd worked with Charlotte the previous spring. But the time wasn't right. It wasn't what the buyers wanted then so it didn't sell particularly well. That was the last collection I did for Annette at Tsaritsar before she was forced to close down the business in February 1975 – a financial catastrophe for her.

After the two New Wave shows, the CEC, who were financed by the rest of the industry, felt bound to respond to various manufacturers' disquiet about the poor return they felt they were getting on their money. The CEC decided to take the New Wave out of its rarified atmosphere and make it the highlight of the Fashion Week at Earls Court. Annette was incandescent. This was exactly what she didn't want. Nonetheless some of the designers felt that for stability's sake they should go along with the CEC's plans. Undaunted, Annette set up a new independent group including Caroline Charles, Anna Beltrao, Ann Buck, Salmon and Greene, Shuji Tojo, Hamilton Cruise, Kay Cosserat, Pinkertons and – again – me. Anna Beltrao was married to a Brazilian diplomat, and our meetings were held in their plush apartment in Park Mansions where, accompanied by a maid and canapés, we plotted the new organisation in style.

The first thing we needed was an official name – so the London Designer Collections was born.

The first show was held from 10-12 April 1975 at the Montcalm Hotel, a small elegant Georgian townhouse a stone's throw from Marble Arch. The exhibition was to be held in the basement – all very 1970s, with acres of chrome, palm trees and dark brown suede walls and, again, the chrome clothes rails. Everyone pooled the resources on their buyers' list and invitations to the top-end buyers were written overnight. Penny Graham and Roger Hutchins organised the shows. Percy Savage came in to handle the PR. I roped in Ninivah Khomo, Rifat Ozbek and Jacques Azagury as work placements from St Martin's to help sew on buttons and do general finishing for me. I'd met them when I'd been asked to do a critique on their work and they all became friends, particularly Ninivah. She was a stunner, half native South African, half white, who made the most of her looks with tightly scraped-back gelled hair, bright-red glossy lipstick and billowing black clothes – very stylish.

Then, the night before the LDC début, the whole of the Earls Court building force went out on strike. They left the stands only half built for the CEC exhibition so the place was in chaos. The LDC was flooded with calls from frantic designers pleading to be able to show at the Montcalm with us. In the end, most of the hotel was taken over with all the extra designers exhibiting in suites on the first floor and everything else going on in the basement and top floor as originally planned. All the manufacturers and buyers came over to see what was going on and loved it. They loved the comfort. They loved the classiness. They loved the clothes.

That October, the LDC moved to the Inn on the Park, where there was room for twenty-five designers to show in the ballroom. 'The Great has been put back into Britain' screamed *Women's Wear Daily* in the US. Suddenly everyone wanted to be a member of the LDC. It was not so easy. Every application was carefully vetted to ensure the existing degree of exclusivity and quality was retained. Finally, Percy Savage decided to set up a separate show for the unlucky ones across the road in the InterContinental called the London Collections. We then asked Annette to set up a proper office, the London Designer Collections Association. This was the first formal trade organisation ever set up for designers. Its establishment marked a momentous step for British fashion and established the pattern it would take in the future.

With all this going on, it seemed the moment for me to settle down and set up my own business. I'd got to a point where I needed to stop jumping around all over the place, consolidate my ideas, provide my life with a bit of structure and exploit all the publicity that I'd had over the previous two years. In 1975, I moved into a house in Shawfield Street running off the King's Road, that belonged to the boyfriend of a friend from Ravensbourne. It was a small two-storey terraced house with enough room for me, Tania Soskin's sister Kira who shared the rent, her cat, and, most importantly, room to start my business. I did the cutting on the ground floor where I slept while the main room on the first floor became the showroom.

Annette was right behind me but thought I needed a good business person as a partner if I was going to have a hope of survival. She introduced me to Anita Richardson. I say 'introduced' but apparently we had met already at Tsaritsar although I don't have the slightest memory of it. Anita had been working there, most recently helping Annette close down the business. I didn't have strong views as to whether or not this was the right move for me but I was so suggestible that I just agreed. I biked round to the house on the Lower Richmond Road where she lived with her husband, Kevin Carroll. She cooked dinner for us, the first of many, and I ended up proposing that we started working together. That's how our long partnership began, although the idea of our becoming business partners didn't arise for another six months or so. Why I didn't remember her, I don't know, because she had a big personality, very friendly, very easy and not 'fashion' – which I especially liked. She was tall, big and blonde, with a great earthy sense of humour. She was a practical businesswoman, particularly good at the production and sales side of things, and she certainly didn't want to steal my thunder. I was definitely still the star of the show.

When the time came, we used the accounting firm of Hill Vellacott to help us with our business plan and accounts, Ivor drew up the legal papers ratifying the company and Mr Weekes, my obliging bank manager at Lloyds on Bromley High Street, gave us an overdraft facility of £1,500. We were in business. The loan bought just enough fabric to produce the first dress range under my own name. Within about a month Anita told me she was pregnant. It didn't seem like the most auspicious of starts but as it turned out it made not the slightest bit of difference to us.

We started selling to a number of boutiques but our options were limited because in those days there were only a handful of shops that stocked designer wear in any serious way.

These customers were obviously incredibly important to us because they provided a way of showcasing the merchandise. Anita worked hard to make sure it happened so over the next few years we developed good friendships with the owners. Among them, was Suzy Gold who owned Wardrobe. She's a clever marketing woman with a pragmatic approach to her business who specifically targeted the working woman and really wanted to help us develop our business. Lorette Shiner had four or five Originelle shops so was the one store who got us doing volume, buying thirty of a style when Suzy could usually only buy four or five. I remember a slip of a dress that we did for her in matte jersey with satin piping round the collar. It was very simple, got a page in *Harpers* and was used by Suzy for advertising. We must have done about 120 of them for her. The obvious problem was the manufacturing of that sort of number. It was hard finding anyone in the UK with the capacity to turn out the quality, and the orders were nowhere near big enough to enable us to produce them in Italy.

We sold across the British Isles, in Dublin, to Pat Crowley, to Joan Ponting in Birmingham, Little Black Dress in Leeds and Julie Fitzmaurice in Harrogate. There was Smudge Whiteman and her husband who owned Chic of Hampstead and the folks at Diagonal in Guildford. In Scotland we sold to Jenners where I remember the buyer fussing: 'Och, I do think we need a sleeve on that one. We don't want to show those wee whiskers, do we?' Get a razor, darling! Our relationship with these people was strong until everything went pear-shaped at the end of the seventies when everybody's business suffered badly.

I clearly couldn't do all the work to supply so many orders myself so we had to employ staff for the first time. We certainly had a part-time pattern cutter who I helped and I cut some of the samples but we also used a number of outworkers to help make up the garments. Anita introduced me to Felix and Judith Wolkenfeld who over the years were to become an essential part of our business. They had both worked with Anita at Angela Gore and Annacat. A Jewish couple, they had emigrated to the UK before the war. They had a young family and a marriage made in heaven. Judith was to become another of my 'mothers' and has been a close friend ever since. She had trained at the London Fashion College to become a superb seamstress while Felix was a highly skilled pattern cutter. When I met them, they ran their own dressmaking business from Blackstock Road in Highbury, where they had a small workroom, essentially a cutting room with four machines, where they worked with a finisher. They produced 'CMT' (Cut, Make and Trim) work. Felix did the cutting while Judith turned her hand to everything.

I'd take them the sketches, fabric and patterns then leave them to it, visiting them about twice during the whole manufacturing process just to check how they were getting on. Occasionally slight changes might have to be made to a pattern or I might alter a detail on a sketch but I knew they were so professional and worked to such a high standard, I could trust them to get on with things. With their invaluable skills, skills that were largely dying out by the seventies, they soon became not only essential to the business but very much part of the family. They were superb at producing small quantities of high quality and I was much happier keeping it that way. We always went wrong when we tried to cope with larger numbers and quality inevitably slipped. This was a constant disagreement between Anita and I in terms of where the business should go. I wanted to stay with high-quality garments but Anita's prime concern was to try to increase the business. Understandably, she was much less interested in the fine detail of the clothes and, in any event, that was not particularly part of her remit.

It was about this time that Victor came back into my working life. I was working incredibly long hours and becoming more competent and confident in my designs, albeit my methods were sometimes somewhat untrained and unconventional. Victor's experience, speed and accuracy were invaluable to me. He came round every Thursday and at weekends. We'd sit puzzling over ways to translate my drawings into wearable garments, listening to music and swapping ideas. One weekend, Victor remembers me putting a skirt on the stand and playing with it until I worked out that by twisting the skirt 180 degrees on the lining, the fabric would spiral round the body and create a harem effect. The jersey also lent itself to making complimentary reversible T-shirts in brilliantly contrasting colours.

In those days I used to do everything on a bike, including delivering to *Vogue*. I'd cycle round to see the girls there – Mandy Clapperton, Sheila Wetton, Grace Coddington, Felicity Clark – taking them a latest sample.

'What do you think of that?'

'Yeah, we like it. Can you do it in white for the shoot we've got coming up on Thursday?'

It was as simple as that. I'd leap back on the bike, belt round Hyde Park Corner and get on with what they wanted. I loved all that. I'm particularly indebted to the editor, Sheila, who was then probably in her sixties, chic as hell with sleeked back grey hair. She was very lady of the manor but with a mouth like a fishwife. Hilarious and very supportive. A lot of the *Vogue* pictures I had in the seventies were thanks to her and Grace and of course they made a huge difference to my business.

One month after the 1975 LDC show at the Montcalm, we had £8,000 worth of orders with another anticipated £6–7,000 to come from appointments in the following two weeks. We met our overdraft limit by buying more fabric to make the orders for the customers we knew would pay within the week. That in turn gave us enough to pay the seamstresses and pattern cutters with enough to invest in more fabric. Hand to mouth it may have been but we were in business and in business we meant to stay. It was at about this time that we brought in Lindy Woodhead to handle our PR. In that business, you're only as good as your last account and hers were top notch – Missoni, Walter Albini, Daniel Hechter. So she was hot and a great person for us at a time when we were getting an extraordinary amount of press coverage in the top fashion magazines, most importantly *Vogue* and *Harpers & Queen*, which placed us just where we wanted to be. She interfaced between the press and the designers, finding opportunities for doing shows and bringing in new customers. She introduced me to Annabel Jones (Lady Astor) who became my first 'nob' client and who used my clothes in the catalogues she produced for her jewellery. Once I was persuaded to appear in the catalogue myself, playing chess with Rachel Ward.

The problem facing Anita and me was that we were running a severely under-financed company. Success in fashion depends on a regular flow of cash. You start every season with a deficit, having spent money making a sample collection and showing it. In those days, however expensive the garments were to produce, a show could add anything between £5,000 and £10,000 to your costs, depending on the location, the models, the accessories, the staff and whatever extras you lay on for the clients, with another £3,000 for an exhibition stand of your own. Today it could add anything up to £100,000. Once the buyers and manufacturers have ordered what they want, you have to buy the fabric, pay for it to be made up, pay for it to sit until the whole order is complete then pay for it to be shipped. Then you sit and wait to be paid. That could take thirty days, sixty days, some times never. All the while you owe your creditors who are beginning to bang on your door.

In the meantime, there's the rent, the rates, the staff to pay and you've got to live. You've also got to pay for the next set of sampling that has to be financed and shown before revenue appears from the previous season. You're almost always treading close to the edge. It can be a nail-biting situation and this front-loaded finance with no certainty of a return is what makes fashion such a high-risk business which banks are loath to touch. However Anita was the one who could charm the bank manager every season and so we kept going.

It was here that we made the first of our bank changeovers. We were introduced to Ted Emerson by Suzy Gold of

Wardrobe. He was one of the old school of bankers operating at a time when managers were given a great deal of latitude to decide for themselves to whom the bank's money should be lent. Hill Samuel in St James's had a tendency to loan to slightly more creative businesses, particularly artists, and Ted was refreshingly receptive to Anita and me. He recalls that I arrived with a portfolio of sketches and press coverage and was very cocky. Anita, on the other hand, was armed with figures and projections. In a way that was how we marked out our territory. We moved to Hill Samuel and stayed with them for many years. In 1981, they even let us hold a show in the bank. Ted left shortly after we joined them but was always there in the background with sound advice when times were rocky on how best to tackle any problem in the prevailing financial climate – invaluable help indeed.

Apart from organising the finances, it can be hard finding the people who'll make the garments to the quality required in the quantity ordered. If, as in our case, the garments are being made in relatively small quantities, it's impossible to get geared up mechanically as a larger manufacturer would. Because it's fashion, everything changes with every season. It's not as if we were making something like a Lacoste polo shirt that remains the same for fifty years. That only requires the establishment of a manufacturing system that can churn them out endlessly. It can't be done with fashion clothing here. In England, we don't have the set-up, the sophistication, the flexibility or the will to allow design ingenuity to be embraced within the production line. That's why the designer market has never properly succeeded in the UK. Big businesses don't see potential in fashion and we aren't good at marketing our ideas and talents. Banks are scared of the amount of pump-priming money and the constant marketing/advertising spend. Really successful British designers make their money abroad, working with big operations in France, Italy and Japan, manufacturing products under licence.

There were times when Anita and I couldn't afford to pay the workers, never mind ourselves. When business was good, we could take people on and when it wasn't, we would have to be ruthless and cut right back, laying staff off where we could or at least reducing their hours. I can remember sitting in Hyde Park, the only place where we could discuss our staff's future without being overheard, trying to work a way through our financial dilemmas. One day I even had to flog an antique light of mine so that we could pay our seamstress Emilia's wages because we couldn't manage without her.

At the beginning, it was always difficult to get credit from the fabric companies or to find willing manufacturers, either because they didn't know our name or because of the small quantities we wanted to produce. However over three or four seasons, people began to like working with us and that we paid the bills so things picked up. We had to learn the business side quickly and how to separate design from commerciality. Despite us always running back and forth to the bank, the business surely began to grow.

All my energies were consumed running it. Then we had word from up north that, not altogether surprisingly, Janet had run away from the Reform School and had been rehoused in some sort of hostel. I was appalled and immediately got on to the authorities.

'Look, all her family are down here. Her sister and brothers are here. I'll give her a job.'

At first the answer was, 'No. It's quite out of the question.'

But I wouldn't give up and eventually they gave way. Janet came down to London in 1975 and was found a hostel in Putney, conveniently close to Anita and Kevin.

Anita and I rarely fell out – if at all. Everyone commented on our closeness. More than our shared obsession with the business she was like a sister to me. Apart from the hours we put in at work, we spent a lot of personal time in each other's company – the two sides of our lives were inextricably caught up together. I was the godfather to her son Jack and was often to be found round at their Putney home having one of her delicious suppers and playing Racing Demon, often with her sister Marian too. Anita was more than willing to offer any help she could so we gave Janet work. She came into the shop every day and worked happily as a general gopher until she left to get married a year or so later. I did make her wedding dress, which I'm somewhat embarrassed to admit I subsequently took back – well, she wasn't in the mindset of heirlooms – and sold to someone else.

By May 1975, we were doing well enough to put the business on a new footing. We moved the workshop and showroom to 9 Walton Street, a chic residential area with various boutiques and small shops close to Knightsbridge. The place itself was quite a dump with little narrow rooms – even the fact it was near Harrods couldn't make it seem any bigger. Meanwhile I moved to fashionable Notting Hill. I even bought my first car – a silver BMW – and I began to enjoy the trappings of limited success and my arrival on the nursery slopes of a long-awaited period of stability. As far as I was concerned, this was just the start of everything I'd been working towards. We were still only on the lower rungs of the ladder.

CHAPTER THIRTEEN

The furnished basement flat that I'd found in Campden Hill Square was to be my home for the next eight years. Barry helped me build a low platform from never-to-be-painted MDF for cushions, the TV and hi-fi in the bed-sitting room. I bought a chrome-legged black laminate table from Habitat, marking the start of my penchant for black furnishings, covered the chimney wall with a floor-to-ceiling mirror and hung a very strong drawing by Colin of a particularly unattractive woman in a black dress. I still have the drawing and only noticed the other day that he'd omitted to ink in one of the sleeves of her dress – strange it never occurred to me before.

The large kitchen contained the usual plus a pine table and chairs to look out on to a patio. It was clean, pleasant, a very good address and seemed the right place to nest. As far as I could see there was only one drawback and that was the spiders. Every September and April, they would find a place on my pillow en route to a warm spot to sleep through the winter and then back again to the spring sunshine. It was a very quiet place to live although I do remember when the peace was shattered in 1975 when an IRA bomb intended for Sir Hugh Fraser, killed Professor Fairley who was out walking his dogs. I had just left the square and was walking up Holland Park Avenue to Notting Hill to get a taxi to work. The explosion was right behind me, so loud but muffled. I think it blew out all the windows on that side of the square. Yes, it was frightening to experience such violence so close to home, but that was life in London in the seventies.

I remember great times there: Sunday lunches, for instance. I'd ask round as many old friends as would fit in. Back then food was either very fancy with a French gourmet twist or the plainer, basic roast meat, veg and a salad with a nod to the continent in the form of pâté and a gherkin or two. I went for the latter. At least that's how I started and was able to conjure up a pretty acceptable meal. As in everything I did, I always wanted to go the extra mile or two to get it just so. Not that it always worked but the intention was there. I've always felt that hospitality isn't necessarily to do with whether you can cook but much more to do with creating an atmosphere that makes people feel that they are valued and being looked after.

I'd also spend a lot of time in the company of Colin who had bought a flat near-by, just off Ladbroke Grove. It was quite a contrast to mine with its high ceilings and tall first-floor windows leading on to a balcony. It was very modern inside with low sofas, a big kitchen and a deck at the back where you could eat. He was very generous and let me use it for entertaining from time to time. I think that he liked having the people that I was becoming friendly with at his table. He understood that my flat simply wasn't sophisticated enough. I recall a dinner I held there with Bianca who arrived in a full-length voluminous cotton skirt and sank into the yellow sofas. Colin could hardly restrain himself from getting out a sketchpad and paint brushes, I wish he had – Bianca certainly wouldn't have minded. Jill Bennett also came to that party with Bill Reed, an American journalist who lived close by and, as I recall, Anita and her husband Kevin, who regaled Jill with stories of past times in the Chelsea Potter. Colin was like a big brother to me and also let me have my thirtieth birthday party there.

Otherwise I'd be hanging out with Marion and Ninivah or with Alva Chin and Grace Jones as they came through London on their way to the Paris and Milan shows. We'd listen to music – Earth, Wind and Fire; Tavares, Candy Statton or Aretha Franklin – drink champagne, put on our glad rags and hit the town. We'd go to Langan's, Chow's or San Lorenzo to eat, usually ending up at The Embassy or Maunkberry's where there was never a shortage of drinks being sent over and quite often no bill to pay at the end. God knows where we all slept – probably we all crashed out in the same bed. Ninivah and I often went to the Sombrero, a night club (not dissimilar to the Cheltenham) in a basement on Kensington High Street where you had to have a plate of salad and chips so they could keep their licence. I can only imagine how fat the local rats became as we never ate the food. It was unquestionably the best gay club around, apart from the sin bins of Earls Court which we didn't frequent. We'd bump into other friends there among them another northern designer, Adrian Cartmel, who was married to Cindy White who later became Rifat's business partner. Sometimes we'd find Robert Forrest, probably the best sales-man in town then working at Browns in South Molton Street, or Kerry Warn who later moved to New York to become the darling of the hair and styling set. The music was great and I spent a lot of time on my own on a little raised section on one side of the dance floor simply listening, drinking and moodily watching the crowd to see if anyone caught my eye. If they did I would pounce! It was quite handy for my flat, only a quick walk up the hill with my prey.

Thinking of nightly trysting places, there was also the renowned Holland Walk that led from Ken High Street up to Holland Park Avenue, where a lot of dogs were walked well into the early hours and a quick hop over the wall suited some. One night I was the recipient of a severe beating by eight policemen, having been set up by the best-looking of their group who acted as *agent provocateur.* To my credit I just took it, remarking only that if they were going to pursue this kind of nocturnal activity they should change their regulation size-ten footwear to something less recognisable. The next day, I passed off the bumps and bruises with some story of having been mugged on Westbourne Grove – I don't know whether anyone believed me but I suspect not. I turned up at the Berkeley Square Ball the next evening in sunglasses to disguise my black eye.

I deliberately kept my life very compartmentalised in London unlike in Paris and New York where everything was much more of a melting pot. Back at Sheffield, Alison Anderson had turned me down, writing me a letter that included something along the lines of, 'I would never go out with you because it would just be another trophy on your belt. You went out with all the best looking girls and I'd only be another in a long line.' I was still doing exactly that, albeit with less regularity. She was right. It had nothing to do with masculinity and everything to do with trophies. Not satisfied with my more clandestine sallies into the gay world, I still had to show I could get the best girl. I guess that was one of the reasons why I went out with Bianca in the late seventies during her divorce from Mick. She and I often went to Tramp together. She was sophisticated and glamorous and, like me, she loved dancing. We'd sit in Johnny Gold's hot spot – first banquette to the left in the dancing side of the club – or dance all night.

Looking back, I see that socially I did tend to gravitate towards black people – Marion, Scott, Marie, Alva, Ninivah, Grace Jones, Michael Roberts, Andre Leon Talley, Andrea and Christina Viera. I made no bones about my preference for black or exotic models, and my music of choice still ran from Tamla through Nina Simone to Ella Fitzgerald. Maybe this had something to do with trying to identify with a group so I had an anchor or somewhere to revert when required. This was a time when black people were beginning to get a better deal, when people like us were seen as role models for the future. What we had in common was non-whiteness and a feeling that this was a definite plus. We could go anywhere, had an identity, and people gravitated towards us. As I became better known and fêted for my abilities, I became more comfortable with my colour. I'd almost defy anyone even to think about raising it as an issue. That may be why I've always said I was never conscious of it as such.

The same applies to the gay thing. At around this time I was a bit over-demonstrative, though photographs don't really bear this out. I did have a fairly active undercover gay life at night but it never developed into a need to declare myself to the world. It was my business and although I may have occasionally been indiscreet, it never seemed something I needed to defend. Again, I didn't want to be part of an excluding, exclusive, self-obsessed group. Having written that, I did however take a very strong line with my landlord at Campden Hill Square who suggested it was unsuitable for me to bring people home but men in particular. Imagine the amount of above-stairs gossip that would have preceded that interview. To give him his due, he said his piece, I said mine, we agreed to accept one another's positions and nothing more was said.

At that time I was also part of the fashion mondaine in the London of the moment – Tina and Michael Chow, Manolo Blahnik, Michael Roberts, Ninivah, Adrian and Rifat. I was being seen in the right places with the right people. And many of the right people were photographed for the magazines with me, wearing my dresses. As a single man who could string more than a couple of sentences together I was in some demand. Tina and Michael held sway over the international set – designers, photographers, actors, artists. Their salon was their

Knightsbridge restaurant Mr Chow's, soon to be followed by others in New York and Los Angeles. It was fabulous. The interior was contemporary Italian, with a green tiled floor, a typical 1970s' pendant standard lamp, a huge Richard Smith canvas on one wall and a portrait of Michael by Peter Blake on another. Add to this the enormous chrome and wood sweet trolley and a nineteenth-century wood and glass screen, which belonged more in a grand hotel, and a huge vase of lilies. The tables with white linen tablecloths were individually and discreetly lit so offered a good degree of intimacy but rubber-necking was definitely encouraged. At one table, you might have Jack Nicholson and Angelica Huston, at the next Karl Lagerfeld and entourage, Diana Vreeland at the next and so on. It was glamorous and eclectic to the nth degree. I was completely seduced by it and given a front-row seat, usually at the best table upstairs with the Chows. I did however recognise that this was a game and to stay in it, you had to play by the rules. As long as you were getting good reviews, you were treated well. This firmly established pecking order was the downside to the whole arrangement. I dislike conditions placed on any relationship so I tended to play the whole thing at arm's length.

The Chows were the new aristocracy. Their lifestyle was aspirational. Their style – born mostly from her style and his money and enterprise – was lavish and international. Michael played with the big boys and built up an impressive collection of art deco that included pieces by Ruhlmann, Dunand, Lalique and so on. Typical of him was the house he owned in Fulham. Externally, it was not where you'd expect the Chows to live, but inside it was transformed into an *homage* to Le Corbusier and filled with fabulous deco pieces. It had its own lap pool and a cinema in the cottage next door. I found him inspirational in so far as he was a self-made man and proceeded to dispose of his wealth in the pursuit of his own interests. As well as living as well as he did, he turned it to profit. In retrospect, he reminds me of the Anton Walbrook's character in *The Red Shoes* – stylish, entrepreneurial, a dispassionate collector with a lot of depth who amassed things that struck a chord with me. As for Tina: she was the embodiment of chic with her collection of Fortuny dresses and other treasures. She did wear me, particularly the early jersey garments, but her heart lay in vintage couture and things that other people could only aspire too. André Leon Talley reported in *Women's Wear Daily* on a buffet for forty odd people in New York: 'When the fashion bunch jumped up at 1am to leave for the club, Chow elegantly jumped out of the Fortuny and into a Bruce Oldfield sweatshirt and culottes she pulled from a tiny Tibetan pouch bag.'

That kind of association was worth a lot. It unquestionably gave my clothes considerable cachet, making them desirable to those who wanted to emulate that international lifestyle. Tina was desperate to be head-turningly different, to be an icon and trend-setter. She always had centre stage.

Paris had found its way into my blood and I seemed to travel back and forth as often and easily as I had hitched up and down the motorway in the Harrogate days. I've no idea how I afforded it. In 1975, Charlotte Rampling called me again, this time to make her costumes in Yves Boisset's *Le Taxi Mauve*. I remember another of those pinch-me moments when Charlotte and I had been put up in adjoining rooms in the Lancaster Hotel in Paris. I suppose we must have been there to discuss the film. I can see us lying on the bed wrapped in the hotel's luxurious white towelling robes, watching TV. Neither of us now has the faintest idea what this boy from Brixton was doing lying on a bed with one of the most desirable women in the world (incidentally, nothing happened). When I visited her on the set of *Le Taxi Mauve* at the National Film Studios of Ireland, I was dead excited to meet one of my idols, Fred Astaire, who was starring with her. Remarkably, he had no interest in talking about dance – so no insights into his relationship with Ginger; that was all in the past.

Astaire was one of several icons whose pictures I had stuck in my St Martin's scrapbook, never dreaming I would one day meet them – Charlotte, Antonio, Pat Cleveland, the Queen, Liza Minelli, Cyd Charisse and Lauren Bacall. I had simply chosen pictures of them along with anything else that interested me in those days – coincidence or fate?

One of the reasons for my frequent returns to Paris was Patrique, someone I had met at the Club Sept. He had a fabulous apartment in the Rue de l'Université: one of those buildings on the first floor with a courtyard planted with chestnut trees. It had spacious high-ceilinged rooms *enfilade*. Patrique was a friend for quite some time. He was someone who taught me more about the good life. He was rich, very handsome, drove a Mercedes and had all the trappings that I aspired to. We'd go to Deauville for the weekend and stay in a smart hotel. It was great while it lasted. The first time I met Jean Michel Jarre, soon to be Charlotte's second husband, I was staying with Patrique. Charlotte had been over for tea and Jean Michel came over to pick her up. It wasn't until a year later that he realised that the apartment actually wasn't mine. He was under the impression that I was this fantastically successful English designer who'd done very well in Paris – I'd have had to have done *very* well in Paris to be living in an apartment like that.

They got married the following year and the wedding was in their mini chateau at Croissy-sur-Seine on the outskirts of Paris. It was a great party but like everything Charlotte did it wasn't a starry affair for the sake of it, it was just friends, apart from Charlotte's parents. Bailey and Marie were the only other English people there that I knew. I remember him being thrilled to meet Jacques-Henri Lartigue, another famous snapper. Of course we all got very very drunk and afterwards I went with Bailey and Marie to the Club Sept for dinner – I made it into the restaurant at last.

Meanwhile the business was growing at a pace and I was receiving increasing coverage in the fashion pages and magazines that mattered. I had always been uneasy about showing my work as part of a large group so eventually I approached my friend Shirley Giovetti who was still at Revlon. She arranged sponsorship from Marcella Borghese cosmetics. Their financial input meant that I could show my spring 1976 collection alone at the Berkeley Hotel with Tina Chow and Alva Chin modelling. It was my first proper solo show. It was quite a tight collection that incorporated sporty shapes in dressy fabrics, giving sporty daywear a glamorous spin for the evening – a theme I was to revisit over and over again. I also used novelty fabrics and silks for the first time with reversible bomber jackets in silk jersey with harem pants and jersey bustiers. Nobody else was doing clothes like these, deceptively simple in appearance yet difficult to make.

Despite more good press we can't have made enough sales for it to be viable so we rejoined LDC to show the next winter collection at the Inn on the Park in March 1976. At this stage, to the frustration of the foreign buyers who had to negotiate their way round the shows, the fashion scene divided into various factions. The CEC decided to show in Birmingham, leaving the way clear in London for the fashion houses to do what they wanted. Inevitably, there was a breakaway group from the CEC showing at Earls Court, with the LDC at the Inn on the Park, the London Collections at the InterContinental and various of the larger designers (Gibb, Bates and Muir) showing privately and at different venues. Despite the apparent chaos, with overseas buyers complaining about the distances between the shows and the demands being made on their precious time, our show was widely praised. My own collection, again in soft jersey, included various separates in theatrical colours: harem pants, Grecian-styled tops, jerkin jackets over bandeau tops, swirly gathered skirts, pants and overshirts and jersey dresses in unusual combinations including flame/mushroom, purple/ fuschia, plum/saxe blue. The aim was, as usual, to add a sportier, more relaxed feeling to evening glamour with the emphasis on interchangeable separates that could be dressed up or down to suit the occasion.

While the general mood in English fashion was for fantasy clothes, I stuck to simplicity and versatility, producing garments that I hoped women would want for their glamour but also their wearability. It seemed to be working. In fact I sold much of that collection to Michael Winner for his film *The Sentinel.* Michael had called me asking me to design a wardrobe for the film but immediately making his position clear.

'I've already spoken to Valentino in New York who's willing to give me the clothes free of charge. I hope you'll be able to see your way to doing something similar. It'll be great publicity for you.'

'I'm very flattered,' I replied. 'But I'm only just starting out and I couldn't afford to do that. I think you'd better take Valentino's offer.'

We ended the conversation on good terms and then, a couple of months later, he called me again.

'Bruce. It was very nice talking to you the other day. I'm not sure I want to go for those costumes with Valentino after all. Come on, you can give me a wholesale price, can't you?'

The answer was of course I could. But I made sure I got the money up front this time. I'd learned from my experience with *Jackpot.* Michael and I remain friends to this day.

Crisis came in October when the Inn on the Park booked a

barmitzvah plum in the middle of the dates reserved by the LDC. The hotel refused to cancel it in our favour. It wasn't easy to find another suitable venue at short notice. The only place that could accommodate us was the Café Royale. It was not a happy event. I felt utterly dispirited by rejoining the group. It was then that I decided to make the final break. I explained in the press:

> It is not because I think I'm too grand but I do not mean to get watered down with twenty-four other people showing at the same time. I prefer to show in isolation. I don't want to be associated with any particular camp. Oldfield buyers seek out people whose designs interest them. This is still the only country to come to for evening wear. France is not able to fill that gap.

I was mouthy even then.

Annette was extremely upset but I was 100 per cent confident that it was the direction I had to take if I was going to get where I wanted. And I still wanted to be the best and the most successful designer in the country.

Breaking away from the New Wave designers was straightforward if painful but to make it in the fashion business, to a certain extent, you have to run with the pack. I had to stay in the wholesale business and show two collections a year during the London Fashion Weeks, making sure I was up there on the calendar as a designer buyers wanted to see, getting the right amount of coverage.

Despite inflation, sales of English designer clothes were on the up. The reasons were various: the arrival of Arab wealth in the purses of the sheikhs' wives; an establishment reaction to punk fashion; the devaluation of the pound attracting buyers from Europe, and, according to the *Los Angeles Times*, a reaction to fantasy, individuality and outrage that resulted in a refined fashion that was both serious and wearable. Jean Muir led the way. But I was only a step or two behind her.

I was primarily interested in making beautiful, wearable clothes. I wasn't interested in following in the design footsteps of the big five – Zandra Rhodes, Bill Gibb, John Bates, Yuki and Gina Fratini – who had all been producing distinctive clothes, but I was interested in being up there with them. I wanted to be innovative without scaring the horses and was particularly interested in designing glamour. I like sensuous, curvy shapes. If anything I had been influenced by the time I spent in America. Having seen the designers like Halston, I had adopted that very pared-down approach to produce simple but noticeable clothes. Forties' Hollywood was totally my period. I always designed from a technique that interested me – anything like smocking, ruching or pleating. The last thing I wanted to be was intellectual. Applying a technique to a fabric gives it another dimension as it encompasses the body. I much preferred the challenge of working that way instead of working to some outside thematic inspiration.

Among my supporters at the time was Michael Roberts, influential fashion correspondent of *The Sunday Times*. He had the same background as me, being half Jamaican, half English. He studied graphics at art school before turning to writing about fashion, later turning to illustration and photography. He was definitely a force to be reckoned with and one that it paid to have on your side. But even if we fell prey to his acid pen, we had at least made it into the paper. He'd often turn up at Sunday lunchtime and sit round the cutting table with Victor and me and tell me frankly what he thought of whatever I was working on. It was always a relief to break off from my pile of drawings and bank accounts as I wrestled with the cash flow – or tried to. Michael had a good eye and kept his ear close to the ground so, albeit grudgingly, I usually listened to what he had to say.

Our next ready-to-wear show took place in the Walton Street showroom with both Jerry Hall and Marie modelling. The event almost didn't happen thanks to Jerry losing one of her ruby ear studs during the rehearsal. She had been given them by Bryan Ferry and had already lost one that he'd had to replace, so she was frantic to find it. We turned the already chaotic place upside down until we did.

Left to me I would rather not show at all but I had to, to get the notice I needed to attract if we were to survive. On the other hand, shows do crystallise my ideas, forcing me to focus on a collection and how it hangs together. It also presents my look for that season and my ideas as to how it should be worn, to the press and buyers, whether stores or individual clients. It was a relief to be able to move away from the impersonal spaces offered by Olympia and Earls Court and the larger hotels. I never liked big runway shows. I didn't see them as the right venue for my clothes and don't to this day. I liked the intimacy of Brown's Hotel which worked well, using three smallish inter-connecting rooms with the runway through the centre. Then, as audience numbers began to expand we moved to the ballroom of the Hyde Park Hotel in Knightsbridge. Spring 1978 sticks in my mind because I had decided to make a few changes and chose entirely classical music. I instinctively knew the whole thing wasn't going to go down well. I worked through the night and walked to the hotel, dreading what was about to happen. In the event, it was worse than I imagined because the atmosphere was horribly wrong – it was a breakfast show and someone forgot to close the curtains. I liked the clothes in that show as they showed a move away from jersey. By adding leather and wool to the collection I was able, for the first time, to show tailored clothes. Although they were soft with nipped-in waists and puffed sleeves – an almost Edwardian silhouette. I could show a more structured approach to dressing. My inspiration had loosely been 'young girls at the Conservatoire' and I had accessorised some scenes with the models carrying violin cases so it was logical to use classical music too. All this was a bit much for some members of the audience but the collection did generate a fairly good press return. That was the last of the big shows as we decided to show even closer to home in the familiar milieu of the restaurant San Lorenzo.

I was learning to go for the staples I knew my customers liked from the previous season and tweak them a bit for continuity but also adding something different to tempt new customers. So I'd introduce some new themes and fabrics such as velvet and satin that I could tailor. I was making unconstructed cashmere tweed jackets, steering clear of traditional methods of fusing and canvassing, using only a soft piece of canvas on the front, lining the sleeves with chiffon so the garment retained its fluidity. Anita would despair. 'God, you and your jackets,' she'd sigh. But I always liked them. Finally I'd stage something to make an impact so that I was assured of getting my point over to the press. More often than not, it was these gratuitous wild cards in the collection that provided us with coverage in the daily press and fashion magazines. I discovered that there was always disagreement over the pictures used. Scandalised, the tabloid fashion editors would hurl invective at the picture desks, usually staffed by men, who would choose the most scantily clad images to illustrate the stories from the collections.

I found the lead-up to the shows a horror story. I'd spend the weeks before working from 7 a.m. until at least 10 p.m., editing the collection, making new garments, altering others. I could never cut off from what I was doing so I'd wake up in the middle of the night convinced that a certain dress wasn't right, trying to work out a way of fixing it. If, at the eleventh hour, I realised

I needed, say, another red dress for maximum effect in a section of the show, I'd often have to make it overnight. Those last-minute additions have frequently gone down the runway without linings or without zips. The effect is the thing.

The day of the show itself was always very charged although as years went by I surrounded myself with a very good team so eventually I only had to orchestrate the big picture, relying on others to take care of the detail. Back in the early days though, Anita and I would be working all hours – arranging the rails, choosing the music, booking the models, sewing on buttons, arranging food for the models, collecting from the airport. We'd eat, sleep and dream each show. As a rule, the shows never went wrong – they were either good or boring. But they always got us extraordinary nationwide and international publicity.

Over the years the wholesale fashion market has changed so that the big companies show their collections to the buyers a year before they go into the shops. When they do a show in fashion week, they can afford to put in 'window clothes' that may find their way into Harrods' or Harvey Nichols' windows, into the pages of *Vogue* or the other fashion magazines or be loaned to film stars or for promotions, i.e., clothes that are not generally for sale in the shops. They have the budget to produce these loss leaders whereas with a small business like ours, what you see is what is for sale. Big businesses need the extended lead-time to produce the huge volume of goods they sell and equally they can afford to stockpile and warehouse units destined for the stores. We have never been able to do that.

Apart from the hard work producing the garments, it was up to us to sell them. Anita was fantastic with the buyers and dealt with all their appointments but as well as the British shows we went to New York twice a year. Sometimes Anita and I went together, but I often went on my own and stayed for the week with Scott. In 1976, We took Joanne Creveling as our New York agent. She was a tall, pushy American woman who knew how to get things done. Her office was in a great position at 730 Fifth Avenue opposite Tiffany's and Bonwit Teller's. She handled a variety of clients from suite 1930 of the Genesco Building: Ralph Lauren cosmetics, furniture designer Angelo Donghia, design duo Pinky and Diana, and myself among others. Her office was a series of rooms with black-and-white tiled floors, white walls and lots of Perspex furniture. It was a good address and whenever I arrived in town, Joanne's assistant, Mallory, would get the press and buyers in to see me.

As ever, fashion was BIG in New York. The *New York Times* dubbed the younger names on the current fashion scene 'the Fashion Comets'. They were the ones who showed up at ready-to-wear collections in Paris, Milan and New York. Some were young designers, some were working as design or photographic assistants, some were simply fashion groupies. For whatever reason, they helped create the buzz each season, clubbing till dawn and staggering into the shows during the day. I was right in the thick of it all, showing my own collection at Saks, being seen at the shows, partying with the rest of them and making the pages of *Women's Wear Daily* as a result. This was an activity I only pursued in New York. Even in those days, I had little time for the fashion set, though I did appreciate the value of being embraced by it, particularly within the pages of *WWD*. That signalled to the buyer from Elizabeth Arden or Barney's that I was in town with the collection.

It was on that 1976 visit that I finally met Michael Winner. He was busy filming *The Sentinel* when he called me again.

'Why don't you come down here? We've never met. I'll sent a car to pick you up and you can visit the set.'

So a stretch limo duly rolled up.

Michael took one look at me and barked, 'You're a good-looking chap. We'll get you in a few scenes as an extra.' Imagine how strange it was when I walked into an LA hotel room some years later, to see none other than myself on the TV in *The Sentinel.* He helped me in the press too, telling them I was responsible for Christina Raines' wardrobe. When asked why he hadn't used an American designer given he was in America, he obligingly answered, 'You can't get clothes for the young American girl here and designer fashions are the worst of all.' Never one to mince his words even then!

Michael Roberts was over in New York at the same time to cover the shows. We hung out together and I remember we visited veteran designer, Charles James, who was living out the last of his days in the Chelsea Hotel. He had a suite of rooms, surrounded by his designs, embittered about some of the cards he'd been dealt. He had had a brilliant career but still nursed a grievance against Halston with whom he'd worked for a short time as a pattern cutter when his career was effectively at an end. He'd challenged the copyright of the patterns and designs he had produced for Halston at that time, which led to unresolved wranglings. There is a fine line between who actually designs what in the environment of a studio. Who is to say that the original design produced on paper by the designer is the same intellectual entity after it has gone through the hands of someone else who has imposed his or her ideas on shape, proportion and line. Charles was most keen to show us a spiral zip that he had been working on for years that wound round a trouser leg. It was so utterly pointless. I left there, vowing that I wouldn't ever become like that.

Anita and I became part of a group of friends that went together to restaurants or met up after dinner to go on to parties or clubs. Among them was Reed Evins, the shoe designer, who had a showy apartment on 57th Street. To my astonishment he'd lie stoned on his Corbusier chaise staring out of his wide-open floor-to-ceiling windows. I had visions of him walking straight out and couldn't understand why it was allowed. We also hung out with Craig Raywood, an interior designer, who lived in a similarly chic apartment over on the West Side that was modern and sparse with grey flannel walls and floor-to-ceiling blinds. It was all white orchids and Baccarat crystal. When I criticised him to Anita for being such a show-off with his wealth, she was very stern: 'If you had the money, you'd have exactly the same things.' She was right. Now I do have some of them.

During these regular trips, I became very friendly with André Leon Talley who went on to become editor at large of American *Vogue* – a fiercely intelligent black guy about 6 foot 6 who looked like everyone's idea of a down-South dandy, the sort you'd see in a bright yellow check suit as an extra in *Carousel*, very camp and self-aware but very self-parodying. I'd hang round the clubs with him and Scott, drifting from one to another into the early hours. As we did, I couldn't help feeling that the world of fashion was inhabited by people who should know better – including myself.

I remember when Studio 54 opened it became an almost nightly destination. If I was in town for just a week, I would want to go there every night and Scott would always oblige. While I was in New York, he was my entry ticket to everywhere just as I was for him in London. There is no way that I would have been able to jump to the front of the queue at places like Studio 54 or Hurrah without 'Good evening, Mr Barrie. One guest, is it?' Studio 54 was an enormous theatre which had been gutted and completely refurbished, the upper balcony seats left in place, most of the stage removed and the entire stalls turned over to dancing and bars. It throbbed to high-energy dance music for all the latest dance crazes and, depending on the night you were there, you might chance upon Diana Ross or Ashford and Simpson lip-synching to their latest hits. The place throbbed to the music of Candy Statton, Barry White, Sister Sledge and KC and the Sunshine Band, and being on the dance floor was like being part of a single entity. Most of the dancers were wasted on booze or drugs (Quaaludes were the fashion then) so inhibitions had flown. It was very democratic so you might find yourself dancing with Diana Ross or someone equally famous. The fact that you'd been let in meant you'd passed muster. Although primarily a gay club, the waiters wearing the shortest of shorts and no shirts, its clientele was both sexes who came to pose, dance and get noticed. It was all about excess in what was otherwise a pretty boring decade. Scott introduced me to a lot of people, many of whom were his clients, one I particularly remember being Roberta Flack whose honeyed voice was as unmistakeable in normal conversation as it is in song. Studio 54 is a phenomenon that has never been equalled for sheer hedonism and cool. It was brimming with Warhol celebrities, Bianca, Calvin, Halston, Liza and Liz (Taylor) all looking for some excitement and I remember on several occasions actually leaving the club at 4.30 a.m. with my small carry-on bag, heading straight for JFK and the 8.00 a.m. flight home to London.

One year, instead of using Joanne Creveling's office, I was invited by Arianna Stassinopoulos and her mother to show the clothes from their house on 63rd Street. It was a smart East Side town house that had been gutted inside, giving a mezzanine floor overlooking the vast drawing room. I had met Arianna the year before when I was invited to a talk she gave in London on Maria Callas. She was a very good speaker and very passionate about her subject. I think she identified with Callas as a butterfly emerging from its chrysalis. Mrs Stassinopoulos was very Greek, larger than life, full of extravagant theatrical gestures. I can still see her throwing rose petals over the mezzanine. They were both tremendously hospitable to the store buyers who turned up and couldn't work out the set-up at all. Once we went out to dinner at Mortimers, one of the discreet and chic upper East Side society restaurants, with a European royal and a very suave Greek gentleman who had something to do with armaments. At some point, I muttered to Arianna, 'It's very strange to be plonked into a situation where you've got a foreign royal, a society writer, a gun runner and me, a lad from Durham.'

'Darling,' she replied, 'you're like me. We have natural intelligence so we can fit in anywhere.'

I liked that. Perhaps it was true.

The same year, I was invited to Los Angeles for the opening of Surya, a new boutique in Beverley Hills. It was owned by a wealthy Thai family who had chosen to feature my collection. Edmund Surya Jaya, the boutique owner, lived in the gated enclave of Bel Air where Sharon Tate had been murdered a few years earlier. It was extreme wealth gathered together, where everyone had big Alsatian guard dogs guarding their vast establishments. The weird thing was that not only did these people isolate themselves from the surrounding community but they isolated themselves from one another too. Neighbours ignored one another. The whole thing was unreal. I couldn't understand why someone so wealthy would want to open a shop – it was a mystery to me. I stayed with Mary Lou Luther, fashion writer for the *LA Times* and her husband of many years, Arthur Imperator. Mary Lou was from Oklahoma and was very much a lady, well-liked, very enthusiastic if engaged but not one to be mean or nasty about anyone. Arthur was involved in publishing a textile trade magazine out of NYC among other things.

At that time I was very friendly with Tina Chow's sister, Bonny, who was the greeter at the LA Mr Chow's. It certainly didn't do me any harm to have her wearing my clothes there. When I arrived I went straight to a show in Saks on Wilshire Boulevard where the beautiful Lois Chiles was sitting across the catwalk from me. We flirted outrageously during the show – not unremarked by the fashion editor of the *LA Times* – and had a short-lived fling afterwards that gave my stay a bit of extra pizzazz. She was another trophy woman for me. I did enjoy flirting with women and although attracted to them, it was always a neck-up rather than a below-the-belt kind of attraction. With men I tended to be immediately attracted by the whole package but the attraction was never sustainable whereas with women, I could maintain friendships because it was uncomplicated by sex. Lois and I went out a couple of times in London when she came over to make the James Bond film, *Moonraker*, so I probably never rose much above being her walker.

Gradually I was becoming better known in the States. My collections were regularly reviewed in the *LA Times* and *Women's Wear Daily* with retailers taking my clothes in Dallas, San Francisco, New York and other major cities. It helped that a very good model, Carla LaMonte, hitched her wagon to us. The fact that she was so good at sales was an added bonus. This can be vital at the trunk shows. The American way was for a designer to be linked to a retail chain like Saks that has numbers of department stores round the country. The designer visits the separate stores with their garments while the stores take responsibility for bringing in the customers and laying on cocktails and the fashion show.

I always preferred an informal show where the model could chat to the customers and Carla was one of the best at that. She looked amazing, long legs and very stylish, and could talk up a storm. Like the other girls, she'd come over to London at collection time and it would be a real asset to have her on our stand. 'Oh, Mr Rothenstein, how are you? Wasn't that party fabulous? Last week in Paris . . .' and so it went. She knew all the buyers, could talk to them about anything and she'd sell the dresses at the same time. She was such a great runway model

42. Joan Collins and me in Beverly Hills. Photograph by Alan Davidson

43. HRH Prince Charles and HRH Princess Diana, polo at Smiths Lawn, Windsor, 1988

44. Diana and Nancy Reagan
in Washington 1985.
Photograph by Tim Graham

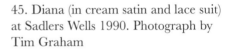

45. Diana (in cream satin and lace suit)
at Sadlers Wells 1990. Photograph by
Tim Graham

46. Diana at the Birthright Ball at the Albert
Hall in 1985. Photograph by Tim Graham

47. Ultimate red carpet occasion 1989. Photograph by Tim Graham

48. Me and Mrs
Thatcher at Downing
Street, *c.*1986.
© News International

49. Me and HRH
Princess Margaret
at a fashion show in
Guildhall, 1979

50. Scott Barrie
in San Lorenzo,
New Year's Eve,
1989

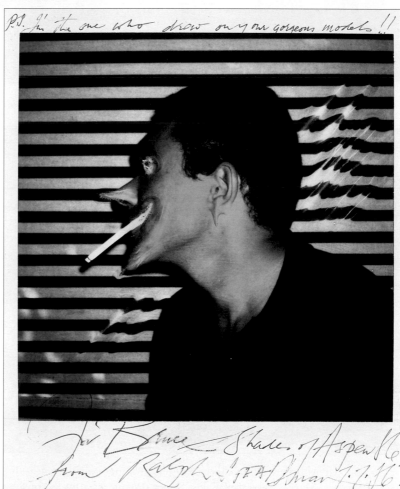

51. Ralph
Steadman
distressed
Polaroid,
Aspen, 1987

52. David Bailey photograph of me and Marie Helvin for *Ritz*, 1970s

53. Me with Barnardo's children at a Christmas party given in the canteen at
Marks & Spencer, Baker Street during my stint as consultant

54. Two decades of fashion shows.
Photographs by Niall McInerney

55. Me with chairs at the Design and
Decoration Building, 1991

56. One of the couture chairs at the
'Decoration, Haute Couture' exhibit, 1991

that she, like Marie, Jerry, Andrea and Pat Cleveland could always guarantee pictures of the show in the press.

Once Carla threw a fantastic party for me in New York at the Liberty Café ice-cream parlour. Faithfully reported in *Women's Wear Daily*, the photographs show leading lights of the New York fashion world turned out in force to celebrate under streamers and balloons. The only disadvantage was that the café was dry so I kept leading a posse across the road to the nearest bar.

Back home, my work and my social life were becoming virtually inseparable. Being seen in the right places with the right people wearing my clothes was all part and parcel of the business. Once when I was asked what I did in my free time, I replied, 'Work, work, work.' And it was true.

Inevitably holidays were few and far between. I did manage to get away occasionally but they were something I never really had time for. I went to Mykonos once with Scott but didn't like it at all. The gay scene there was far too heavy for me. It demanded total immersion every moment of the day. I get bored too easily. Other than that, it's exhausting because there are demands on you to look good all the time too. There were long hours spent on the beach perfecting the tan. I'm not interested in going in the sea, probably put off by my inability to swim for any distance and by my earlier encounters with deep water. I'd lie there listening to music I'd brought on tape – anything sung by Maria Callas, compilations of arias by Verdi and Puccini. My interest in opera had been born when I saw the film *Sunday Bloody Sunday* with Peter Finch, Glenda Jackson and Murray Head in 1971. The film exerted a certain fascination for me because of my own sexual ambivalence at the time, but more importantly I was seduced by the quartet from *Così Fan Tutte* that accompanied it. I had never heard it before, checked at Covent Garden to see if it was on, went one Saturday matinée and sat in the gods. I was on my own and as I relaxed in my seat this beautiful, lyrical music washed over me. That was the start of it all. My record and tape collection grew quickly as I spent a fortune on classical recordings – picking up again on what Constance Gilbey had introduced me to in Sheffield.

The hotels in Mykonos were ghastly back then but I do remember a wonderful bar called Castro's where I first heard Mahler's Fifth. It looked rather Venetian and was in a small village street perched on the edge of rocks overlooking the sea. It was the most beautiful setting, as I sat on the terrace looking out to the horizon, listening to the Adagio, sipping a vodka tonic with people murmuring round me. It was quite mesmeric.

One summer I went to Turkey, spending the first four days in Antalya, a resort in the south, getting a tan. I then went up to Istanbul where I hung out a lot with Rifat. His parents lived in a stunning Venetian stone mansion on the banks of the Bosphorous. I'd gone there for lunch one day and we were messing about by the water when Rifat said, 'Hey, there's a party today. Let's take the boat there.'

'What, a barbecue?'

'Yes, it'll be chilled. You know the sort of thing, dahlink.'

I didn't but so what? That didn't matter. We got in the boat and chugged round to the friend's house – a beautiful Russian wooden house – dressed in Speedos and a shirt. We moored and made our way up to the house to discover that this was no barbecue, but a party with everyone in their best kit and us looking like the hired help. Well, the hired help of the hired help. But nothing fazes Rifat and he just carried on as if it was the most natural thing in the world. True it was his natural environment and maybe people were used to his eccentricities, expecting him to turn up like that. But for me, Mr Formal, I was completely uptight and couldn't wait to make my escape.

More often than not I holidayed on my own. That way I knew

I could be assured of getting the sort of break I wanted without having to compromise. I like comfort and I stayed in fabulous hotels in Taormina, Positano, Florence. All places where there was an air of genteel respectability, a faded glamour, where you're expected to behave in a certain way and you're treated well. On my own I read and read and plugged myself into my music but I always looked forward to returning to London and the business, sometimes cutting my holiday short to do just that.

As the seventies drew to a close we began almost imperceptibly to change the direction of the business and I began to diversify my designs. I like designing for occasions, outfits that are meant to be noticed. The shops liked exactly the same as they had the season before but with a slight turn on it. My problem was that I wanted to do things that had more character. In the winter '79 collection that we showed in San Lorenzo, I continued with the jersey dresses but added full-skirted taffeta dresses with plunging necklines, tailored duchess satin jackets worn with sequinned pants, see-through georgette sequin sheaths and fifties'-inspired strapless bustier dresses in sequins or silk faille. Some of the new fabrics I was experimenting with were easier than using the jersey because it's not necessary to do a lot with them for effect. But the construction was a lot more complex. I can remember the number of pieces that went into the sequinned dresses and bustiers I was producing. In the boned bodices alone you would need to multiply them by three layers with the outer layer, the interlinings and the linings, and then imagine sewing the sequins back on to cover the outside seams. These were complicated techniques that really only lent themselves to couture.

I had moved on from doing jersey exclusively and the prices were rising. At this point, my clients numbered Annabel Astor, Charlotte Rampling, Jacqueline Bisset, Jane Seymour, Victoria de Rothschild, Joan Collins and Bianca Jagger, while high-visibility models such as Jerry and Marie and important fashionistas like Grace Coddington and Tina Chow were often seen in my clothes. Looking back through my press files I find it interesting to see how I was positioned back in the seventies. I got an extraordinary amount of coverage on both sides of the Atlantic and was always the one English designer to be consistently mentioned alongside the top international designers. Despite all that I don't think I let it go to my head, although others might disagree. I was always pragmatic, only too aware that hype meant everything and nothing. It was great while it lasted but it could be over in a second. The Bendels lesson had hit home seven years before and had lost none of its potency. I knew I couldn't afford to be complacent and perhaps that's why I eventually began to think about changing the direction of the business altogether.

CHAPTER FOURTEEN

It still amazes me that the business survived those early years. All I can think is that both Anita and I were quite good at predicting the vagaries of the market. We could tell when something was going wrong and managed to do something about it quickly. I still have that ability – touch wood!

In June 1978 we realised that things weren't going well for the market in general. We ruthlessly cut right back on the workroom and the number of staff. By the end of 1979 the trade was suffering from 'a summer of unsold stock'. The *Telegraph* reported that, among others, Bill Gibb was rumoured to be having financial problems. On the other hand, thanks to our foresight, only a year later we were reported in the *Telegraph* again as 'bouncing back from financial worries with the sexiest collection ever'.

The fan motif I had begun experimenting with the previous season became a big feature of this, my spring '80 collection, decorating shoulders, waistbands or on a pleated taffeta bodice. Most importantly I used more haute couture materials in slightly less formal ways, so a taffeta ball dress might have a pair of sequin stove-pipe pants under it or be given a sporty neckline treatment such as a granddad collar – just something to defuse the formality. There was a lot of jersey but it was the first collection where the dresses looked more couture than ready-to-wear. The fabric was drawn into a single 'knot' from which a fan or cockade sat proud – on a shoulder, at the waist, on a hip. The excess cloth draped across the body and cut into a dress, trouser or top, giving the appearance that it had simply grown organically out of the fabric of the garment. I used duchess satin and faille, the fabric of classic evening gowns. It was a bravura performance that got very good reviews and a lot of coverage. It marked a new direction for me.

Anne Price wrote in *Country Life*:

> From a truly big line up of talent in Britain, one name stands out above the rest this season. Many people did not like his autumn collection, some said that it was odd and even ugly, a few admitted they could not understand it, but Bruce Oldfield hit the nail straight on the head when he gave us short skirts, wide shoulders, long straight dresses and black brocade outfits reminiscent of the fifties. The doll pinks, dolly blues, grey and parchment satins contributed to the extraordinarily different feeling portrayed in this collection. A change that is already being felt in France by the most sensitive in avant-garde designs. Layers disappeared from Oldfield's life some months ago and his gift for true innovation in a field as diverse as fashion must mark him down as a designer whose word we must trust and whose ideas must be taken seriously albeit they are avant-garde and he may make his changes a season ahead of time.

There's an adage in fashion that it's no good if you're a season early or a season late with your designs. I thought she summed that up quite nicely.

Despite Anita's ambition for us to increase the wholesale side of the business, I felt we should be going in the opposite direction. As far as I could see, there was no logic behind us continuing to do exclusively wholesale without outside financial backing. Besides, we owned the business 50/50 and because my name is my business, I didn't feel I could afford to reduce my shareholding. So outside finance was *not* my first choice. A change of direction was unavoidable. Anita and I were such good friends that I think she knew deep down that I would have the last word. Let's face it, there's not a lot anyone can do with the person whose name is over the front door. He's bound to have an instinct about where he wants to go. If he doesn't want to design jersey ready-to-wear frocks, then he's not going to do it with any conviction or credibility against his will.

By the end of the seventies, the business was in any case veering towards made to measure. I was still getting plenty of pages in *Harpers* and *Vogue,* with the shows being reported favourably throughout the national newspapers and across the US, but I was feeling increasingly frustrated. How long could I go on doing variations on a draped skirt? I wanted a change and was more and more interested in working with more structured fabrics and making more structured, glamorous evening wear.

In fact, I have in part to thank the magazines for our eventual move away from wholesale. Whenever they photographed one of our dresses, they had to credit a shop where the readers could buy it. As a result, we'd often have to credit shops that didn't actually stock the dress but could call in the sample if required. It worked all ways. The magazine got its picture, the shops were keen to have the name Bruce Oldfield on a show-card in their window and we got the publicity. Things began to change when, in 1981, we moved from Walton Street to three floors of 41 Beauchamp Place. Upstairs we had room for a staff of seven while downstairs, the L-shaped showroom smacked of controlled frenzy as Anita and I did everything from answering the telephone, sewing, fitting, advising and even packing deliveries. We were kept so busy that we hired Georgina

'George' Alexander Sinclair as PA to Anita. It was only a matter of time before I nicked her for myself. She's been part of the family ever since.

Now we had the much needed pattern-table space for the private customers and as importantly space for machinists. So gradually, we began to credit the dresses as available to order from our own showroom. As a result, people started coming to us directly to buy or to borrow. That's how the system works. Either you lend the samples to the right people as long as they're brought back in good condition – which they're not always – or you decide on a core group of women who you want to wear the clothes and make a decision to sell to them at wholesale prices. After all not everyone can fit the samples. The great advantage to me of selecting such a group of women was that they would talk about the garments, would be seen out and about in them and would be photographed in the society and fashion pages wearing them. It works to this day as as it did then. Having a major celebrity or notable member of society in your dress is the most potent selling tool going. I didn't need to tell clients that it was incumbent on them to tell the press who they were wearing, they knew it was part of the quid pro quo. For example, I remember Melanie Griffiths wearing a pale blue beaded evening dress of mine for a shoot with an independent photographer who then sold the pictures to a couple of magazines. I gave her the dress. She then wore it to the Inaugural Ball for President Clinton at the White House and was interviewed live on CNN's *Larry King Show*. He asked her, 'Tell me, Melanie, whose dress are you almost wearing tonight?' She replied, 'Why, that's Bruce Oldfield, my new designer from London, England.' Need I say more.

I particularly liked the idea of having a relationship with the client and seeing the garment all the way through from the initial idea, so offering couture as well as ready-to-wear seemed an obvious and lateral way to go. It was no surprise to me to find that couture is perceived as being less fashionable than ready-to-wear, but it was a perfect vehicle for my self-expression. We'd make a collection that was sold into the shops but if somebody wanted one of the garments made to measure we'd do it. A customer might want a dress they'd seen in *Vogue* but might want it with sleeves, or longer or shorter. It was always the case that the press and the private clients would choose the more interesting things from the collection, most often the things I was passionate about. Because our overheads were relatively low we could charge retail prices instead of putting on a full couture mark-up. So it worked all round. Anita came round to my way of thinking that we were on a hiding to nothing if we limited ourselves exclusively to the wholesale market. People were expecting more of a couture service so there was eventually no alternative but to set up in retail ourselves, as customers kept asking for more glamorous and more structured garments in a greater variety of fabrics.

At this time we were introduced to Dominique de Borchgrave, a Belgian aristocrat who had been involved on the periphery of the British fashion scene for some years. She was to act as agent in her native country for myself and couturier Victor Edelstein. As well as this, she also introduced London-based clients to us in return for clothes. This was, and continues to be, a fairly usual arrangement at this end of the fashion business. She accessed and could 'sell' the notion of 'Bruce Oldfield' to women at social gatherings that I couldn't reach. As she was extremely stylish and looked very good in my clothes, it was a good arrangement.

London is made up of a great number of tribes and the key to penetrating them is to find one person who can carry the torch for you, then the rest will follow. We had our best ambassadress to the Greek community in Mrs Chrysanthy Pateras whom I still affectionately call 'Mum'. We did an unusual dress for her daughter, Nini, in the early eighties. It caused something of a sensation because instead of a veil, the dress incorporated a cowl neck at the front which became a hood in the back. The dress, cut on the bias, fanned out at the hem into a froth of chiffon ruffles. It was very Art Deco, very Ginger Rogers, and one of my favourite dresses of the time. Its success ensured a swelling list of Greek clients. Another key figure was Munirah Alatas, a gorgeous-looking Egyptian – a perfect size 10 – married to a Saudi businessman, Ahmes Khalifa. They lived in Wilton Crescent with their two children and had a huge group of international friends from the Middle East, Europe and America.

The importance of these ladies cannot be over-estimated. The English client tends to dress in couture for special occasions only, so the opportunities to wear dressy clothes are limited. In other cultures, including many European ones, there are more opportunities to dress up, so their patronage was crucial. For instance, middle-eastern wedding parties were rarely mixed so you could end up with a wedding in Jeddah where, apart from the bridegroom and the close male family members of both bride and groom, you might have 900 women wearing the latest Oldfield, Valentino or Versace. Oh, to have been a fly on the wall.

Munirah introduced me to Minal Sagrani, a beautiful Indian woman who came in one day seeking 'a jacket that will go around my buttons', and out of her bag spilled a handful of diamond, sapphire and emerald buttons. 'Which do you think are prettier, the diamonds or the sapphires? I've got rubies too. Could you make a black-and-white jacket? Then I could just change over the buttons.' When I'd picked my jaw off the floor, I immediately agreed we could. Later, during the eighties, I had a great time devising necklines for Annabel Goldsmith's fabulous Londonderry necklace and glorious cleavage.

But the real way to get clients is for a designer to go out and become part of their circle. In my case, it wasn't a deliberate move but a purely organic development. Dressing these customers was different from dressing stars. It had nothing to do with publicity and more to do with acceptance of your merchandise within a social group. Annabel Astor, one of my first couture clients, was good for me because she understood the commercial side of business. She hadn't always been a viscountess and managed to steer a happy course between her social position and the needs of her jewellery shop, Annabel Jones in Beauchamp Place. Her business also benefited from her inside knowledge of the lifestyle of her target customer.

I couldn't help but be aware that I was moving a long way from my roots, mingling with people who had no real idea of my background or how far removed they were from it. This was particularly brought home when Annabel invited me to a house party on Jura, an island off the west coast of Scotland. The idea was that we roughed it in cottages almost identical to the ones in which I'd been brought up. They thought this was great entertainment whereas I couldn't think of anything worse to do by choice. It was far too close to home for me, bringing back those years of struggling to make ends meet in Barmoor. Although the whole event was very low-key, I couldn't enjoy it. The idea was that during the day, we went out armed to shoot anything that moved then, by night, we'd eat it. I wouldn't handle a gun by choice but I did go stalking in plus-fours borrowed from Guy Morrison, another of the guests. It seemed easier to do that, just walking and keeping down so the animal couldn't get my scent. My more blood-thirsty companion seemed astonished that this protesting townie could walk at all but I pointed out I'd been putting one foot in front of the other for the last thirty years. It wasn't difficult. When I got back to base I explained my predicament to Annabel who took it in extremely good part and I was helicoptered back to civilisation before twenty-four hours were out. We laugh about it now.

I was really enjoying life at this stage and felt I'd moved into another gear. All my life I'd moved out of one circle into another, almost willing myself into situations where I had to make adjustments. I've always been very adaptable in that way. Living so high off the hog may have been far removed from Barmoor but over time I picked up the social niceties that went with it – not always skills I'd needed while growing up. To begin with, I was very aware of not knowing which knife or glass to use and so on, but I kept my eyes open and took in what everyone else was doing. Partly I was keen not to show myself up but also, because I enjoy entertaining, I wanted to do it all myself when I asked friends round. I like doing things properly and the structure of it all appealed to me. I also like knowing how it's done and that if I don't do it, it's because I choose not to, not because I don't know.

My first experience of establishment opulence came when I went to do a charity event in Dublin and was invited to stay with the Iveaghs at their home in Phoenix Park, Dublin. The thing I remember most was the extraordinarily lavish setting and the enormous stately house. In the morning, I was woken by the butler knocking at my door.

'Mr Oldfield, shall I draw your bath for you?'

'Yes, please.' Blearily.

'How would you like it?'

He returned and stood there holding a dressing gown, expecting me to get out of bed. I didn't know what to do and all I could wonder was whether he'd be standing there when I got out of the bath, ready to towel me dry. It was all very J. P. Donleavy. I had the distinct feeling that I was going to wake up and it would all be a dream. This was living in the lap of luxury all right but what appealed to me was that it was so discreet. It was rather like stepping into the eighteenth century with gracious woodland, grazing deer and sheep and a ha-ha preventing the cattle wandering up on to the lawn.

Another great friend whom I met at this time was Romilly Hobbs, who owned the delicatessen Hobbs in South Audley Street. Our companies had been invited to Hong Kong as part of an exhibition of Elegance and Excellence put on by the Hong Kong Trade Development Council and the Board of Trade. Neither of us sold a thing from our separate stands but we immediately clicked over my ironing board and spent many happy lunches and dinners whiling away the time – even when confronted by the most gruesome local delicacies. She, Anita and I would sneak away from some of the formal functions to amuse ourselves elsewhere. Soon after our return she married Alistair McAlpine. She was another perfect and stylish size 10, and I made her some memorable dresses over the years, my favourites being a white beaded dress for the state opening of parliament and a grey silk taffeta coat that went with a strapless dress. I also succeeded in making her my least favourite thing that I've ever made for anybody. It was a particularly horrible pink and purple sequinned maternity outfit that didn't really suit her. Notwithstanding, our friendship grew as did mine with Alistair and I frequently spent weekends with them at West Green, their house in Hampshire.

The first time I went there I was bowled over by the scale of it all. It was a beautiful small William and Mary mansion decorated in a period way because it was owned by the National Trust. I remember every second Sunday the gardens were open to the public who, although they didn't have access to the house, would press their noses up against the windows to see what was going on inside – rather disconcerting when we'd be having lunch in the garden dining room. When the McAlpines entertained, it was lavish but stylish: lots of flowers, more often than not picked by him; copious amounts of very good wine; pedestals overflowing with limes, nectarines and peaches;

exquisite antique Venetian glassware. It was rather like my Paris experience of seeing food displayed in a completely different way. It wasn't just to fill you up but it was decorative and opulent. Despite being quite small the house had an exceptionally large drawing room, a double cube. Oliver Ford, the interior designer, had created a very ornate setting with lots of chinoiserie, period furniture, wall-mounted china plates and orchids gracing tables draped with tapestries. A tremendous collector with a most eclectic eye, Alistair's study resembled The Old Curiosity Shop. I've rarely met such an impressive character. Everything gelled in the house because of his interest in it. I found it quite inspiring.

I'd go down some time on a Saturday, we'd have a pub lunch and watch TV in the evening. Because Romilly's job was cooking, she didn't particularly enjoy making elaborate meals at the weekend so the three of us would relax together like couch potatoes. Then the next day, a real mix of people would arrive for lunch – diplomats, politicians, designers, architects. For me it was a wonderful respite from the fashion business. They asked me down for Christmas sometimes, so I'd go down on Christmas Eve and then, when they dashed off to Chequers on Christmas Day, I'd be left to a very classy salad, or I'd disappear home.

By the mid-eighties I had got used to being surrounded by this kind of privilege. I was asked to endless balls and dances and went to as many of them as I could face, often having dressed the hostess as well as several of the guests. I used secretly to dread going in case something had gone wrong with any of my dresses. One of the first big society events that gave me a taste of the level of lavishness was a twenty-first birthday party held by Mrs Philip Harari for her daughter Shona McKinney. The Drill Hall in Westminster had been transformed into a carpeted Caribbean island. The ceiling above the dance floor was hung with greenery, bananas and grapes, while pink and white lighting played through the dry ice. As for Mrs Harari's dress. I delivered it half an hour before the party was due to start. Something went wrong with the zip so I had to sew her into it. At the end of the evening I had to leave her husband to unpick her.

Diana Harari has two sisters, Cherry Hambro and Ruth Fitzgibbon, both just as statuesque and stunning as she. It seemed that no social gathering was complete without the presence of one, two or all three of them. Between their bitter complaints about how expensive I was, I enjoyed the patronage of all three for many years. A few years ago, I received the ultimate accolade of being asked to do a wedding dress for Ruth's daughter. It was a wedding I won't forget in a hurry as Fiona Sangster and Gail Ronson pitched up wearing the same outfit. They had bought them from my ready-to-wear shop so I wasn't to blame, but it did make a good picture in *Hello!*. The third sister, Cherry, was the one who struck the fear of God into everyone with her booming voice but I always found her a pussycat who just loved people standing up to her. I remember making her a one-shouldered blue silk gazar dress. Gazar is a difficult fabric to use because it's very stiff and has a mind of its own. So Cherry wanted it to do one thing and I wanted it to do another – a struggle of the minds – but between the gazar, Bruce and Cherry we finally got there. It was one of my good dresses and we had a happy Cherry Hambro.

Sonia Melchett's fabulous Black and Gold Ball in the Orangery at Holland Park was another do to remember. The place was festooned in black velvet and gold flowers with an enormous black marquee lit by hundreds of fairy lights and dancing to the Pasadena Roof Orchestra till dawn. I was very well represented there with Dominique de Borchgrave, Marguerite Littmann, Emma Soames, Sophie Hicks and Lady

Aberdare all sporting me. Dominique was in black silk taffeta, looking fabulous. We'd sewn a string of white dressmaker's weights (bought by the yard from Peter Jones) round the hem of her dress so it would hang better. Unfortunately it began to unravel so I was chasing round the dance floor trying to pick the weights up before someone slipped on them and broke their neck.

I was also dressing Baroness de Portanova then. She and her husband, Ricky, were Texan, larger-than-life characters who'd come to Claridge's every year and host a huge party there. They were part of a very wealthy group of people who travelled the world. They'd move from Texas to New York, then be in London for the London season on to the South of France and then Venice. It was a regular pilgrimage for them. She had a bosom fabled for its size and her husband once said to me in his assumed English accent, 'You're the only man I know who can keep my wife's bosoms where they should be.' Some compliment.

My life continued to divide into very different strands. I moved from one to the other with the greatest of ease. I could be at Rocco Forte's wedding in Rome and then back on the Sunday night with Bianca or Astrid Wyman and the rest, at a London party, spending the next weekend at West Green, stopping off for a drink in some bar or other in Earls Court on my way home.

Society wedding dresses began to play an important part in my business. The first one was in 1975 for Irene Forte. Another early one was for Bianca Juarez for her marriage to Hamish McAlpine. It was made of cream corded lace with a little bolero and a lace veil that had been her mother's wedding veil. Hamish and Bianca were among the first of my client friendships and we saw a great deal of each other. They had the lifestyle that I aspired to but were roughly the same age as me and a good time with them was always guaranteed. I'd often go round to their Chelsea home where, on one occasion, I remember the surreal experience of watching the siege of the Iranian Embassy on TV while hearing the explosions only a few rooftops away. Their lodger was actor Rupert Everett, now a confirmed sophisticate but who I remember looking more like a reject from *The Rocky Horror Show* with his sub-bondage clothing, leather cat suits and studded neck collars.

I was particularly good friends with the Dellal family at that time too, having made the wedding dress for Suzy who tragically died soon afterwards. Lorraine lived near me in Sheffield Terrace with her husband David, a gregarious good-looking property dealer with a penchant for the high life who sadly died earlier this year. I spent a lot of time with them, getting to know a lot of pop industry people along the way. She went into business with Bernadette Bishop who was married to the photographer John Bishop, making very iffy suede dresses under the label No Scruples. They dressed all the pop stars' wives and partners, passing those who wanted something a bit grander my way. After divorcing David, Lorraine, an inveterate pop groupie, subsequently married Simon Kirke, the drummer from Free – remember 'All Right Now' – and moved to Sheen, close to great friends Ronnie and Jo Wood. She too gave great Sunday lunches and despite their distance from the centre of London had an impressive turn-out of the great and the good who, like me, had probably been at Tramp until late the night before. Once at Johnny Gold's famous club I sat for several hours chatting with Marvin Gaye. It wasn't quite like the animated encounter I was to have with another hero, Joni Mitchell. We were two black guys bonding in a white club in Jermyn Street.

Among the regulars on the scene were Christopher Reeve and his partner Gae Exton, Bill and Astrid Wyman, Dave Gilmour, Sabrina Guinness, not forgetting the Australian contingent of *Rocky Horror Show* producer Michael White, Little Nell, Lyndall Hobbs or Gael Boglioni. The great thing about Lorraine was that, despite being extremely wealthy, she went out of her way to be ordinary. She was great fun to be around and we were very close friends until she moved to New York in the late eighties.

It was at about this time that the Princess of Wales hove into view. The Palace had asked Anna Harvey at *Vogue* to master-mind the Princess's wardrobe, so various designers were asked to send a selection of outfits along to the *Vogue* offices where the Princess would make her choice. We made her a very sharp rust Venetian wool suit that she wore when she returned to London from Balmoral, and then when she turned on the Regent Street Christmas lights for Christmas 1981 she wore a blue velvet culotte suit of ours. Naturally, we were excited to add her to our list of clients but at the time we had absolutely no idea it was the beginning of such a long and well-publicised relationship. Neither had anyone an idea of her eventual transformation into one of the best-dressed, most glamorous women in the world.

As we became busier and busier, I was also being called on to make odd TV appearances and to judge various fashion competitions both here and abroad. One of these was a black fashion design competition run by South African Breweries. I was in two minds about accepting because apartheid was still in force. Even considering it meant I got some stick. However, I felt I wanted to support the people who had entered the competition, disregarding any questionable working practices of SAB. The whole thing was interesting and slightly worrying because, although it was never mentioned, it was understood that I was to be treated as an honorary white and that made me very uncomfortable. I remember the PR was constantly apologising for the nation's state of affairs. It was brought home to me several times. I stayed for a week in Cape Town and Johannesburg. Once, at Cape Town's Mount Nelson Hotel, I was walking through the gardens to the pool when a gardener shouted, 'Hey you, man!' He certainly hadn't mistaken my colour and thought I shouldn't be there. He took some convincing that I was a guest. Another time I was in the bar with some Dutch people who were rather loudly saying what they didn't like about the place when we were rounded on by a Scotsman who blurted, 'If you don't like it here, get back to England. We really don't need you here.' I just felt, Oh sod off, sunshine.

This was all part of a fairly jet-setting period in my life. I was back and forth from the States a great deal and I went to Europe frequently. The promotional bashes sponsored by Reid and Taylor, a Scottish wool manufacturer were great fun. Every two or three years they'd give their invited designers the cloth, always fabulous wool, to make a range of clothes. They'd then take over Leeds Castle, a palazzo in Venice or a schloss in Vienna and fly in planeloads of designers, models, press and buyers. The guest list usually included Princess Margaret too. It was a peculiarly British event wherever it took place. We used to call John Packer, the organiser, Bonnie Prince Charlie, so fond was he of swanning round in a kilt and cape. Meanwhile Princess Margaret would be knocking back the scotch, very much the prima donna while we'd be entertained by Pavarotti and/or other singers and musicians of his calibre. At the Venetian event, I was on a vaporetto with Jeff Banks and a designer friend who worked for Simpson's Piccadilly. He was loudly criticising his boss when the door opened and who should walk out but . . . his boss who simply said, 'You're fired,' and turned on his heel. Brutal.

I remember that Zehave Dellal, wife of Jack Dellal and mother of Lorraine and Suzy, took me under her wing, suggesting I pack a case of samples and she would take me to the best shops on the Côte d'Azur. I arrived with my suitcase stuffed with garments. She was under the misguided impression that all I had to do was turn up without an appointment and all doors would be opened to me. Would it had been so easy. We'd screech to a halt in her Mini outside a shop, I'd leap out with my case and go in. Once she'd parked she'd come and help me with my French. Unfortunately she couldn't make the distinction between being a customer and a saleswoman, so spent much of the time riffling through the scarves on display, commenting on them rather than assuming the humility of someone trying to sell something. It was an experience though.

In 1983 Peter Morton, the man who started the Hard Rock empire agreed to let me do a show in his LA restaurant, Morton's, the epitome of style. I had to pay for the tea, the catwalk and the models but the invitation would read 'Joan Collins requests the pleasure . . .' I'd been making clothes for her privately since I'd done the costumes for two very iffy movies, *The Bitch* and *The Stud*, at the end of the seventies. I dressed her a lot for openings and we got on well. I met Peter Morton's wife, Paulene Stone, through Joan, and knew him in London, so it all fitted together. I flew to LA on my way to stay with Marie in Hawaii for a short holiday, popping in to meet with Joan, who was living up in the Canyons somewhere with her new husband, Peter Holm. The show itself went well. I somehow simultaneously dressed models, greeted guests and dealt with the press. These were *Dynasty* and *Dallas* days, so we got a lot of coverage thanks to Joan inviting her co-star Linda Evans along with all the other women who made up the Hollywood scene. The only heart-stopping moment came when Joan made a late entrance and promptly fell off the runway. Peter Morton was having kittens as he envisaged the law suit but she just picked herself up and went on. She's a great trouper.

The life in LA was great. I was there for a week without much to do so was bumming about going to the beach by day, doing high-society things in the evenings with Joan and Jackie Collins and Linda Evans. One evening I was Joan's date at Spago, a very high-profile restaurant, where we sat at a round table with Billy Wilder and Larry Hagman and their wives and Kim Novak. Hagman didn't like smokers – so it was bad luck that he'd been placed on a table with me and my Benson & Hedges habit and Billy Wilder with his cigar. As a heavy smoker I was struck dumb at the sight of Hagman pulling out a couple of small battery-run fans and putting them on the table, angled to blow any smoke away from him. Only in Hollywood . . . I have to confess to a twinge of satisfaction when he underlined a point he was making in a story by banging his fist down so hard that the table rose into the air, upending most of what was on it into Mrs Wilder's lap. I like to imagine that Wilder and I shared a little pleasure in Hagman's extreme embarrassment. Some sort of come-uppance, I felt. And very funny too.

I was thrown into that glossy international Los Angeles set and it was fun being surrounded by so much glamour. We were very, very social indeed. At a party given by Larry 'Hustler' Flynt, I was almost struck speechless to find myself sitting next to Joni Mitchell who for me completely outshone the rest. I still have all her albums. I think she was bemused by the fact that I knew the lyrics to her songs better even than she. She was great to talk to and what impressed me some years later when I met her again in Mr Chow's was that she remembered our first encounter.

I'd agreed to give a lecture at LA County Museum of Arts Costume Council. When I'd agreed to it, it seemed an agreeably long way off. As it rushed towards me, I became distinctly less relaxed about it. Fortunately Marion was living in West Hollywood then and he helped me with the show at the Museum while Sarah Reed (of Ravensbourne days) had made up my slide box for me. I was amazed that I could stand up and speak but I'd made the mistake of thinking that the slides and a model would automatically prompt me into speech. Wrong. The audience seemed not to notice any awkwardnesses though and the show turned into quite a pleasant informal question-and-answer session.

It was a very glamorous time, completely different from everything I was getting to know so well in England. I enjoyed the experience of being lionised thanks to my connections with Joan and the Princess of Wales who, by this time, had become a regular and well-publicised customer. During this time there was also a huge crossover of Hollywood girls like Jacqueline Bisset, Jane Seymour, Lois Chiles, Shirley Anne Field, Stefanie Powers and Barbara Bach, all of whom became clients and some of them friends. Barbra Streisand, small and curvy, was another very good client as was Faye Dunaway, second only to Bianca in her fastidious attention to detail. She would stand at a fitting scrutinising every fold and crease, then go over the back of the dress in the same way with a little hand mirror.

I never planned a collection to the nth detail. It was a much more organic process than that. I remember meeting a buyer who said, 'Oh gee, I can't believe you don't sit down before a season and plan exactly what pieces are going into a collection. I mean. That's what everyone does.'

'Well, call me stupid but we don't.'

'But who merchandises your collection? You must have someone who sits down with you a few months before making a collection and points out what you need to include and what to drop.'

'Nothing of the sort.'

It's true that we didn't have a very businesslike way of doing things, either because of Anita's inability to motivate me in that direction or because of my obstinacy in not wanting to go that way. I imagine I always had the last word. The great thing about

Anita was that her open personality made her a very good sales person. She had no side and because she hadn't designed the stuff herself she remained much more detached from the process than I would. She was endlessly patient with the retailers if they didn't like something, whereas I'd be more likely to give them short shrift.

In the spring of 1982 I had been asked to make two maternity dresses for the Princess of Wales. Unfortunately I was reported as justifying my choice of a less sack-like design than was then common by saying, '. . . that bump I was trying so hard to conceal could be the future King of England . . .' That provoked sufficient embarrassment that I had to apologise to the Palace. I learned my lesson: discretion is the better part of royal dressmaking. I was forgiven and, by the end of the year, the Princess was back in shape and back on the job and I was asked to design for her again. It was just as rumours of her bulimia were beginning to circulate. She wore a blue off-the-shoulder dress of mine to the Birthright Fashion Show and that's when the talk really started. None of us had noticed anything out of the ordinary. I'd lunched with her at a discreetly positioned table in San Lorenzo and never given a thought to how little she ate. After all, if you're in the fashion business, you can almost never be too thin.

Dressing her was quite different to dressing the divas who were going to swish parties. This was more a question of dressing a young woman who, to an extent, was relying on us to steer her straight, knowing we wouldn't let her down in the concept of the garment, the way it fitted and the way it was made. She was a very good-looking woman who knew where she was going, but not necessarily in terms of style. She'd already had a few tasters of what the press could be like – think of those pictures of the sun shining through her skirt, or of the much-photographed Belville Sassoon's bustier dress. She realised that she was attracting more comment than anyone had anticipated so was on her guard. Sometimes too much on her guard, perhaps. She was suggestible but also quite tough. I should maybe have been more directive in the fittings but we were bound by her desire then not to show too much leg or cleavage. Apart from the press, she had to think of the protocol demanded by the occasion. She was young, unsure of herself and quite unsophisticated. It was our job to give her that sophistication and help her develop her own style. She wanted the glamour that we could give her. And she got it.

At last we were doing well enough for me to be able to move myself out of cramped Campden Hill Square and buy a place of my own. Ninivah was moving from her ground-floor flat in Redcliffe Gardens off the Fulham Road, so the opportunity came to buy it at just the right time. It was a really comfortable warren of rooms with high ceilings but I was after gracious living with lots of light and space. I redeveloped the space into two very large modern rooms with a big kitchen off. It didn't have to be all done at once so it gave me the opportunity to be creative and to develop the place as I wanted it. For me this was nothing to do with investment but more to do with coming of age. I was thirty-three and had stayed in Campden Hill Square for far longer than I'd imagined. This was a chance to have something like the living spaces of so many of my friends in New York, Paris and London. At last I could entertain in the way I really wanted to. I much preferred it to going out. People come and go in life, especially in a life like mine. I move very rapidly through uncharted waters and submerge myself in different groups of people and different activities. But although I moved through all these different worlds, I still cling to the same home values. My long-term, tried-and-trusted family and friends have always mattered most to me whatever other circles I moved in, and enjoyed moving in, thanks to the business.

The only thing that marred this period was the international awareness of AIDS and the massive government campaign in this country. I was scared stiff both by it and its implications. Going back and forwards to New York, of course I was very aware of the spread of the disease and alarmed by the statistics and the prevailing attitudes that were so overwhelmingly against gay men. It wasn't great to be gay. Not just because of the potential threat to one's life but also because of the implications it had on the business side of things, making it difficult to borrow money without an AIDS test or to take out a mortgage. It seemed expedient to be discreet about my sexuality although I confess that from this time on I didn't engage in sex in any significant way. Of course I had boyfriends during the eighties but I didn't carry on the kind of lifestyle I'd enjoyed in the previous decade.

But once again, it wasn't just me that was ready to move, the business was too. With the couture side booming, it was time to get a presence again by doing ready-to-wear. I wanted to give women the immediate gratification of buying something off the peg without having to wait for a couple of months. Other designers were opening their own shops in London so we decided to take the bull by the horns and follow suit. Anita was more guarded than I was but as far as I was concerned this would be just the beginning. I had dreams of empires with shops rolling out in other countries. In those days I had the optimism of youth – anything was possible.

CHAPTER FIFTEEN

The shop opened in June 1984 at 27 Beauchamp Place where it remains to this day. We raised the funds by participating in the government's Business Expansion Scheme that gives tax breaks to investors who put money into small businesses that would otherwise be less appealing as investments. It came at quite a cost to our equity in the business since we had to give away a substantial block of shares. With hindsight, this wasn't such a wise move. It pretty soon became clear that the share-holders were not prepared to go beyond their initial outlay and invest more money to develop the business. We were stuck in a business relationship that was going nowhere – a position that lasted for nearly seven years.

Anita had the inspired idea of taking on Ros Woolfson from Shandwick Communications to handle our PR. We'd met her some years earlier when we were all staying at the Gotham Hotel in New York for Fashion Week. She was extremely well connected in the British fashion industry with particularly good contacts in manufacturing so she understood exactly what we needed and how to get it, although I know she was frequently discouraged by how low the British designers were rated internationally. It was rare for British designers to meet their European counterparts then. But Ros organised a dinner on behalf of Selfridges for Karl Lagerfeld and got me along to that. Similarly, much later, when she was involved with the opening of Emporio Armani in 1988, she introduced me to the man himself. Both were seen as photo opportunities by the press. Otherwise she was to be very successful at managing my press profile to the extent that she even got me on to the *Nine o'clock News* – that was a real coup.

The shop itself was great. There was an architectural concept behind its design with pink and grey granite paint-effect walls to suggest huge slabs of masonry and glass shelves for displaying accessories. I had my office at the very back, where I'd sit smoking away until I heard a customer that I recognised. Then I'd come out and pounce. The only down side was that I could get trapped in there if someone I didn't want to see came in. The shop was managed by Marie Todd, a very capable young woman from Durham, and Neila Souissi, a French Algerian, who I'd spotted working in Ashley and Blake. There was a small alteration workroom downstairs but we kept No. 41 on for some time.

The first week we opened was very exciting. We were incredibly busy and the stock virtually walked out by itself. The girls downstairs were constantly making new garments to keep the rails full. Even after the initial rush, the buzz in the shop was constant. New customers wandered in off the street and gradually we built up a regular clientele. The couture clients were all a pleasure to deal with in the main but there was inevitably the odd tantrum. I remember when one regular customer arrived on spec demanding to see me, Marie told her I was busy. We kept a very careful appointment schedule. However she refused to take no for an answer. Marie brought her dress up for a fitting but she refused to deal with anyone except me. In the end I had to break off what I was doing and went out.

'Listen, I'm with a client who made an appointment to see me. If you want me, I'm afraid you'll have to wait.'

She immediately took off the dress, screwed it into a ball,

tossed it in a corner and stormed out. I was recently asked if I have any difficult customers. The answer's easy: 'Only once.' I'm not going to throw out someone who's spending thousands of pounds but I wouldn't encourage her back.

I love the story of the adventure of Lady X's bra. She was having a dress made but because of the low neckline we had made a slight alteration to her favourite bra. Her driver picked up the dress and drove off with it before we realised that the bra had been left behind. By the time we caught up with Lady X she was in the Hassler in Rome and furious. As if there were no lingerie shops there. However the only thing we could do was courier the bra to Heathrow, book it on a flight to Rome and organise someone at the Hassler to collect it from the airport in time for the occasion. The bra's weekend break must have clocked up a good £200. However Lady X was pleased and has remained a client to this day.

Various minor disasters occurred in the shop that the staff thought they kept from me but I suspect there was very little I didn't know about. I was well aware of the drama when a cup of coffee (strictly against the rules of the workroom to have one by your machine) was spilt all over the panel of a finished wedding dress. The bride was coming to collect on the Saturday. Fortunately the dry cleaner's round the corner completely removed the stain and the bride was none the wiser and I didn't need to be told. For obvious reasons, brides are often the most nervous clients. I remember one poor girl fainted and went down like a tree before anyone had time to catch her. When she was picked up there was a perfect pair of red lipstick lips on the carpet that stayed there as a reminder for months. Once the wrong dress got bagged up and sent to a client for her fortieth birthday party, she was holding in Spain. On the following Monday morning, an irate husband turned up threatening to sue us but fortunately calmed down with the offer of a refund. My brute strength was needed a couple of times: once when a rather generously proportioned client sat on a chair that disintegrated under her weight and I had to help her off the floor with the staff stifling their giggles in the background. She did make up by spending a lot on her wedding dress. Another time, the mother of a bride got locked in the lavatory downstairs. When someone eventually noticed her shouts for help there was no alternative but to get me to kick the door open.

At this point, we were getting heaps of publicity. The shop received plenty of column inches in all the right places both here and in America. Paramount Pictures even made a short feature called *The Dress* about a magic dress bought by a woman played by Phyllis Logan. It was a backless, red matte jersey dress with a draped front and bugle beads on the shoulder and much of the film was shot in and out of the shop. It even won a BAFTA for the best short of the year. The garments were getting pages in *Vogue, Harpers, Tatler, Cosmo* and receiving national coverage during Fashion Weeks. Of course the best ambassador I had was the Princess of Wales – the most photographed woman in the world. The press were rapaciously interested in what she had worn, what she would be wearing, what she might be wearing. The one thing we could never do was comment on speculation about what she would wear for an occasion. We could only confirm a dress was ours once we'd seen a photograph. Though in those low-tech days, it was often hard to distinguish the detail in a blurred fax. One of my proudest moments was when the *Times* trumpeted DIANA WEARS OLDFIELD on their front page.

By this point I seemed to be considered a minor celebrity in my own right and, thanks to Ros's strict management, was frequently invited on to TV chat shows, doing *Wogan* two or three times, *The Late Show* in Ireland, and appearing in *In At the Deep End* in which Paul Heiney tried to fathom the ways of the design business. I guess I was in demand because I came over in a way that people seemed to like. It was the start of quite a prolific TV career. Becoming a well-known face was a mixed blessing. It used to annoy me when people muttered, 'There's Bruce Oldfield,' or, worse still, asked for an autograph. I learned to take it in my stride although it was odd when some-one made eye contact. Were they cruising or simply recog-nising me? Tricky one. I could have put a stop to it but my celebrity was my only advertising budget and as I was good with the media, I milked it – and continue to do so.

In 1984 I had attended a Barnado's special appeals function at London's Royal Garden Hotel. In the course of the evening I suggested to the head of their aftercare section, that we put on a Gala Fashion Show to raise money for them. At last I reached the stage where I felt comfortable with my upbringing. After all without them . . . At the same time I broached the subject of seeing my file again. In 1983 I'd raised the matter and had received the evasive reply:

> I gather you were wondering about the file we have here on you . . . You and many people are anxious to know about their early life, and we shall be only too happy to get the information extracted from our records and arrange to see you for a chat.

This wasn't what I'd wanted at all. I wanted to see the file for myself. It wasn't that I was keen to find out about my mother. Yes, I was curious but no more than that. I think then I was more interested in what had been written about me over the years. Certainly after my renewed request, a report was written about the evening in which the head of aftercare wrote:

> [Bruce] very much feels he should see his file. He wants to know basically what people thought of him and

> although he has many happy memories about his time in Barnardo's, he has some unhappy thoughts about his problems.

What problems? I have no idea what this refers to. Nonetheless, the seed was sown more firmly in both their and my minds, although I wasn't to act on it until the following year.

Instead, my thoughts became entirely focused on how we could produce a gala dinner that would be much more than a fashion show. It had to be a whole event and a money spinner – a far cry from our usual more modest shows or contributions with other designers to other fundraising events. I wanted to take it out of the realms of the tired format of long auctions, indifferent food and C-class entertainment. For me this was a sort of coming-out with Barnardo's. I had never made my background public until now. With the Princess of Wales as President, it couldn't have been better timed. Not only did I have to come up with a spring collection but we had to organise the whole thing. It was the first charity fashion event I can remember that had been held on that scale. It was a logistical nightmare. To begin with we set up a committee chaired by Lady Forte. We met in her house off Belgrave Square and discussed our plans. I find committees are always problematic so I felt it was better to be autocratic, making the decisions and telling them afterwards. In fact I think the members were happy not to be bothered with all the fine detail. Otherwise we would have spent months debating menus, invitations, lighting, music, guest presenters, the band and so on.

The only place big enough to cater for the sort of event we were imagining was the ballroom of the Grosvenor House Hotel, fortunately owned then by the Fortes. Of course getting the Princess to come would be a huge scoop but in the event that she couldn't attend, we made sure we invited an extraordinary star-studded guest-list. We sent the invitation to the Palace in October and waited. Eventually, in December, they contacted us to inform us that the Princess was delighted to accept.

As far as designing the collection went I knew I had to stretch myself. The show, though probably twice as long as a standard show of fifteen to twenty minutes, would follow the usual format, starting with daywear and ending with the glamorous evening dresses and, in this case, a wedding dress. The biggest problem was that the staging had to be enormous to cater for the band who were playing later on. It was all hands on deck for the organisation. We brought in Harvey Goldsmith who'd so brilliantly orchestrated Band Aid at Wembley to stage-manage the event and Michael Rosen to produce the actual show. Dame Edna graciously agreed to run the raffle with the help of Charlotte Rampling and Shirley Bassey while Kid Creole and the Coconuts were booked to play after dinner. Having such a professional band with all its high production values was extremely unusual at a charity ball back then. A raft of prestigious sponsors was lined up. I made the calls and Anita and Ros put the whole thing together. They had to come up with the raffle and auction prizes, organise the seating plan with Romilly while Anita and I chose and tasted the food and organised the decorations. The committee was worried that the ticket price was too high at £100, but between our database and the committee's, we sold the lot. We aimed high and it worked.

As the day drew nearer, nerves were fraying. I'd given up drinking for three months to make sure I would be completely in control but the cigarette intake was rocketing. We were making dresses for a number of clients to wear at the event, among them Charlotte, Shirley Bassey and Joan Collins. Most unpredictable of all was Dame Edna who'd turn up at the shop as Barry Humphries causing havoc as he answered the customer private line at the back of the shop, then barking orders at the staff downstairs over the intercom.

All the fine detail had to be left to the last minute. We'd done the British casting for models in February and optioned about forty girls who we were expecting to see in dribs and drabs as they came in for Fashion Week. As usual, George and I only made a final decision the day before the show when we'd exhausted our options. We used all my favourite girls: including Wendy Medway, Hazel Collins, Amanda Cazalet, Camilla Cecil and Cathy Brooks. Then one model didn't turn up because she'd got a lucrative last-minute fashion shoot and another was stopped at immigration and sent back to New York. But, no point in flapping. This sort of thing is par for the course so we swiftly revised our choice and called round the agencies to get British substitutes. Although I'd been working on the hats with Viv Knowland and jewellery from Slim Barrett for a couple of weeks, the finished articles only arrived at the hotel at the same time as the models. As for the shoes – my old friend Johnny Gairdner, who was PR for Charles Jourdan, supplied them.

The day before, Ros and Anita were dealing with TV crews and reporters, all anxious to get a scoop on which celebrities we were expecting and the dresses they'd be wearing. George had to sort out Kid Creole's band who had arrived without a work permit. Kid Creole was unhappy with the hotel he'd been booked into and had to be moved. The models were complaining about being booked into rooms with no bathrooms so had to be moved. Shirley Bassey's tickets hadn't arrived. Joan Collins' dress didn't fit. A couple more models didn't turn up. The workroom was stretched to the limit, completing alterations and extra garments for the show. As usual I spent a sleepless pre-show night worrying about everything that could go wrong.

On the day itself, Ros had booked me on to Breakfast TV as guest of the day so I was up at 5 a.m. I had to sit chatting with Frank Bough and Selina Scott, trying to look nonchalant, knowing I was dashing back to Beauchamp Place to meet Joan Collins who was arriving for a final fitting complete with TV crew. After sorting the dress out to Joan's satisfaction, I spent time in the workroom, making sure the dresses were exactly as I wanted.

Grosvenor House was swarming with press, all trying to nobble a fitter or machinist to find out what the Princess would be wearing. One of the more enterprising journalists phoned the ballroom pretending to be someone from the workroom. Fortunately they were sussed. The models hadn't arrived until lunchtime because the set boys had only started building at 5 a.m. and were still at it. They had enormous trouble with the 20-foot cinema screen at the back that first wouldn't fit and then wouldn't go up, almost causing the entire set to collapse. This was much more the province of a pop stage than a fashion show, but it did add to the drama with whatever was going on on the stage played on to the screen. Meanwhile George oversaw the fittings and checked the girls in a line-up, adjusting positions according to height, changing outfits and shoes until she'd achieved a cohesive look.

Thank God for experienced models who know how to make the most of a garment, how to keep moving so no one can see it's too big, how to angle themselves for the photographers, how to stand with their hand in the right place to stop a skirt falling down. But inevitably there were still last-minute alterations that had to be made on the spot. We'd been working on the set with the designers and staging company for months and had come up with quite a complex structure that of course the models hated. There were various entrances and exits from the back and sides so they had to be well rehearsed – at least two hours instead of the more usual half an hour for a straightforward catwalk. Michael gave them all a pad and pencil and made them write down their moves scene by scene, yelling at them when they went wrong and making them go over it again and again until it was right. As usual, George made sure that the dressers had a list of which dress went with which accessory and how to do up anything out of the ordinary. As they dressed, the models were to re-read their instructions for their next entrance and be reminded again by whoever sent them on. Michael ran through a selection of music with me until we got a final choice that we were happy with. I wanted something up-beat, easy to walk to. Donna Summer's 'The State of Independence' provided a strong finale. All of this was being done with a film crew hovering over our shoulders, producing a documentary for the news programmes. The workroom was making garments up to the wire so that a number of them, including the final wedding dress, didn't arrive until a few hours before kick-off. Caroline Charles generously allowed us to use her workroom up the road in Beauchamp Place to cope with the last-minute alterations. When I arrived at the hotel at 3 p.m. in a taxi with four others in the pouring rain, I had ten outfits on my lap that I was rushing into the rehearsal.

By six o'clock, the final fittings were done, the models were rehearsed within an inch of their lives and we were all exhausted. So when Kid Creole said he wanted not only the stage but half of the dance floor as well, I couldn't be bothered to argue.

Olga Polizzi, Lady Forte's daughter, had laid on hotel suites for Dame Edna and the rest of us to change in. Then a huge sense of relief swept over me when the doors opened and we began the evening with a private reception for the committee and Princess Diana who arrived at 7 p.m. on the dot, looking quite the fairytale princess in the backless pleated silvery blue lamé evening dress I had designed. There was nothing more I could do except get on with my role as host. Backstage there would be a scene of controlled chaos. I knew from George that over-excited models were dashing about in curlers trying to get into the room to see who was there or flirting with Kid Creole backstage. The obligatory glass of champagne (just one makes them perform better!) only made them more determined to escape the confines of the dressing room.

As I led the Princess down the stairs to our table, I felt it was the start to a very special evening. The room was perfect. Each candlelit table had a large display of white tulips at its centre supplied by Lynne Lawrence. Wherever I looked in the sea of tables, I could see friends and famous faces. My family was there, Anita and the team were there and so were an enormous number of clients.

First of all was the fashion show. The staging itself was quite amazing. Images from Hitchcock movies were projected on to the screen between sections with appropriately eerie music. The girls had to walk up a series of staircases at the back of the stage, appearing on the highest level and then descending the stepped ramps from level to level to the dance floor. To make any kind of impression, we needed lots of activity – so lots of girls were necessary in each group. The show began with all of the girls out at once wearing jersey separates and dresses in what had by then become my trademark outrageous colour clashes. You really needed sunglasses to cope with the magentas, oranges, sulphur yellow and turquoises. These combinations always worked well, confounding people's expectations. You just break the rules. It's fun. There were shapely waisted suits with curvy peplums, very broad shoulders and pencil skirts in red, white and black. Then bold prints for a day at the races. This was followed by a black-and-white section of cotton voiles, stretch sequins and crêpes, a sophisticated 'resort' look of bras, ruched hipster skirts and billowing voile toppers. Then came a group of tailored dresses and jackets with 'panier' pockets at the hips, perhaps the miss of the show, and a small group of lace dresses with large bands of duchess satin threaded through. Because the stage was so big, the evening dresses had to have scale too so, notwithstanding the enormous shoulders prevalent at the time, I also designed what was to be called 'the armadillo dress' as it consisted of yards of red taffeta circular skirts ruched into a tiny waist, the bodice consisting of ruched batwing sleeves tightly sashed and bowed at the waist. Shoulders everywhere were large and padded with tiny belt-accentuated waists. I remember Hazel dropping her earring and, unfazed, waiting till her return to the spot to elegantly dip down, scoop it up and replace it – a very cinematic moment. Whatever muddle there had been during the day was now slick, well-paced and looked terrific. Michael and the rest of the team had done a fantastic job. The finale brought the most alarming moment when the bride picked her way down the steps surrounded by dry ice and darkness. Her mission was to come down, cross the dance floor and present the Princess with a bouquet, but the poor girl could barely see where she was putting her feet. She made it, but only just.

Watching the video recently, I recognised at least six dresses worn subsequently by the Princess of Wales, including the dress she wore at Prince Harry's christening, the red and white suit worn to meet the Reagans at the White House, the black and white suit worn to the Melbourne Cup and the red evening dress she wore to the Birthright Ball. There was also a red pleated dress with a gold embroidered midriff that Romilly wore to Rocco Forte's wedding plus the beaded chiffon number gathered on to padded shoulders and draped below the hips on to a columnar skirt that was worn by both Princess Katherine of Yugoslavia and Eileen Bond.

Over dinner, I remember the Princess hinting that all was

not well in her marriage but I really didn't want to pursue this conversation. It wasn't the moment.

'It's not quite how you think, Bruce.'

'What do you mean?'

'Well, it's not a bed of roses. Not quite as much fun as it's made out to be.'

'Aren't you happy?'

'Some of the time. Is your life happy?'

'It is at the moment. Err . . . more bread, Ma'am?'

My after-dinner speech was as short as I could respectably make it before handing over to Dame Edna who took on the role of MC with aplomb, deftly managing Charlotte, Christopher Reeve and Shirley Bassey who were doing the tombola, then carrying off the auction so successfully that she managed to get Lord Forte to bid £1,000 for the flowers in the room. Unbelievably he was trumped by Peter Stringfellow who paid £5,000 for the lot. Heaven knows what he did with them all. Edna concluded by asking for a 'little bit of shush' before reading her Ode penned specially for the evening:

> When Bruce first ran his chilly tape
> From my slender ankle to naked nape
> I asked him, 'Of all the girls you've dressed,
> Tell me. Possum, who's the best?'
> Bruce gave me one of his famous grins
> But, alas, his mouth was full of pins.
> Yet, I doubt if his answer would give you a shock
> As you gaze at me now in this stunning frock.
> But I must be as generous as I am able
> To those poor runners-up in the Oldfield stable.
> You all look gorgeous. You've all done your best.
> It's not my fault I'm better dressed.
> But tonight's event is no mere charade

Of glamour pusses on parade.
As I am an actress and chanteuse
I've been given a job to do by Bruce.
He said, 'Edna, please write a few talented verses
To make those silly old hubbies put their hands in
    their purses.
It's within your powers as a megastar
To remind us all how lucky we are.'
As we gobble our champers and avocados
Let's think of the work done by Dr Barnardo's.
Let me tell you my secret for satisfied living
It's giving and giving and giving and GIVING.
What a relief to know that your donation
Won't be squandered away on administration.
I think of young Bruce as though he's my son . . .
But if I get too emotional, my mascara might run.
So welcome to this Barnardo's Beano.
I'm glad I didn't wear my Valentino.
But a spooky voice inside my head
Made me slip into this little number instead.
And darling Bruce would get such a shock
To spy me in a rival's frock.
But isn't this Oldfield number bliss?
I know women who'd kill for a dress like this.
Bruce's top clients all agree
It's an honour to be upstaged by me.
But the Barnardo's boys and girls all know we all know
They are the stars of this glittering show.
With our generous help, their feet will be planted
On the road of life we take so much for granted.
So turn your minds, Possums, from food and sex,
The fashion tonight is BIG FAT CHEQUES.

*

The fund-raising concluded, the dancing could begin, led by the Princess and myself. I think she regretted having said anything earlier and simply wanted to lighten the mood.

I didn't relax until 3 a.m. the next morning. When I got up after a few hours' sleep, it was to see both the Princess and me splashed all over the papers. Later in the day, the Princess dropped by the shop unannounced so that she could thank everyone in the workroom. Her readiness to give thanks where due was something I always liked about her and of course it made her very popular in the workroom. The letters that arrived over the following days were testament to the hard work that had gone into making the evening a truly memorable event. Later I was invited on to *Wogan* to present a cheque for £104,000 to Barnardo's. The money was used to buy, refurbish and set up a house in Darlington for five severely handicapped children and their carers.

The whole event received the most amazing coverage that ran for almost the rest of the year. It was a major PR coup and really put us on the map. Looking back at it now, particularly at the well-circulated photograph of the Princess and me at dinner, I realise that it was a quite extraordinary moment. There was the future Queen of England and there was me. Rarely would you have seen an image like that – a designer with such an important client. I don't remember any of the others she used being photographed chin-wagging with her and I certainly can't imagine a scenario where Norman Hartnell would have sat next to the Queen. The fact it was allowed to happen marked a new age. Of course the fact was it was good for her to be seen actively promoting her role with Barnado's, good for Barnardo's and good for me. It presaged all sorts of similar events. The media loved it and it ran and ran. It put me in an unassailable position whereby I gained career credibility that stood me in very good stead for the future. I'm also sure we attracted a lot of new customers because of it. It still surprises me when I look back at the pages of press cuttings, the Grosvenor House represented the pinnacle of my career to date but it also marked the start of a new career after a kind of apprenticeship. Everything was happening for me. That night was just the start and we would go sky high. I knew it.

CHAPTER SIXTEEN

After a short break, it was back to a huge and very flattering media flurry in July when it was widely rumoured that Peter de Savary had bought the distinguished couture house of Norman Hartnell and that I had been appointed to run it. I had been in confidential (I thought) discussions with them but the first I heard of the fuss was when Ros called me. She'd had a call from Ann Chubb on the *Telegraph* who had phoned from Paris asking her if there was any truth in the rumour. We decided not to confirm or deny but the story spread wildly out of control to the extent that a BBC TV crew pitched up outside the shop, complete with their then royal correspondent Michael Cole. I called Ros to the rescue. She made it clear that we weren't going to invite them inside but there was nothing we could do to stop them filming outside the shop. And so it was we appeared on the main BBC news once again.

But why on earth would I have moved? Anita and I were trying to build up our own couture house. These old couture houses had had their days in the twenties and thirties but never really regained their former positions after the war. Hartnell was probably the strongest but all that was left was an enormous piece of real estate on Mayfair's Bruton Street with a beautiful, if faded, first-floor showroom and a warren of thousands of square feet of empty workrooms. There was one small workroom that continued to make things for their last remaining client, HM

Queen Elizabeth, the Queen Mother. This was not like being offered Chanel where there was still an ongoing business with a long heritage and a big budget that you could do something with. Of course, we looked at the possibilities. Who wouldn't? But Anita and I were very clear about what we did and didn't want to do. We were both convinced it would be a bad move. However, remaining diplomatically silent got us acres of publicity.

Meanwhile the Barnardo's wheels were grinding forward and I had a call from Roger Singleton, the chief executive, inviting me to come to the Head Office to read my file. This was unprecedented. Roger explained to me that he had been going to weed through it himself on my behalf so that he could pick out what he thought would be relevant to me. After he began, he realised what a ridiculous exercise it was. He was convinced by what he read that there was no reason why I shouldn't read everything for myself. This really was the start of the Barnardo's organisation thinking afresh about access to files. He realised that something had to be done with this vast historic legacy of hidden information particularly since Barnardo's was coming under increasing pressure from me and others like me who wanted to see what had been written about them and what information had been kept from them.

By letting me read my own file, he was breaking Barnardo's rules at that time. It's interesting to me that Roger remembers the experience because it was influential in his own thinking about the changes the organisation needed to make. It was not until the nineties that people were finally permitted to have copies of their files as well as the originals of their birth certificates, baptism certificates and their school reports. So it was that, at his invitation, I caught the tube out to Barkingside one summery day to find out more about who I was and what the people who cared for me had thought of me. I don't think I was very impressed with the file although it was a surprise to read quite how deeply involved Edith Blair was in my welfare. However, it didn't spark any feelings for my birth mother except perhaps to make me realise that she wasn't an entirely bad lot – more a victim of her time and circumstances. But to be honest, I wasn't too concerned. I was far too tied up in my own little world. Reading about my background didn't fire me to search further for my real family. The characters I read about seemed to have little to do with me. It wasn't until another twelve years had gone by, when I was a much more mellow individual, better able to cope with things, that I set the wheels in motion again, and determined to find out what had happened to Betty Lally, my mother. Instead, I went back to London and got on with my life.

The publicity that had been engendered by the gala seemed never ending. When the Princess of Wales visited Italy on a state visit later in the year, we got almost as much coverage from the fact that she didn't wear me as if she had. The press were buzzing with excitement about her choice of outfits when she visited the Vatican and La Scala. In fact she wore Jan Vanvelden but was reported as explaining that her decision not to wear the gala dress was down to its backlessness: 'People didn't know where to put their hands. When they are guiding you they sometimes touch bare flesh. It's rather embarrassing.' However, I was pleased to see that she made up by wearing a blue-grey suit of mine to see da Vinci's *Last Supper* and a dark-blue and white one on her visit to Rome.

To my delight, another cherry on the cake that year came from Suzy Menkes, then fashion editor of *The Times*, the most respected editor in the business, now of the *Herald Tribune*. She chose a strapless black crêpe and gold lame dress from the collection as Dress of the Year for 1985 for the Museum of Costume in Bath alongside a man's suit by Scott Crolla. It was quite an accolade.

Anita and I decided that it was time to look again at how we could build the business both at home and internationally. My idol then was Armani whose empire had proliferated around the world but who never allowed standards to drop. But without external funding – hard to get in a country where, to a venture capitalist, fashion is a dirty word – that sort of ambition was a pipe dream. We had to look at opportunities we could realistically optimise. Having the Princess as a client obviously did us a huge amount of good and now was the moment to build on the current interest in the brand. We decided the way to go was to extend it by taking on selected licensing deals with the aim of making 'Bruce Oldfield' more of a household name. This was a practice followed the world over by brands that wanted to expand their reach and revenue without necessarily incurring costs themselves. Pierre Cardin, the French couturier, amassed a huge fortune and deep disapprobrium from the French fashion community (as if he cared) by the less-than-careful way in which he used his name. Anyone could buy something with his branding on it. Factory workers from Columbia to Timbuktu could sport trousers, ties, shirts, socks, umbrellas, all with the Cardin logo. To be so indiscriminate obviously reduces the credibility and aspirational value of the brand which, unless you are about to shut up shop in the near future, is not smart.

Designers like America's Calvin Klein tackled the problem in a very different way. His main licences – men's jeans and underwear – were promoted so strongly and with such integrity that it didn't matter that they dominated his brand because, although mass market, they had design credibility and were aspirational. He was able to use the vast returns from this lucrative licensing to create high-visibility fashion collections and to embark on one of the most successful American fragrance licences of the twentieth century.

We didn't have to go out soliciting thanks to a number of companies who approached us. This was Anita's field and she chose very carefully which we should take on, weighing up what they wanted from us and how we would gain through the association. She had a very clear view as to which were the right deals so I was guided by her as we turned down umbrellas, slippers, duvets, anoraks, you name it. All I had to do was design the goods with my assistant's help, decide on the colours and themes, oversee the sampling and watch the royalties roll in. At least that's what I thought. But it turned out to be an enormous call on my time, largely because I like to do everything well and insisted on checking every last detail. It was also to be a source of continual disagreement with the other shareholders. They felt that the money belonged to the company, whereas since the work depended on my skills alone, I felt I deserved a larger share. The difference we could never overcome was that while the European and American model of licensing would be simply to brand the product with the designer's name, the UK companies insisted that their name should appear on the branding too. Bruce Oldfield for WHOEVER. This wasn't a route I favoured. My idea was to strengthen the brand of Bruce Oldfield and make that the peg on which to make the sale. However this was not to be, so we had to be even more careful that whatever names we were associated with were of a sufficiently high calibre not to compromise us.

The range of furs we did with Birger Christensen was logical from the glamour angle and we launched the first range in September 1985. Ros introduced us to Charnos, another of her clients, and our first range of tights appeared in 1986. That was a particularly happy arrangement because the Bruce Oldfield hosiery sold well. Slightly against my better judgement, I toured the country's department stores to sign packets of tights, finding queues that reached out of the shops and round the nearest corner. It was extraordinary the number of people who turned up. A very strange experience. There was a black pair of tights with a seam and a little bow that I gave to the Princess of Wales. She wore them somewhere and the press grabbed hold of the story. Ros was having a coronary, anxious people would think we were cashing in. She had to ring round the stores to ensure they didn't unwittingly sell any stock to the *Sun* or the *News of the World* in case they used it for a readers' offer.

The lingerie line I did with Charnos a little later wasn't great and didn't last. Over the next two or three years we did shoes with Rayne, several seasons of a very successful range of cashmere designs with knitwear specialist Murray Allen as well as ranges of shirts with Hilditch and Key and spectacles with Pilkington Products. Each of them stretched me as a designer and increased our presence as a household name.

The one that got away was Nike, the sportswear brand. One day Anita got a call from Brendan Foster, ex-athlete and TV sporting presenter, who was involved with the giant American corporation. They wanted to do something slightly different and were keen to do something with a British designer that could be 'rolled out' across the US. We had many meetings where terms were agreed and design and marketing concepts were worked on. I spent quite a lot of time going backwards and forwards to New York where I was given Nike House to stay in whenever I liked. The range they wanted was to be slightly retro – I suspect the top brass were hedging their bets on the longevity of their very successful sportswear lines (which I could never fully understand). They were looking for cross-over garments that people would wear going to and from the golf clubhouse or the tennis courts, not necessarily what people would wear for the sport itself. Boy, did they get that one wrong. However, I wasn't being asked to judge the marketing wisdom of such a move, simply to come up with the concepts and designs to facilitate it.

Out of the blue, I had a call from Oregon asking me to drop everything and to come to Los Angeles for a meeting with Mr Knight, the CEO. Flights were arranged and my suite was booked for a week at the Beverly Hills Hotel. I arrived, had a lunch meeting with Mr Shlusser, a lawyer for Nike, who told me that he'd be in touch. I then spent most of the following week by the hotel pool or visiting clients and friends in Malibu and Beverly Hills, occasionally bringing people to the hotel for lunch where I could simply sign the cheque. It was a great holiday. I was fascinated by the goings-on round the pool where every next sunbed had a starlet and every cabana a would-be director or producer. The paging system always caused a stir. 'Mr Rothenstein. Paging Mr Rothenstein. A call from Paramount.' Everybody was instantly rubber-necking to see who this Mr Rothenstein was. I tried it myself, getting friends to ring. 'Paging Mr Oldfield. Paging Mr Oldfield. Miss Collins on the line for you.' It worked like a dream. At that time, Joan could do no wrong. Her ratings as Alexis Carrington in *Dynasty* made her one of the most recognised faces in America. I was pleased for her. She had always treated me well, probably because I supported her in the days when the too-terrible *The Bitch* and *The Stud* brought her back into the public view.

The following Monday I had my next and final LA meeting where Mr Shlusser informed me that they wanted to get out of our contract. All I had to do was name the figure I wanted for compensation. Naturally I wasn't about to discuss that with him there and then so it was agreed that when he was in London in a few weeks' time, he would sit down with me and my advisors. There followed a strange meeting at the office of my solicitors, Lewis Silkin, who had advised me on all my licensing deals. Anita and I were sitting with our lawyer Roger Alexander and in came Mr Shlusser. A figure was mentioned. He jumped up, red-faced, blustering, 'I'll see you in court,' then stormed out.

End of meeting. It was like a scene from *LA Law*. Anyway, we never had to experience any more bravura performances like that and we settled on a very handsome figure.

By the end of October we had shown our new collection and were gearing up for Fashion Aid on 5 November, following fast in the footsteps of Bob Geldof's Band Aid to contribute to the end of world hunger. The whole event was extremely well organised, thanks again to Harvey Goldsmith. All the top designers had a spot of between twenty and thirty pieces, almost a mini fashion show each from Yves St Laurent, Calvin Klein and Giorgio Armani to Rifat, Scott Crolla, Jean Muir, Zandra Rhodes and myself. It was at the Albert Hall so had around 5,000 in the audience with a huge runway down the centre of the arena. It was great fun because the designers had licence to go wild. Katherine Hamnett's section was themed like a Hindu wedding; Rifat's was Italian Riviera time with him appearing wearing one of the dresses; Joseph was Egyptian themed; Anthony Price delivered Jerry Hall to the runway in a vast gift-wrapped box and she proceeded to give the best performance of her career to rapturous applause; Issey Miyake had models coming down from the ceiling on ropes while Bodymap had Boy George and David and Elizabeth Emanuel had got hold of Freddie Mercury. I put on a really glamorous, sexy show to Diana Ross's Reflections. The dresses were black and gold from the winter collection. To create a real impact on that massive 90-foot runway, we'd made some extra gold dresses especially. The models sashayed round well-oiled bodybuilders wearing the briefest of towels with Bruce Oldfield sewn on to them. Camp, maybe. Effective, definitely.

Only days afterwards, I flew to Perth for Australia's social event of the year. Alan Bond's daughter, Susanne, was marrying American radiologist Armand Leone. It began when Susanne and Eileen her mother had come into 27 Beauchamp Place some months earlier. I remember them particularly because Eileen 'Red' Bond was a great character who turned up wearing a white floor-length mink coat in the middle of summer, with an enormous diamond ring that was twisted into her palm out of the sight of potential muggers. We discussed what they wanted, I did some drawings and we talked again. At first they wanted 'romantic', then they wanted 'romantic but grand'. Finally I said, 'Can we stop beating about the bush? Do you want this to look grand, over the top and seriously deluxe?''

'You've got it, Bruce.'

'Well, why didn't you say so in the first place?'

'Because we thought you'd be a bit more savvy and get there quicker.'

So that's why the dress was totally over the top, as big and beaded as it could be. I've done similarly ornate dresses subsequently but mainly for my Middle Eastern customers. This was to be something Australia had never seen before. I was also dressing Eileen, the bridesmaids and making Susanne her going-away outfit. In the end I designed a total of thirty dresses for the pre-wedding parties, the event itself and for the going away. So it was quite an event for me.

I flew to Perth with the dresses a few days before the wedding. I stayed in Alistair McAlpine's Bishop's House, a beautiful colonial building in several acres of formal gardens in downtown Perth, nestling among the skyscrapers, many of which had been erected by McAlpine himself. He was there for the first night then left me to go to Broome, a pearl-fishing town further up the coast where he had become something of the local lord of the manor. I never ventured there myself after hearing tales of frogs that spit venom, funnel-web spiders and all sorts of anti-social nightlife. There was quite a racy set in Perth in those days. One minute they were millionaires, the next they'd lost everything. The wedding was the social event of the year and there were a great many associated parties and barbecues. I spent as much time as I could on my own, simply walking along miles and miles of beach although every night I'd get roped into something. The locals were keen to get inside the house and weren't disappointed with Alistair's eclectic collections of Australiana, including a number of works by Sidney Nolan.

The wedding had originally been planned for Perth Cathedral but Eileen was so incensed by the Bishop's refusal to fit them in at 5 p.m. that she took the whole shebang to St Patrick's Roman Catholic Church in Fremantle where she and Alan had been married. She had the altar repainted white and adorned it with red brocade, recarpeting the confessional and aisles with green carpet and festooning the place in red and white flowers on the day.

The day of the wedding, the Bond mansion was a scene of complete mayhem with the exception of Alan Bond, sublimely cool and collected, sitting in his bedroom, wearing his dressing gown watching a black-and-white Tarzan movie while waiting to perform his starring role, perhaps mulling over just how much money he'd spent on the wedding. I was either ironing or helping to dress the whole party – bridesmaids in blood-red taffeta, Eileen in black and gold and of course the bride in ivory and gold. The car pulled up to take Susanne to the wedding. But instead of the Vanden Plas Princess I'd recommended, they'd hired a 1920s' Rolls Royce that gave us entirely the same problem as the Princess of Wales arriving at St Paul's in that too big dress in that too small coach. She emerged like a crumpled butterfly from its chrysalis with no time to straighten her wings. However we managed somehow to squash Susanne in beside her father. I came along in the car behind so I could leap out and help tidy her up at the other end. The church was mobbed, everybody anxious to get a glimpse of Australia's equivalent of royalty. Susanne looked stunning, like a fairytale princess from *A Midsummer Night's Dream* and the excited reception she got from the crowds confirmed it. Her ivory silk taffeta dress had a heavily gold-beaded bodice included a heart with the initial A in its centre. Another heart with the initial S was near the hem. Over a slim underskirt was an enormous taffeta skirt and train gathered to a V into her tiny waist. The top skirt's eight-foot train was detachable for the reception and dancing.

After the ceremony, a splendidly lavish reception was held at the Bonds' home on the banks of the Swan River. No expense was spared. There were tugs, spraying plumes of water on the river; a half-hour firework display in which the bride and groom's names were fierily intertwined in the night sky; the red carpets were resplendent with monogrammed initials and led the way under illuminated palms into the pink, white and silver marquee. Like something from *The Arabian Nights*, the ceiling and walls lined with parachute silk dotted with thousands of twinkling fairy lights; dozens of chandeliers and arrangements of white Christmas lilies, peony roses and orchids. The attention to detail was staggering with gold thread complementing the bride's dress woven into the tablecloths. A 2.4-metre high *croquembouche* wedding cake took pride of place and each guest received a commemorative medal. The speeches were made and telegrams from Bob Hawke and other Aussie notables were read out. The dozens of bottles of Krug were downed to the music from the floating bandstand until an announcement: 'Unless you are wearing a bathing costume, it would be wise not to use the dance floor.'

The dance floor, suspended spectacularly over the beach, had collapsed! Undeterred, the partying continued on dry land until well into the small hours, long after the bride and groom had departed by dinghy. Breakfast was served as dawn broke.

I got back to England, completely dead, on the morning of

the Birthright Ball, which was held at the Albert Hall. Michael Howells had designed the event like a massive banquet so a single row of candlelit tables stretched along the tiers and in the boxes of the auditorium. It looked fabulous. The Palace had asked if Anita and I would take one of the few tables on the dance floor next to the one taken by the Prince of Wales, presumably so we could help look after the Princess. She wore my favourite of all the dresses that we made for her – a very sexy red silk crêpe sheath knotted at the throat, the customary square shoulders and V-back-neckline.

It was a fitting end to an incredibly successful year.

CHAPTER SEVENTEEN

By 1986 we had given up 41 Beauchamp Place but needed more space for the workshop and indeed for us. Anita found us a small building halfway between Putney and Redcliffe Gardens in a scruffy backstreet off Fulham Broadway. Argon Mews was a little cul de sac with the LEB directly opposite us. It had its own parking bay that nobody respected so either there was never anywhere to park or, if you found a space, you were guaranteed to be blocked in by someone else. I wasn't keen to move the office and workshop there but I could see it answered our need for space and it was more convenient for Anita, since she didn't need to come to the shop very often and she and Kevin were still living in Putney. To me, it was a bit of a retrograde step going from Knightsbridge to Fulham and I didn't relish the idea of having to tear between the three addresses – even if it did mean there was room for me to have an assistant.

Bruce Robbins was a student I had previously come across while doing a crit at the Royal College of Art and subsequently I had nominated him in one of the Sunday supplements as a designer to watch. He left the RCA and went to New York where he worked on a variety of licensed products for Donna Karan. On his return, I snapped him up to work in the Fulham studio because he had gained such good experience. Debbie Little joined us a little later, introduced by Howard Dickinson, a friend in Paris with whom she'd worked at Cerruti. Judith agreed to come and manage the workshop from the start. After an accident, her husband Felix had been unable to work so made it sense for them to close down the Blackstock Road operation they had run for so long and for her to come to us.

In an earlier life, the building had belonged to the DHSS, only too evident from the wheelchair access and elaborate fire escapes. It was large and gave us the luxury of a big office for Anita, which we filled with contemporary furniture and a very pre-possessing desk; an office for our accountant Keith Frazer, and a huge room for fabric and stock cutting where Jill, the production manager, held sway. Upstairs, at the front of the building, was a very large and light-filled room that I divided in two with sliding screens. I occupied the front part and George and Bruce shared the back. We had to call Bruce 'Robin' or 'little Bruce' to avoid confusion and George was always just George. The enormous workroom accommodating the pattern cutters and seamstresses was Judith's domain. There always seemed to be a good atmosphere and everyone was kept extremely busy. Some clients preferred the anonymity of the place so a number of fittings were done there as well as in Beauchamp Place. The Princess of Wales came down soon after we'd moved there. I had sent her about six sketches and she wanted to go through fabric possibilities for the different occasions she had in mind. We looked at some options that I'd picked out downstairs, then hefted the rolls she was interested in up the stairs to my office. The barefoot princess insisted on carrying them as well.

'We can't let you do that, Ma'am,' Judith protested.

'Oh, let me,' she replied. 'In the Palace, they don't let me do anything.' It was this sort of unaffected behaviour that made her very popular with everyone. She insisted on meeting the staff and would often send flowers after she'd worn a 'Bruce Oldfield' to show her appreciation of their work.

One time she came for a fitting but as she came in, Anita's Jack Russell, Tailor, shot out to see who it was. I heard Anita roaring, 'Get in my office, NOW.'

'Yes, of course,' said the Princess and shot in there almost as fast as Tailor.

Anita was mortified although the rest of us, including the Princess, thought it was hilarious.

Most of the fittings were done at Kensington Palace by Anita, Judith and me. The first time we went, we weren't sure about the form so decided to go to the tradesmen's entrance at the back. We were met by kitchen staff who then informed the butler, an enormous man with a big, booming voice.

'Mr Oldfield,' he intoned, 'a man of your distinction and talent must never use the back door to this palace again!' So we never did.

We'd do the fittings in her sitting room, dumping everything on the three-seater sofa and putting up the long portable mirror. The room was very light and comfortable, lit by the long windows behind her desk. To the side there was a smaller round table that held her collection of china. Our appointments always had to be held when she wasn't fetching the children from school. Then she'd give us an hour and a half – long enough for three fittings, a coffee and a chat. Once when I had left the room so the Princess could dress, I was sitting perched on a window seat in the drawing room when I heard the unmistakeable voice of Prince Charles in the corridor. I had to resist the urge to step behind the voluminous curtains and hide. Another time he interrupted one of the fittings, looking at his wife and asking me, 'Have you seen the Stubbs exhibition at the Tate?'

'No, Sir.'

He disappeared for a few minutes, returning with the catalogue of the exhibition. Pointing at a duchess astride a horse, he wondered, 'Do you think my wife would look good in something like that?'

A full seventeenth-century riding outfit? It wasn't quite what we'd had in mind.

'I'll see what I can come up with, Sir,' I promised.

I never felt the Princess was entirely at ease in her position, at least at that point in her life. She disliked pomposity and used to call me 'oily Oldfield' when I was being particularly ingratiating. Half the time, I didn't know how to deal with her, whether to be normal, telling her not to slouch, or whether to bow and scrape because however friendly she was, she never let down the regal front entirely.

She was growing far more aware of her importance as an ambassador for British fashion. She would search the mirror, worried that her shoulder pads were too big or that the skirts were too short. Most women have something they dislike about their body, however irrational. As a couturier you learn to look at certain areas and cut your cloth accordingly. The Princess had a thing about both her shoulders and knees. As far as I was concerned her shoulders were a gift because they ensured everything hung so well. As for her knees? They looked like anyone else's to me. These anxieties and the restrictions of protocol meant that while she was the most fantastic advertisement for us, there was also something of a double-edged sword about dressing her. It involved inevitable compromises and an awareness that much depends on how women exit cars without revealing too much and the like. I might say, 'Let's slash it to the waist,' and she'd counter with, 'Let's slash it to the shoulder blade.'

We found ourselves in a bit of a *Catch 22* situation. On the one hand, Anita and I wanted the publicity but, on the other, we spent ten years avoiding direct questions and avoiding making direct statements about the Princess of Wales. 'Never deny, never elaborate,' was our mantra. I think we stayed in the vanguard of her dress designers for such a long time because we observed the codes. Even when she and I were splashed all over the papers together, we continued to say nothing. We still got dropped by her in the end though!

She was not the only British royal we dressed. One of my fondest memories is of one of the members of the royal family arbitrarily deciding to do her exercises in 41's showroom. Just as she began to stretch, an open-topped tourist bus drove slowly by, pointing out the stops on the Diana tour, and a group of open-mouthed tourists gazed in disbelief at what they were witnessing. The only difficulty I sometimes had was having to persuade other members of the family that they didn't want exactly the same dress as the Princess of Wales had worn at a previous function.

Susan Sangster was another regular visitor to Argon Mews. She would order dresses and come to be fitted on her way to Heathrow en route to the Isle of Man. We always used to ask what time her flight was so that we could fit round her schedule and her reply was always, 'Oh, it doesn't matter.' It took ages for us to twig the fact that she had her own plane but was too modest to mention it.

A memorable wedding of that period, almost immediately after the Bond wedding, was that of Jordanian Alia Tabbah to Prince Feisal, the second son of King Hussein of Jordan. Alia would come to Argon Mews getting dresses for the numerous parties surrounding the wedding. I remember one similar to one I made for princess Diana, with a ruched midriff section and floating skirts in red and white polka-dot chiffon. Alia wanted a fairytale wedding so we made a romantic full-skirted white taffeta dress, the skirts and sleeves festooned with embroidered flower garlands. On the day, they drove through Amman in an open car. It was the wedding of the decade and I only regret that I wasn't able to attend. We have remained good friends over the years and Princess Alia loaned me the wedding dress to put into a retrospective of my work at the Laing Gallery in Newcastle in 2000. We also dressed her bridesmaids, both of whom I was subsequently to make wedding dresses for in 2002 and 2003.

We were still constantly on the move, whether doing fashion shows in far-flung places or crossing the pond in search of the Yankee dollar. In May, we took the collection to Singapore to do a show under the auspices of Christina and BS Ong. As we had been doing business for many years with their boutique in Singapore, Club 21, we had built up a good relationship with them. BS and Christina were on the way to becoming extremely big players in the global fashion market. Already with interests in hotels, they were soon to take on the franchise of Giorgio Armani in the UK, subsequently adding other international names to their stable of big fashion franchises. Owning the franchises meant that they were responsible, under the artistic constraints and dictates of the designer they represented, to create approved retail sites in approved territories around the world. Depending on how the deal is structured, the franchisee would have to finance the real estate and the fit-out of the premises and sometimes guarantee a minimum turnover on the site while the design company would supply the merchandise. This would mean that designer X's shop on Sloane Street may not have belonged to him, but the simple fact that it existed would raise his profile, kudos and visibility to the clothes-buying public and could encourage other franchisees to open similar outlets in other territories. This made the franchisees very powerful and a tiny handful of wealthy individuals could colonise streets such as Sloane Street, Bond Street and Brompton Cross and turn them into high-rent oases almost over night. The point of all this is that BS and Christina were on our hit-list as potential partners to replace the current shareholders. It wasn't to happen because they really only wanted established brands with an established retail heritage. We also submitted a proposal to Robert Sangster, flying to the Isle of Man to go over it with him but it didn't come to anything. They made much better friends than business partners.

As well as arranging flights for Anita, George and me, the Ongs also arranged one for Kevin so he could come along, help with the show and join us on a little sailing trip they had planned. I remember they took us in two boats to Tioman island in the South China Sea. We were on board for most of the day so we had plenty of time to relax and get quite merry. I must have been, otherwise I would never have agreed to swim ashore. Of course it was much further than it looked. I eventually made it to the shore, getting horribly cut on the coral while behind me the Ongs' daughter was fished out of the water by the dinghy.

Back on dry land, when it came to the show we realised the Chinese models were too small for the clothes. We had to use falsies as well as a cleverly devised waist-thickening belt that the girls strapped on so that the clothes would at least be anchored at the waist. We did have one model who was slightly larger than the rest and particularly gorgeous. It wasn't until Kevin almost broke her arm getting a bracelet off that we realised that she was a transvestite.

Another highlight of the eighties was being invited to the International Design Conference at Aspen, Colorado, a forum for the design industry. It spreads its net over practically every field where the design process is employed, from architecture through theatre and film design, product design, fashion design and so on. Because of the breadth of the subject, the conference attracts a wide array of first-class talent, which was why the mix was so eclectic that year. To get David Hockney,

Eva Jiricna, Roy Strong, David Puttnam and other luminaries around the table together is quite a meeting of minds. George and I travelled to Aspen, which is 5,000 feet above sea level, a problem for anyone like me who smoked. The conference that year had been arranged by Pentagram and was celebrating the best of British design. During the week the audience heard talks from the participants. George and I put together a fashion show featuring a number of British designers.

We'd shipped out the clothes two weeks earlier but Katherine Hamnett insisted on sending hers out later. She was opening the show but when the clothes failed to materialise, we had to improvise. I took the conference T-shirts, white with a Union Jack on them, and, with a pair of scissors, I customised them on the spot – just like being at art school. The rehearsals had to be done late in the evening because the talks went on in the tented auditorium during the day, so we had plenty of time to amuse ourselves. The models were staying in chalets complete with outdoor jacuzzis where they were romping about in the buff until the outraged neighbours sent in the police to restore a bit of propriety. Of course the police loved such an unusual disturbance and spent the rest of the week acting as a cab service for the girls. I went to several of the talks, but also spent time reading and drawing. Most of the time I was nursing a headache brought on by the altitude so I felt permanently hungover as well as alarmingly breathless. Not so the models who carried on smoking even around the oxygen cylinders back stage.

George and I travelled home via New York so that I could show her the city for the first time. We shared a room at the Westbury on Madison Avenue. After dinner on the first night, I crashed out, leaving George to go to a club with our agent. The next day, we did the full tourist bit in the morning from the Empire State Building to the Twin Towers. We lunched and shopped in SoHo where I discovered a fantastic 1920s' bust, sculpted in clay, fired and then the surface of the face and hair lightly coloured and buffed. It weighed a ton, but George convinced me that I should buy it and carry it back on the flight that afternoon. I gave in (she wasn't the one carrying it!). It sits in front of my desk today.

Anita and I were keen to break into the Japanese market. We were already selling a small number of clothes into Tokyo but wanted to expand. Japan is a huge market with a tradition of licensing and franchising. Because the Japanese body is different to the Western body it makes sense for the clothes to be manufactured out there. The great advantage to us was that there would be no financial outlay. You provide the designs, they do the rest. And you pick up the royalties. That's the theory at least. We were approached by Mitsui, the trading company, who invited us over to meet potential manufacturers. If we struck a deal, Mitsui would take a share too so it was in all our interests for the idea to work.

We flew out the day of the stock market crash in 1987. It had been heralded by the hurricane that had swept across Britain leaving havoc in its wake. The augurs were not good. However we stayed in the Akasaka Prince Hotel in Tokyo, typically smart, central and impersonal with beds that were way too short for me. We spent our time doing photo shoots of the clothes we had taken with us to show potential partners in the major cities. I saw for myself that what everyone says about Japan being another world is true. I was fascinated by how developed it had become since the war while somehow managing to retain so much of its history and tradition. I saw for myself that the industry was not in any way Japan-centred. It seemed to have no confidence in its own products or designers so the Western product was King. The exceptions were Hanae Mori, a very grand couturier, the very talented Issey Miyake, and the cerebral and celebrated Rei Kanawabo and Yohji Yamamoto.

The trading companies were happy to spend a lot of time and money on building on and hyping up the legacy of the brand they were to bring to the market. It was quite a surprise to see labels that were not necessarily so important or trendy enjoying huge status in Japan. Some of the classic names like Norman Hartnell, no longer a brand name anywhere, had a perfume, In Love, still available in Japanese stores. Burberry (two decades before their recent reincarnation by marketing supremo Rose Marie Bravo) was everywhere, their distinctive check found on anything from golf bags through key-ring holders, handbags, slippers and ties, each one an individual licence granted by the trading company who controlled the brand locally. The sale of clothing was not necessarily the prime concern, as in the European business model. The clothes would be used as a loss leader, bringing awareness to the brand. It would be the consumer's entry point into the brand and where a lot of money would be made. The idea was that accessories bearing an aspirational logo would bestow on the consumer a feeling of having arrived. The stores were vast temples to consumerism, Times Square or Piccadilly Circus had nothing on the garish neon hoardings heralding the latest must-have items in stock that covered entire façades of department stores.

Both Anita and I came away anxious to get a deal off the ground. We spent quite a lot of money working with a venture capitalist in the City who was skilled at putting together this sort of joint venture. However, in the end Mitsui didn't go for the idea, partly I suspect because we didn't have much of a heritage but largely because of the Crash. Something that eventually would affect us all.

Back home during this period, I was receiving quite a lot of public recognition. I'd been picked as Northern Personality of the Year by the Variety Club in 1985 and then was given an Honorary Fellowship at Sheffield Poly a couple of years later.

Ros was working hard too. She had masterminded my development as a 'personality' alongside my renown as a fashion designer. I was invited to choose my desert island discs, where I was able to play Marvin Gaye, Joni Mitchell and Aretha Franklin next to Mozart and Beethoven. I made *My Favourite Things* with Russell Harty and filmed *A Journey In Fashion*, the story of my life, with Tyne Tees TV. I remember the making of *My Favourite Things* with particular affection. Russell was a hilarious companion whom I'd met through Kenny Everett. Together with a film crew, we tracked down my favourite things, among them Durham Cathedral for my favourite building; Croxdale Church for the hymn 'O thou, who comest from above'; the V & A for Elsa Schiaparelli dresses; a trip down the Thames to see the bridges that I find so inspiring; New York for its instant buzz; the films of Rogers and Astaire; fashion drawings of the 1940s. I was also asked to be one of the final judges of the 1986 Whitbread Literary Award. Predictably, there was quite a lot of eyebrow raising about the choice of a fashion designer. One of the other judges exemplified the worst of the literary world in their high-handed attitude. I pointed out that I might not write books but I could read. Of course it did attract the attention of the press because there I was, an 'illiterate dress designer' judging the country's number-two book award.

I have to admit that I did find it a killer reading all the submissions. I took myself off on holiday to Lanzarote to do it. The place I chose was ghastly. I've never seen anywhere more brutal looking. It's one thing getting sand in your sandwiches but grubby volcanic sand is something else. I left as quickly as I could and flew to Madrid and booked in at the Ritz. That night a party in the ballroom somewhere below me went on until the small hours, succeeded by a strident car alarm that went off at regular intervals for the next two hours until the traffic on the

57. Jemima Goldsmith and Imran Khan, 1995. Photograph by Harry Page

61. Me and Marie Helvin at Versace opening party on Bond Street. Photograph by David Koppel

62. That **Kiss**. Joanna Lumley and me at the wedding of the decade in *Absolutely Fabulous*

63. Noemi Cinzano and me

64. Susan and Fiona Sangster
wearing my hand painted
parcos at Jane's Harbour,
Barbados, 1994

65. Me repairing Fiona's zip
in a dress to be worn that
night. Melissa Lilley, Sue's
daughter looks on

66. Me and Guy Sangster at
Cobbler's Cove drinking an
infamous Cobbler's Cooler
with disastrous results

67. Caroline Charles and Malcolm Valentine at my 50th birthday at San Lorenzo's
68. Sarah Reed and Desmond Biddulph
69. The late Robert Sangster, Kevin Carroll in background

70. William and Annabel Astor

71. George Sinclair

All photographs on this and facing page
by Hugo Burnand

72. Lizzie Walker, Barry and Anita.   73. Christine Lambert and partner George

74. The other family. Cousin Jennifer and behind her, husband Stuart, Aunt Enid, me and Aunt Joan with husband, Len Collier

75. Linda and Amy Li

76. Romilly McAlpine

77. Babe looking regal
at home in London

78. Staff and friends at lunch party at the Mill

raised ring road near by built up in volume. The concierge told me the Rastro opened at 8 a.m. so with some relief I dashed into a cab through the fog only to discover it opened at 10 a.m. I redirected the driver to the Prado but it was shut. The whole thing was a disaster, typical of my holidays, so I ended up taking a flight home in the early afternoon. But somehow I did manage to finish all the books and I remember Kazuo Ishiguro's *An Artist of the Floating World* was a very worthy winner.

Thinking back to it now, Redcliffe Gardens was a flat that I really loved, the two twenty-five feet long rooms linked by a slender seven-foot archway, light flooding in from front to back. Having lived in a glorified bedsit for the previous eight years, it didn't bother me to have my bed in the less formal of the two rooms with an open plan kitchen off that. It was all about open spaces and multi functionality. I kept the place very simple with floor to ceiling roman blinds covering both the windows. Storage cupboards covered one entire wall and a huge bookcase filled another.

Around this time I began to collect paintings, starting off with an odd allegorical picture of a woman, naked from the waist up in a neo-classical setting, typical of the 1930s, one panel of a tryptich by English artist, Braida Stanley Creek. I found out more about her from a contemporary fellow artist and student at Farnborough Art School, Ursula McCannell, who contacted me following an article in the *Express*. I went to see her and bought several more paintings by Stanley Creek. My favourites among these were a self portrait (she was a dead-ringer for Bette Davis) and a portrait of her 'muse', Miss Frances Outram. Both showed great skill in the strength and directness of the characterisation, her use of colour and her stylised composition. I then found a pair of portraits by society painter Cuthbert Orde of the artists Cedric Morris and his partner, Arthur Lett-Haines, painted in Paris in 1925. They again appealed to me for their extreme stylishness. It was the beginning of my continued interest in not only the painters, but the writers of the inter-war years. Whenever I get the chance I'm off to the National Portrait Gallery to visit the twentieth-century rooms where they have a fine collection from this particular period.

Life was good. My outgoings were relatively low and my income was beginning to show distinct signs of improvement. My broadening horizons also gave me an increasing feeling of confidence. Looking back at photos of that period, there seems to have been a steady stream of parties and dinners. As usual, I held a big party for my birthday and there they all are: Linda and Patrick, Barry, Anita and Kevin, the extended family plus friends I'd collected along the way. It surprises me looking at the photos that although the birthday cake might have been a gift from Romilly, neither she nor Alistair would be there. My friends seem to be compartmentalised. I have never mixed and matched them, which I find very strange. The other striking thing about these pictures is the longevity and continuity of some of the friendships, perhaps not friendships with any significant provenance, simply people who have moved along similar planes with me throughout the decades, paths inter-twined, other friendships and experiences shared; those are the ones that endure: Lizzie Walker, Vanessa Delisle, David Reeson, Felicity Bosanquet, George, Ninivah, Jacques Azagury.

In 1986 I commissioned Michael Roberts to shoot a double-page ad for *Vogue*. He used my flat as a studio and found a girl who looked incredibly like Princess Stephanie of Monaco and had her cavorting around with a half-naked male model. She wore quite a few different outfits including a pleated lamé coat made from the same cloth as the Princess of Wales' gala dress that appeared the following season (which is how I can date it). Michael's cheeky montage got everyone talking, thinking that I also had the Monégasque princess as a client and that she was willing to appear in an ad for me!

During that period we did quite a few series of ads in *Vogue*. Goodness knows how we could afford it, though the accountants at Condé Nast would probably have tales to tell on how long it took us to pay off the debt! Using photographer Neil Kirk we did a series of shots incorporating the licencees. The pictures were taken in the gracious surroundings of West Green house, much to the displeasure of the photographer who was unhappy about everything that day. The look we were after was a genteel Englishness, probably not dissimilar (though not intentionally) to what Ralph Lauren would propose. I'm never sure how potent advertisements are. They cost a vast amount of money both in the origination of the image, photographers, location and model fees, make-up, hair and stylists fees, travel costs and insurance. And then you've got to buy the page space in the glossy magazine and negotiate the position in the mag that it will subsequently appear in.

When I decided to leave Redcliffe Gardens, I bought a fabulous flat in Elm Park Gardens just off the Fulham Road. It was twice the size and was a ground-floor lateral conversion across two houses. I had my own front door, my own doorstep with windows on either side so it looked as if I owned the entire house – very grand. Suited me. Shelagh Sartin, a friend of Colin's, helped do it up for me in spite of considerable problems with the neighbours below but sadly we fell out over money. I loved that flat and lived very simply. The basement of the house was divided into two flats. The first was inhabited by a pair of ladies, one of whom worked nights for the BBC; the other was owned by a gentleman with exceptionally acute hearing. Between them it mean that life was lived at times on tiptoes. After the seventies, Barry would come in and out of my life sporadically. He moved into Elm Park Gardens with me for a few months before he eventually left for America where he's lived ever since.

I was doing well in those days from the licence deals, the business was doing well and I only had myself to spend the money on. Having said that, Anita and I were always lurching from one financial crisis to another, largely because we let the overhead run away with itself. Anita did try to curtail my spending. I've still got a letter from her remonstrating with me over buying a new second-hand car. But I remember pointing out that it was only my third car and it was second hand whereas hers was new. Wasn't she the pot calling the kettle black? I had bought the latest one because the last had been stolen. At the time Barry was living with me so I'd assumed he had taken it for some reason, so didn't take much notice at first when that it wasn't there. When I did eventually get round to calling the police and reporting the theft of my 'cashmere colour' BMW635 CSI, the guy said, 'Not that tatty gold job you've been driving for the last couple of years.'

'Tatty gold!' I repeated. 'How do you know?'

'Another of my jobs is standing sentry at Kensington Palace so I've let you into the palace many times.'

Over the years, I went to several weddings in Jordan. They are always lavish occasions whether royal or not, and quite often are held in beautiful gardens, in one of the big hotels or in the grounds of one of the fabulous palaces. I was always struck how, in many Arab countries everything with any history has been swept aside to make way for the new – quite unlike Japan. I particularly recall going to Princess Sumaya's wedding, having made her dress for one of the wedding parties. One night before the wedding, there was a very good party at the Dead Sea at least one and a half hours outside Amman. As we descended the winding roads that seemed to be hewn out of solid rock, we could see the three minarets of the Jerusalem skyline in the distance. A bus took us to the Sea where we swam – so salty it was a bit like floating in slightly congealing chicken stock. We stayed in the water until sunset when everything was suddenly bathed in red light reminiscent of a scene from that epic Charlton Heston film *The Bible*. It was spectacular. Once we'd washed the salt off, dried and changed, there was a big feast set up in tents on the beach with a roasted goat turning on a spit. We sat on low benches on long camel-hair runners and big cushions while the food was brought in to us. In the distance twinkled the lights of the villages bordering the left bank.

Another nuptial event I remember, but for a different reason, was the wedding of Alia Rifai, daughter of the Prime Minister of Jordan. The reception took place in the gardens surrounding the pool at the Amman InterContinental. I remember watching the hem of the bride's dress becoming dirtier and dirtier as she strolled among the guests. The dinner for 300 people was held at her parents' house. There wasn't enough room in the marquee for the bridal train so Alia eventually removed it and it was stuffed under a table. Some bright spark found it, thought it was a tablecloth and sent it off to be laundered. It was completely ruined so we had to make another.

Around this time, apart from business and the licences, I decided to have a flutter with Marks & Spencer, where Paul Smith already had a men's wear consultancy. Everything I did at the time received rafts of publicity thanks to Ros and her network of journalists. By this point we'd been good friends with many of the fashion editors for some time, among them Jackie Modlinger on the *Express*, Liz Smith on *The Times* and Ann Chubb in the *Daily Mail*. They'd all supported us over the years – we needed them and, from a story point of view, they needed us. So when I agreed to be a consultant with M&S the headlines screamed, DI'S FAVOURITE DESIGNER DESIGNING FOR M&S or BRUCE OLDFIELD HAS DESIGNS ON THE HIGH STREET. It was all press hype but it suited all of us: M&S because it looked as if a successful designer was joining their ship and me – well, it was lucrative.

In fact, I never designed anything for them. That wasn't the arrangement. They operated a complicated system that involved scouring the collections around the world trying to spot the trends and colours they would offer their shoppers the next season. A book was compiled each season, beautifully drawn with colours and concepts. It was given to the major manufacturers who then used their own in-house teams to come up with the designs they thought M&S wanted. That's where I came in. At this point, the consultants would go to the Baker Street head office and advise on the merchandise proposed by the manufacturers. It was difficult for me because I was making clothes for several of the manufacturers' wives so I was anxious to be impartial. In fact, the manufacturers weren't allowed to label the items so I could remain quite independent. The problem as far as I was concerned was that they were always aiming at the lowest common denominator. They'd insist that only one style could be offered to cover the size range 8 to 22. Therefore the same design had to encompass both a 30-inch and a 46-inch bust. Of course it couldn't work. It should have been obvious that two styles were needed and considering these garments were being produced in thousands of dozens, they would still have been an economic proposition. I tried and I tried but nobody would listen. These designs went back and forwards to the manufacturers for more adaptations – I don't know how they put up with it. I worked there for a year and a half, when my contract came to an end.

One of the most exciting things we were asked to do was to participate in the 1988 Australian Bicentennial Wool Collection show in Sydney. Jean Muir and I were the two British representatives in a huge fashion show that took place in the Sydney Opera House. The other international designers made an impressive line-up: Versace, Missoni, Kenzo, Sonia Rykiel, Claude Montana, Donna Karan and Oscar de la Renta. George and I flew out a week ahead of time to do all the fittings and rehearsals. I remember we decided against Elle MacPherson, unlikely as it seems today. In our defence, it was in the pre-supermodel days when the models were either international runway girls or girls who didn't walk well but who the camera loved. To our eye, Elle belonged in the latter group. She didn't then have the curvy figure that we preferred. Somehow though, she made it back into our line-up and looked fabulous

I have no idea how the whole event came together. It seemed totally chaotic. We had an Australian choreographer whose ideas were constantly being thwarted by the designers who had their own concept of how things should be presented. I very quickly got bored with the rehearsals and left them to the capable George. For once in my life, I kept a brief diary (most of which is lost) but a few snatches give some idea of the goings-on:

THURSDAY 21 JANUARY

Arrive Terminal 4. Thought I had a lot of luggage – one limo for me and PA Georgina, another for luggage – but Jean Muir's husband Harry arrives with seven trunks! Bit worrying, what can be in there? BA very helpful – no excess to pay – and twenty-four-hour first-class flight relaxed and pampered. Arrive Sydney 11.30 p.m. Friday 22nd. Swished off to InterContinental Hotel and a suite on the twenty-fifth floor.

SATURDAY 23rd

Woke up to a grey sky. Hey, what is this? I though Australia was the land of the sun. Whisked off by limo on sight-seeing drive around northern beaches – Palm Beach, the Sydney stockbroker belt – stunning. Had lunch at Berowra Waters Inn, a fabulous restaurant hidden in dense bushland accessible only by a ferry across a lake. Heavens opened for a one-hour, spectacular tropical downpour – thunder, lightning, the works.

Back to the hotel where we fixed up compact disc and speakers and relaxed before dinner with Cameron Allen, the composer of the show score, and Chrissie Koltai, the choreographer. Dinner at Around Midnight, a newish trendy dinner club in Kings Cross. Had to walk back – no taxis in sight as Sydney overflowed with visitors arriving for the Bicentennial. Asleep by 3.00, awake at 4.00, valium . . .

SUNDAY 25th

Bright sunshine over Sydney Harbour. Have great views of Bridge, Opera House and Botanical Gardens. Amazing how busy it is on the water, the roads and in the air. Helicopters, seaplanes, blimps – jets above, liners, yachts, tankers, tugs and endless private boats – also little yellow, green and red ferry boats which look like something from a Disney cartoon, and people – so many tourists. Took a closer look at the Opera House. It is truly spectacular. Hard to believe that something built in the last twenty years could manage to retain its credibility considering how many modern buildings quickly become dated. Odd that they forgot to build a car park though!

Dinner with Angela Neville and Billy Keating – picture lover with a love for Sydney and things Australian. Met briefly with Dire Straits' John Illsley – such a star-packed city.

Signed an autograph for Sharon from Cape Town . . . went to bed feeling that I had arrived.

MONDAY 25th

Up at 7 a.m. – first fittings at Opera House on Australian and international girls – atmosphere a little strained between the two groups of girls but top model Pat Cleveland was soon mixing in. Left George there and went up to hotel suite for first round of interviews. Seven that morning between 9.00 and 11.30, pretty gruelling as I kept feeling I should be asleep. Twenty-five floors below at Government House, the Prince and Princess of Wales were leaving on their first engagement amidst much flag-waving and enthusiasm. What is she wearing? Jasper, I think . . . Someone muttered Catherine Walker but it does *look* like Jasper's.

THURSDAY 28th

. . . Party at Royal Yacht Club given by Bernie Leser. Followed by a dinner for thirty at Lady Fairfax's mansion. First time I had encountered what is described as Sydney 'Old Money'. There's not a lot of it about. Interesting way to entertain, disco after the starter, followed by an operatic recital – then the main course, etc. Must try it in London.

FRIDAY 29th

Tempers getting frayed down at the Opera House. Models seem to be a bone of contention with much blame being laid at the feet of absentee Gianni. Try not to get involved, anyway I'm on first so get the pick of the girls. Donna not too happy about her music – it keeps running out before the end of her section!

A lot of screaming and sulking going on but it soon blows over albeit temporarily due to the ministrations of Vincent Matthews – ace arbitrator of the Wool Board. Considering the egos involved it, in fact, runs remarkably

smoothly. Ingrained national characteristics are sometimes more responsible for flare-ups than logistics of
rehearsing nine designers on the same stage in a period
of six hours.

Nipped off to the zoo with George to do a *Breakfast
Time* with Anne Diamond and a quickie interview with
Caryn Franklin for *The Clothes Show*. Accepted invitation
to dinner with Australian Designer Adele Palmer at
Buttons.

The show itself was fantastic with a choreographed dance piece
to Cameron Allen's composition before every section. Michael
Parkinson was the compère on the evening with the show being
beamed into millions of homes in Australia and the Pacific
Basin. He was less than complimentary to a couple of the
designers whose response to the brief at hand – ie, design a
collection using wool (our sponsors were the Australian Wool
Board after all) and incorporating specific Australian cultural or
geographical references – was apparently to ignore it. I had
come up with an aboriginal collection and Jean Muir's was a
fabulous Great Barrier Reef marine collection. When I was
congratulated on my use of red, black and yellow, traditional
aboriginal colours, I refrained diplomatically from revealing
that I'd hit on them by complete chance. Eyebrows were raised
when a French designer announced, 'I was inspired by the
magnificent colours of the tropical birds of Australia,' then
proceeded to show twenty black cocktail dresses. Eyebrows
twitched again when the Italian who closed the show with his
latest collection of fabulous evening dresses, literally hot off the
Milan catwalk, threw black wool stoles (purchased that afternoon in Sydney) over his models as they went out on the runway
in an attempt to ward off any criticism of no wool content.

Beforehand I'd had very mixed press. The one glowing piece

seemed to provide an excuse for commentators to have a go at me. However, after the show, everyone sang the praises of Jean and me simply because our designs were more Australian than the rest. Suzy Menkes wrote a lengthy complimentary profile of me in Australian *Vogue* – fantastically prestigious. Back home the *Mail* headlined the event with SUCH ABORIGINALITY BRUCE! while Colin McDowell in the *Guardian* dwelt on Jean Muir's and my restraint compared to the more disgruntled and volatile visiting designers.

We were in Sydney for Australia Day when we got up early and took our limos to Alan Bond's mooring to join his floating gin palace, *Southern Cross*. Each designer had a white limo at their disposal. It might have seemed extravagant to take it to Tamarama Beach but it would have been wasteful to hire a cab, *n'est ce pas?* We made the most of it. The boat was vast, all white, chrome and glass. A non-smoking zone but the champagne began to flow at 9 a.m.!

We made our way out into Sydney Harbour as the Tall Ships hove into view on the final stage of their celebratory round-the-world passage. The harbour was awash with anything that could float, makeshift rafts, canoes, you name it . . . One thing was certain and that was that Bond's boat was the centre of attention, with Alan and Red basking in the crowds' adulation, in part due to Bond's success in the 1983 America's Cup.

Over on the shore, the Prince and Princess of Wales were engaged in the formalities of the occasion. It was quite spectacular, with the ships, the fireworks, and helicopters buzzing around carrying camera crews. On board we watched TV as a mini-crisis unfolded in one of the smart suburbs. Susan Ranouf, Robert Sangster's second wife, had locked herself into the family home that had been in dispute since her most recent divorce and was stylishly under siege by both police and the press. Once we'd escaped from the activity in the centre of the harbour, we found a place for lunch and a swim – although Susanne discouraged us from the latter. Just the word 'sharks' was enough. It was a fabulous day, although we did manage to get minor sunstroke for our troubles – so it didn't end on such a high note.

Then it was back to grey old Blighty where, despite the overt success of the business, cracks were definitely beginning to show in our relationship with our shareholders and to some extent in the relationship between Anita and myself. As we faced the continuing pressures of being an under-financed company, in straightened financial times once again, we were to respond typically in our diametrically opposed ways. But not just yet.

CHAPTER EIGHTEEN

It's always difficult to recapture a success but Anita and I were keen to try. 1988 marked a relaunch of Barnardo's, spelling out how the organisation had changed from the old days when I was a boy. Social legislation since the war meant that Barnardo's and their like had been made to rethink their traditional roles. While doing so, they had a continuing commitment to children who were still in the old system where Barnardo's took on the role of parent. The emphasis shifted away from looking after children in foster and residential homes to supporting them within their own homes, families and communities wherever possible. They were in constant need of publicity to generate more much-needed money.

This seemed the ideal moment to mount another fundraising gala for them. We relied on the same format, with expensive tickets and the presence of the Princess of Wales, this time accompanied by Prince Charles. The event was held in the Grosvenor House Hotel, a sell-out just as before, and was quite as starry with a strong mix of showbiz with royalty. The Princess wore a purple crushed-velvet off-the-shoulder dress that was used that year for the official portrait by Norman Parkinson. She and the Prince were going through their well-publicised rocky patch and it showed. The tension between them was palpable.

Remembering that she had given me cigarettes at the last gala, I took it as *carte blanche* that I could smoke.

'Do you mind if I smoke, Sir?'

'It's your lungs, Bruce.' He's only two years older than me, for heaven's sake.

The high spot of the evening was a specially choreographed piece in the fashion show where Marie and Jerry entered the stage in white siren dresses, strutting their stuff as only they could do, prompting wolf whistles from Jack Nicholson and Michael Caine who were on the table next to ours. Dawn French and Jennifer Saunders ran the raffle and had insisted on wearing samples (size 10s), strapped and taped together as a 'pretend' fit – they looked like couture bag ladies. They were very funny but a remark about the 'fluffy little princesses on the top table' did not go down at all well with the Princess of Wales who visibly stiffened. Then, instead of dancing the night away as before, she was taken home by the Prince as soon as he could respectably make the break. He seemed ill at ease the whole evening and the Princess remained subdued. None the less we raised £215,000.

Shortly afterwards Anita, Kevin and I went to the Prince's fortieth birthday. Ladies will not be wearing tiaras, announced the invitation. Anita had a black velvet dress made and was looking very glam. There was a huge reception downstairs at Buckingham Palace before the guests processed up a grand marble staircase hung with pictures to where the Queen, Prince Philip, Charles and Diana were waiting in a receiving line. The thing I remember most was, as I got nearer to the top of the stairs, realising for the first time that the Queen was so petite. I admired the way they shook hands with a not-too-tight grasp but tight enough to tactfully but firmly push you on down the line. The party was held in the west side of the palace where the State Dining Room had been given over to dancing. The Dark Blues – a band with great vocalists that could copy any sound – and Phil Collins provided the music as we danced under some of the masterpieces from the Royal Collection. When you were tired of that, there was the disco in an Arab tent at one end of the Picture Gallery. I remember dancing next to the Queen, unable to figure out why she carried her white handbag on to the dance floor. She was, after all, at home. At least she didn't dance around it! Otherwise the Blue Drawing Room, the Music Room, the Picture Gallery and East Gallery were provided with tables and chairs for relaxing, chit-chat and refreshment. The only person I remember meeting was Harry Secombe but I have no recollection of what we talked about.

As the invitation didn't include dinner, the guests had all eaten beforehand. So we danced until breakfast when I sat at the same table as Princess Anne, so informal was the whole affair. It was an odd experience, rather like being in one of the Great Eastern Hotels – high ceilings with lots of gilt, pilasters and chandeliers. The food was a typical English mix of scrambled eggs, grilled bacon and sausages. Those old days in Harrogate's Granby Hotel came flooding back.

Despite the problems that were brewing in the business world in general, we had to try to keep the show on the road. As far as our public image was concerned we were still getting plenty of pages in *Vogue* and *Harpers & Queen*, and the shows were extensively covered in the press both here and in the US. At this point we launched licences with Murray Allen and Hilditch & Key. There was something quite satisfying about a piece of knitwear emerging from a machine – quite different from producing couture dresses. As the main reason for any company becoming a licensor was to improve their manufacturing and sales capacity, they would be reluctant, at the outset of a new business at least, to invest in machinery to produce more contemporary products. They really were competing with modern styling and techniques that were coming out of the Far East but they chose, or perhaps were constrained, to continue making old-fashioned-looking knitwear on old-fashioned machines. Despite this, we produced several good ranges that began to make headway in certain areas. The good thing about Murray Allen was that they were prepared to invest in promotional activities, went to the trade fairs and understood how to place the product. As for Hilditch & Key, they did great men's shirts, but although they wanted the added value of my name, they weren't set up to sell blouses for women. Both ventures faded into obscurity within a couple of years.

By 1990, the writing was on the wall for most of our licensors. Everyone was cutting back. A return to core business was essential if you were going to survive the next few years. In order to bring in some much-needed revenue, we made a deal with Dewhirst, a very successful family-owned and family-run clothing manufacturer in the North East. I had been familiar with their work on the tailoring side at M&S. Pru Dewhirst was a client and she thought it a good idea and set the ball rolling. I remember in the early days of talks, Pru and I had dinner in Annabel's where my grey Armani sports jacket was considered too racy for the august surroundings. I was asked to wear one of the house navy blazers which turned out to be a Dewhirst jacket from M&S. Such a coincidence. Pru proved it to me by showing me their manufacturers code in the inside pocket!

We agreed that we would use Dewhirst for this new line. I was quoted in the *Independent*:

> The finance has never been forthcoming . . . we make business plan after business plan but the banking institutions won't listen . . . If Dewhirst is prepared to put its manufacturing capabilities behind me, then perhaps the banks will be prepared to come to us with an open mind . . . Haute couture should be part of the advertising budget – that's how they consider it in Paris . . . I used to

be cocky and tell journalists I would have a fashion empire by the time I was forty. Well, I've pushed that back to fifty now.

Although it was a licence, it was to be branded 'Bruce Oldfield 1992' in a move to expand the brand laterally. We called it 1992 because it struck a chord with the European Union imminent in 1992, and I felt I was associated with the date in people's minds, having been roped into the TV campaign to promote the launch of the DTI European Single Market Business Awareness Offensive. The photographer Terry Donovan had called me one day on spec to see if I'd come down to take part in a shoot he was doing for the government. It was very good for my profile as it meant my appearing on posters, billboards and forty-five-second ads. But, with the best will in the world, our game plan was bound not to succeed. The wrong people were sewing the garments and the sales people were selling it into the wrong shops despite Anita doing her best to re-educate them.

I had got to know the Sangster family during the eighties. Susan Sangster had become a close friend and a great ambassador for me, always photographed at Ascot wearing my suits. I remember her once ringing up to ask for an evening dress that she need in three weeks' time after she'd had a baby. We asked what size she though she'd need.

'Make it an eight.'

'Don't be ridiculous. You'll never get into an eight, three weeks after having a baby.'

But she did.

Robert and Sue Sangster were a great support to me when business was really bad and were generous enough to invite me to Barbados for Christmas 1991. I went slightly apprehensively given my unsuccessful track record with holidays but I needn't have worried. The Sangster home, Janes Harbour, is a beautiful, coralstone house in the style popularised in the forties and fifties by Oliver Messel. It's a great mix of classic comfortable English and Bejan indoor/outdoor style, with large airy triple-height rooms, some formal but mainly low comfortable furniture that can take wet costumes. It was a lifestyle unfamiliar to me but I grew into it very quickly. I was usually the first up, having been first to bed the night before and would take long walks along the beach front as the neighbouring Sandy Lane Hotel began to wake up with staff raking the sand flat and arranging sun loungers. I would stroll past the enormous houses of the very rich indeed, the morning shift of security men still bleary-eyed from too much of the night before. It's always struck me as a shame that these homes are built open to the elements but surrounded by ten-foot security fences – which rather defeat the object. I loved those solitary walks. When you're staying in a house full of people, often couples with children, it's good to have a little time on your own. I'd get back to the house in time for breakfast that was set up in the open-air dining area closest to the beach, the butler ready with fresh fruit and anything else I fancied.

The daily routine was centred round the pool, with the Caribbean Sea only a champagne cork's distance away. Leisurely lunches were washed down with Domaine Ott Rosé and followed by golf for those who enjoy it (that seemed to be everyone except me). I'd prefer to go for another long walk along the beach or to collapse on a lounger preparing myself for whatever the evening had in store. At sunset, the mosquito tablets would be plugged into the wall and the incessant chirping of the tree frogs would begin. Drinks were served in the bar at 7.30, swimsuits exchanged for cocktail dresses and 'resort smart casual' for the men. Definitely no jeans. We might eat dinner at home in the candle-lit coral-stone loggia, the huge glass table decorated with exotic plants and flowers, or we might go to one of the island's top restaurants such as the Cliff or the Lone Star. Sometimes the whole house party would be invited to dinner at Heron Bay, the spectacular home of Anthony and Carol Bamford where we'd mix with their house guests, or to Dermot Desmond's penthouse apartment at the Sandy Lane. Whatever we did, wherever we went, it would be the best food accompanied by the finest wines and a serious hangover to look forward to the next day. The usual game played on these evening sorties was to see who could get home the earliest, Robert or myself, neither of us being fond of very late nights. Robert usually won, being the more practised, but he did live there six months each year and I was only there for a week.

I remember a terrible accident once when we went for lunch at Cobbler's Cove. One of things they are famous for is their Cobbler's Coolers, a kind of rum punch. If you can drink three and walk round the pool without falling in, you get a free meal. So Billy McDonald, who was staying with us, decided to make mine extra strong. After lunch Guy Sangster, Robert's oldest son and I were messing around and he threw a piece of chocolate cake at me. In return I smeared him with it. I look back on all this with amazement because it's so out of character – mine, anyway. He put his hand into an ice bucket that he was going to empty over me but there was a piece of broken glass in there that sliced through his artery. Mad panic ensued. He was bleeding like a pig. Fiona, Guy and I all piled into 'Lunchtime's' (so-called because he's a legend in his own one) car with his wife Margie O'Sullivan. Guy sat in the middle and I held his arm up, pressing on what I dimly remembered was a pressure point having made a tourniquet out of my T-shirt. We hurtled through Bridgetown, jumping every traffic light – it was like something out of the Keystone Cops. By the time we got to the hospital, we were both covered with blood and nobody could immediately tell which of us needed treatment.

In the mid-nineties, the Sangsters lent me their place in Mougins for a couple of weeks in the summer. They were happy to have someone using the otherwise empty house, perched up in the hills behind Cannes, overlooking the sea. I would chill out there, inviting friends to join me and enjoying cooking for them and generally entertaining. At last, I'd found the kind of holiday that I liked. I discovered the pleasures of being away with friends. It was a lovely house too and I liked the fact that it was in my care and that I could make sure my guests wanted for nothing.

It was very different to a holiday in June 1990, when Linda came with me to the South of France where I rented another house in Antibes. She was scared of flying so, as the plane banked over the glittering Mediterrranean, revealing all the opulence of the fabled Côte d'Azur, which I hadn't seen since the early seventies when visiting Charlotte, Linda missed it all. She kept her eyes tightly shut, her knuckles white.

Quite different from the luxury I would become accustomed to at Mougins, this place was rather ramshackle, with a pool, a garden and a stable block that had been converted into two or three guest bedrooms. We had a very relaxed time, not bothering to cook but going out in the evening to eat and drink too much. While we were there Anita called excitedly to say that the Palace had contacted her to ask whether I was likely to accept a formal offer of an OBE. As if they had to ask.

I threw a good party for my fortieth birthday that year, taking over Morton's in Berkeley Square thanks to the owner, Howard Malin. I invited about ninety friends. All the old crew were there, including Scott who came over from New York, Barry and Linda. The highlight was a surprise 'Happy Birthday' sung fairly drunkenly by the Sex Aids (aka Jane Lomas who'd made the documentary *A Journey in Fashion* and her ex-husband, Nick Hurt) with apologies to Irving Berlin.

Brucie, dear birthday Brucie,
Here's the only press release that slipped past Ros
And we have no doubt that she will be quite cross
But we journalists are never at a loss.

Brucie, dear clever Brucie,
At last the Queen has recognised your fame
And we thank God it's OBE, not Dame,
But it's Other Buggers' Efforts all the same.

You dress Duchesses and dollies
And sometimes gangsters' Mollies
But after fourteen double Stolys
They tend to look the same.

Forty, naughty forty,
And though we know you like a sortie or two
We dare not say just where, or you might sue
And so might George and sweet Anita too.

Brucie, juicy Brucie,
We're pleased that you count us among your clique
And we hope our song won't cause a fit of pique
Cos we need our discounts, dwahling . . .

For dining out and dancing
For climbing and advancing
Social life enhancing . . .
Chic to chic.

Going to the Palace to get my OBE was a very important day for
me. You were allowed two people to come with you so I took
Judith and Linda. Anita and I had been there several times so I

thought it would be a wonderful opportunity for the others. I made Linda's suit and Judith made her own in one of our current styles. When I reached the Queen, she asked me if I still made clothes.

'Yes, Ma'am,' I replied, 'and for a number of your family.'

Afterwards Anita joined us at Launceston Place for a celebration lunch.

That November, Marie Helvin threw an amazing party for my OBE at Christine and BS Ong's restaurant, Zuma, on Sloane Avenue. There was a great turn-out, Jerry sporting her engagement ring from Mick for the first time, Simon and Yasmin le Bon, Ronnie and Jo Wood, Jean Muir, Michael White, Lizzie Walker. Anita and George had got together with Marie to help on the guest list and a great time was had by all. It was sweet of Marie. She and I had been close ever since the early days. After she and Bailey separated, we'd go to parties together. We enjoyed each other's company but we were also aware that we'd always end up getting good pictures in the press. We were like bookends and the reason we went to all those parties was simply just to keep in. It's what you do. For a long time, Marie was my muse. I have plenty of pictures of her trying things on and giving her verdict – suggesting variations and improvements. She had often modelled for me but I remember watching fascinated when she modelled for Bailey. He was shooting a mail shot for me. She remained absolutely still unless instructed to move a part of her body just the fraction of an inch. Their teamwork was remarkably precise and the results were little short of perfect. Bailey included me in a picture in this session. I lay shirtless with Marie draped over me in a Bruce Oldfield dress. He let me know in no uncertain terms that modelling was not my strength!

That Autumn, we did a show in Claridge's. It included the 1992 Diffusion line, knitwear and Bruce Oldfield ready-to-wear. It was a fun collection, very large because of the various elements all of which had to have their fair share of the limelight. Wherever possible we tried to intergrate the sections so that the long white cotton jersey T-shirt dresses from the 1992 collection might be worn with a geometric cotton cardigan from Murray Allen and so on.

I also returned to America that season. It was back to Bendels for the first time since I'd been sent packing. They had been taken over and this time I was limousined around in style. We showed at their stores in Cleveland Ohio, Boston and in New York. It was a typical trunk show except there was no back-up stock in the stores. They hadn't had the bottle to place an order beforehand so we had to hope for orders.

Despite the outward signs of success, financially things were going from bad to worse. Business was poor and our overdraft was high, accompanied by an extortionate rate of interest and various punitive restrictions, debentures and personal guarantees. Both Anita and I were drawing salaries. One day she came to the flat and proposed that if I paid her £x, she would leave the company. There was no doubt that our business relationship had run its course and we saw the future of the company in different ways. I accepted gratefully. I had been constantly having rows with my fellow shareholders. The immediate problem was that, as I saw it, they had facilitated the opening of a shop and that was all. They had not tied me up for life but the shareholding structure made it feel that way. In 1985, I'd published an illustrated book, *Season*, that went behind the scenes of the business, taking the reader through the stages that led up to the Winter 1985 collection. It seemed to me that a large proportion of the revenue from that and from the licencing deals really belonged to me rather than the business. But they were adamant that it should be the other way around. I was also disappointed that there had never been any more money made available to us for expansion, that they weren't prepared to do anything with the business. The whole experience had been very disillusioning for both Anita and me. It had made us disinclined as well as unable to push forward, knowing there was no funding there.

A few weeks later, for some inexplicable reason, Anita changed her mind about leaving despite the fact that things were very tense between us. We had reached a point where she would write to me rather than speak. She and our accountant would sit in a gloomy enclave in her office muttering darkly. I'd walk past and we'd ignore each other. There was a lot of bad feeling – just as if it was a marriage breaking up.

Susan, the daughter of my old headmaster, had been a client for some years and advised me to talk to her husband, David McErlain. He's a sound businessman with a very clear head and he advised me on exactly what I should do, step by step. Anita was one of those steps. I had to talk to her, to tell her that the status quo couldn't continue. There wasn't a question of options. Either she stayed and the company went bust – and she got nothing – or she went and we negotiated a settlement. It was money I didn't have but I had to find it to survive.

By this point, I felt Anita recognised there was no alternative solution. She was beginning to see a future in becoming freelance, selling wholesale collections for different designers and exploiting her fantastic talent for cooking. Our friendship had been incredibly close over the years and we had been part of a family with all those who had worked so loyally with us. It was an extremely difficult break-up for both of us and it took quite a while to recover. We didn't see each other for three or four years and even after that, it was never quite the same.

A summit meeting was held at Great College Street, the home of Alistair McAlpine. He, Rocco, Olga Polizzi, Anita and I were to discuss the future of the company. Again I'd been expertly briefed by David as to what I should and shouldn't be prepared to accept. If the business was to fold, it spelled disaster for me. As far as I was concerned, they had to relinquish their shares to allow me to go out and find other means of finance. As long as they held 48 per cent, there was no equity left for any other potential backer. We had a very heated debate in which I metaphorically waved my OBE, stamped my foot and said I was not going under. After so many years of hard work establishing the business with my name above the door, I was not going down easily. They investigated every possible avenue and decided to hand over the shares so that I could move on alone.

This meant I would have to entirely reinvent both myself and the business. The grisly situation brought out my most determined streak. My only means of survival was to cut my overheads dramatically. The first thing was to give up Argon Mews knowing the rent was to be quadrupled. With it went most of the staff, regrettably including Judith and George, so that I could run the whole operation from the shop and basement workroom at 27 Beauchamp Place with Marie and a few machinists. My next move was to sell Elm Park Gardens. It was the only way I could buy back the company 100 per cent. I rented a small, manageable two-bedroom duplex on Hester Road on the south side of the river on Battersea Bridge. The drawing room had sliding doors that opened on to a wide balcony overlooking the Thames. By night, I'd look out longingly at the winking lights of Chelsea that seemed tantalisingly close across the water. I'd been pushed south of the river again.

The final disappointment was to be dropped by the Princess of Wales at about the same time. We had been making less and less for her as the eighties drew to a close. Although she did continue to use British designers, she was also beginning to include some of the international line-up too. I imagine she wanted a change – quite understandable. It happens. We have to be sanguine about our customer base. It moves all the time and renewing it is a crucial part of the business. The only irritant about not making clothes for her any longer was that it was quite a visible loss as far as everybody else was concerned. I wasn't offended personally or, if I was, it was only momentary. What I was more anxious about was the impact it might have on the business.

But I knew from experience that I wasn't defeated yet. This sort of challenge gears me up for the fight. The slate had been wiped clean. There was a bit of a debt to be cleared but that's nothing unusual. I was on my own and I relished the future.

CHAPTER NINETEEN

'In 1990 I almost went bankrupt, made momentous decisions both in my business and private life, and took a risk which is paying off now in spades, thank God.' *Vogue*, September 1994.

For me the nineties were largely a time of retrenchment, consolidation and reinvention. Reinvention is a must if you're to survive in the same business for a sustained period. I think my attitude was typical of the more general global mood of quiet and deliberation that followed the excesses of the eighties. To put myself back on track I went underground, which meant going to far fewer parties for a while. I took the business back to its core and strengthened it, concentrating on a smaller clientele and investigating new opportunities that would stretch me. Fortunately, I had a great deal to fall back on. My customers and friends stuck by me. The fantastic press and publicity that had followed me since I left St Martin's had done its trick and carried on into the new decade.

The great thing was that the national press did not make a noise about my downturn in fortune. I received only positive reporting. But if success or relevance in fashion is judged by the amount of pages in *Vogue*, I certainly had lost my position. And it possibly didn't help that I decided not to do any shows for a couple of years. Although it's always nice to have pages in the fashion glossies it may not necessarily help you sell things but it does keep your name up there. So God bless the rise of the celebrity magazines, because my coverage in *Hello!*, *OK* and *Tatler* has not diminished.

During the 1992 General Election which took the Conservatives, this time under John Major, back into power for the fourth time, I was prevailed upon by Tim Bell to tie my banner firmly to the Tory masthead and support the Prime Minister. This entailed pitching up at rallies with other medium- to high-profile faces in the entertainment, media and sporting worlds. I even wrote a piece for *The Sunday Times* outlining my simplistic yet firmly held views on the future of Britain without a Tory in the top job. I was to be hoist on that particular piece of intransigence a few years later in a live interview in Sydney one week before the landslide defeat by Tony Blair, where I declared to an eager Aussie day-time TV audience that the Tories would win. The interviewer retorted that I was probably the only person in the English-speaking world who held that particular view and moved swiftly on to the next item – tenderising kangaroo steaks.

One interesting event resulting from my political activities during that period was an invitation to Chequers to lunch with some of my fellow Tory supporters. As usual I got Sam, my regular driver, to take me as at that time I didn't own a car, living so close to work. Security was high, the underchassis was scanned for explosive devices, sniffer dogs riffled through the contents of the boot. We were declared clean and moved on. The drivers, much to their irritation, were told to go to the local village where the pub provided adequate food. 'It wouldn't have happened like this in 'er day.' 'Proper lady she was.' 'Slap up meal for all the drivers.' 'Knew how to treat people she did.' And off they grumbled. Gentleman John Major personally greeted me at the front door, escorted me to the gents himself and went to some length to show me the least circuitous route back to the main drawing room where the Champagne was being served. I admit to feeling that perhaps all the cars and drivers we'd seen had been going to some other party, so intimate had been this encounter with the PM. I wondered if it was just going to be me, him and a few others. I was relieved therefore when I entered the drawing room to find a sea of faces, some familiar. Over lunch, I had a bit of a run-in with the wife of Tim Yeo. She was sitting on my right when I'd moaned that we couldn't smoke. She asked me tartly whether I would have if we'd been allowed to. I said, like a shot, 'Without any consideration for my fellow diners? I'm afraid so.' We didn't have a great deal to say after that little encounter. After lunch, we all went out on to the terrace overlooking the lawns – some smoked.

It was time to think of new ways to diversify that would bring in some much-needed cash. I'd often toyed with the idea of getting into men's wear and I did a collection on paper that Colin illustrated fantastically well. Tim Lamb did all the graphics for me and Meredith Etherington Smith did the words. It was a great collaboration. The illustrations of the garments were overlaid with acetate inscribed with literary quotations of the '. . . when a man is tired of London, he is tired of life . . .' kind. The next step was for me to try and sell the concept. I went off to Milan where I stayed with Scott, then took my folder on the train to Turin where I had arranged an interview with manufacturers GFT who produce Armani among others. I hadn't done this kind of selling since my early days in Paris, flogging round the couture houses. I got there early to find no one was expecting me or even knew who I was. In their London office, I was always treated with some respect but sadly that attitude didn't travel. We managed in a mixture of my pidgin French and their broken English but it was a complete waste of time. One of them said tentatively, 'We do need someone to design a second resort line for Valentino. Would you be interested in that?' No. It wasn't quite what I had in mind. I've no idea what went wrong. I ended up catching the train back to Milan and that was the death of what we'd seen as such a promising initiative.

One new experience came early in the decade when the *Sunday Telegraph* Magazine's editor, Kathryn Samuel, asked me to preview the Winter 1990 collection due to be shown at Claridge's that March. The unusual thing was that I was to take on the role of photographer. I flew to New York for the shoot. As ever, I was anxious the licensed goods shouldn't seem like a poor relation to the couture so presented them together, including cashmere leggings and hip-draped twinsets from Murray Allen, a taupe and cream wool suit from the 1992 collection, a hand-smocked velvet coat in place of increasingly non-PC fur and some over-the-top couture pieces. We immediately hit a problem when the German model who turned up was too big for the clothes but we rapidly found a replacement in Kristen. Thanks to the different agendas of the stylist, photographer and editor, fashion shoots often produce great pictures but you can't always see the dresses. The designer's never there. It's usually the fashion editor and the photographer who dictate the result. So I was busy making the clothes look good, creating the mood and projecting an image of who I had in mind as the person who would wear these clothes as well as creating an artistic image. But I had no idea of the technical detail you have to watch for. Working with me were Jessica Craig Martin, the stylist, Christopher Colbeck doing hair-and-make-up and a photographer's assistant who did all the light checks and handed me the cameras. Together we had to create the right mood by adjusting the lighting, changing the pose and watching the model's eyes to see whether she looked at all tired or strained. Christopher was ever vigilant and warned me that the model we used had a tendency to get a bit puffy round the eyes. 'You've got to watch out for it because it's better and a lot cheaper to get it right now that to spend time retouching the photos later.' It was much harder work than I'd imagined, but I enjoyed the response from the model. After all, I was doing what I always aim to do – making her look good. Although as far as taking the shot was concerned, all I did was click while the assistant set the technical side of it up, but the results were quite fun and, I'm glad to say, run by the magazine.

I was staying with my old friend, Shirley Giovetti, in Sutton Place and was invited to the Council of Fashion Designers of America awards. Held at the Metropolitan Museum of Modern Art, this was an event like the Oscars – not to be missed. I had to pull together a black-tie look at short notice – a trip to Armani did the trick – and was told that Michelle Herbert, a client and wife of the owner of Pantone, would send a car. When it arrived, I kept it waiting for twenty minutes. To my horror, when I eventually went down, I discovered that Michelle had been sitting in it all that time. I had no idea. So the evening did not get off to a very good start. The dinner was held in the Raymond and Beverley Sackler Gallery, where we were surrounded by ancient Assyrian treasures. It was extremely dramatic. At one point I was talking to Dr David Schaffer, Anna Wintour's husband, when Anna came over and stood with her back to me, so close my toes were almost touching her heels.

'Darling, look who's behind you,' her husband pointed me out.

'Oh, hello,' she said, turning on her heel and putting out her hand, before turning away again. It was the most extraordinary social encounter and has mystified me since. After all, I am unmistakeably me. Did she really not recognise me?

In 1992 another opportunity to design something new came along when I agreed to design all the clothes for the Pirelli calendar. Nothing like the other soft-porn calendars hung on garage walls, these had been the brainchild of Pirelli in 1963.

With great quality photographs and a certain allusiveness of style, it had rapidly gained iconic status. It was sensual, glamorous and unique – a collector's item even then. I'd designed for them once already in 1985 just after Pirelli brought the calendar back after nine years of it being out of circulation. The photographer in '85 was Norman Parkinson. The location was Edinburgh. The designers were all from the fashion world. Each of us was invited to create something for a specific month. Our brief was only that whatever we designed had to incorporate the Pirelli tyre track. My dress was a gun-metal bugle-beaded sheath with an asymmetric hem and a dangerously low back. The tyre tread snaked round the body in black bugles. I gave a copy of the final calendar to Prince Charles who looked slightly nonplussed. 'Mmmm. Not sure what the wife'll think, Bruce.' He later told me he'd hidden it from her in one of the downstairs loos.

In 1992, I was briefed to design the clothes for the whole calendar – all swimwear, so another first. Again, it was a question of somehow incorporating the tread design. I was surprised that I had no interface with John Claridge, the photographer, but simply had to design my costumes which would be taken as the starting point of the shot. Very flattering really. I got Colin to sketch all the designs for me to submit to Pirelli's ad agency. Once they were approved, I got started. For the necessary degree of titillation, I decided to use a few risqué elements, asking a rubber fetish manufacturer in Manchester to produce some rubber-moulded 1930s'-style bathing trunks. I stencilled the tyre tracks on to them and cut them out. Different manufacturers produced a chainmail bikini and an over-sized zip puller with tyre treads as teeth running up the front of a bathing costume. We used diamante body jewellery with a fantastic skirt made from crystal beads with the treads incorporated as a bead curtain – and so on.

I relaunched myself in February 1992 with the first of many shows at Anton Mosimann's private dining club in West Malkin Street, Belgravia. The venue suited me perfectly, almost like my own private 'salon', with the added bonus of fabulous food and wine on top. The shows were intimate and very glamorous. It was perfect for ladies who lunch and for me to show the clothes as I like to. There was champagne, I schmoozed. Business was good and all was well with the world.

That was the year I did a show at Lord and Lady Cavendish's home, Holker Hall, in Cumbria, a beautiful neo-Elizabethan house surrounded by gardens and parklands close to Morecombe Bay. I stayed with the irrepressible and life-enhancing Juju Wattenphul and her husband, whom she affectionately referred to as 'the King'. Juju was unforgettable, a booming and warm hostess who with her swept back brown hair, white face and big red lips had something of the gothic about her. Rather like a nineteenth-century grande duchesse. I'd met her at a party in Belgrave Square and she'd been on the scene enough for us to become friends. They lived in nearby Rusland Hall, an elegant Georgian house set in its own grounds, so far from the road and any sign of modern life, that it was like retreating into the eighteenth century. I remember sitting in the bath, looking out of the low sash window across the unspoilt grounds. It was exquisite. Not long afterwards when I was asked by *Country Homes & Interiors* to come up with my 'fantasy supper', I had to set it in Rusland Hall, inviting Braida Stanley Creek, Gerald Manley Hopkins, Coco Chanel, Marilyn Monroe and Karl Lagerfeld to share its pleasures with me. Quite a gathering.

That same year, Noemi Cinzano happened into my life. She popped into the shop one day: blonde, infallibly suntanned, very funny, clever and great company. She was Cinzano of the eponymous wines and spirit label on her father's side and Agnelli on her mother's, so she was comfortable, shall we say.

She had recently moved to London, having bought a beautiful Georgian townhouse in Fulham which was being decorated by John Stefanides.

For the life of me, I couldn't figure out why she wanted to be in Fulham rather than Chelsea or Knightsbridge but she was part of a large group of young wealthy, often titled and independent Europeans who did not want to live on the same streets their parents would have chosen. They were what was laughingly called Eurotrash, definitely a misnomer. They were young, confident, extremely well connected, well dressed and sociable with a handle on languages that enabled them to sail effortlessly through most situations.

Our relationship was very close indeed though strictly platonic. We lavished extravagant presents on one another and thoroughly enjoyed one another's company. Her father's beautiful 1930s' yacht called *The Gael* was kept in the Caribbean. At the drop of a hat, Noemi would dose herself up with tranquillisers to overcome her fear of flying, then hop on Concorde for Barbados. I might be staying with the Sangsters in Barbados and Noemi would call from the boat on spec: 'Bruce, Bruce. I'll send the plane. You fly down to Union Island where the boat will come to pick you up and take you to Bequia.'

So I would.

There she'd stay, Queen of the island, at the Plantation House Hotel, armed with her walkie-talkie for instant communication with her crew and islanders who made her life. She'd wander round the island and everyone knew her. She was something of an old hippy and loved the laid-back quality of the island life. Given the choice between Mustique, manicured and hardly a black face in sight, or its neighbour Bequia, she would always choose the latter. She didn't want to attend stiff dinners and cocktail parties but preferred the freedom and relative anonymity where she could indulge in whatever took her fancy.

I loved her attitude. She was running her ex-husband's wine business so spent a lot of time commuting between London and Italy. I would accompany her when I could get away, and we'd spend great times with her friends, me hardly speaking any Italian but communicating in a mix of English and rusty A-level French.

Shortly after meeting Noemi, I was introduced to a couple who were to be friends and business associates for quite some time. Nori Nemoto, a Japanese businessman, and his partner, Myko Hamaguchi, a famous Japanese singer, who had decided to develop some business interests in the UK. They had bought a flat in Mayfair and were looking for the details that would make their visits to London comfortable and above all, stylish. Their decorator, David Champion, brought them to me late one afternoon and we hit it off instantly. I made many dresses for the diminutive, doll-like Myko. Nori wanted to wear the same sort of clothes as me so I ended up taking him to my tailor, Timothy Everest, over in Spitalfields. My shoemaker, Oliver Sweeney. I introduced them both to the pleasures of Hermès for their accessories and earned Brownie points from the Ongs by taking Myko for a big shopping spree for everyday outfits at Armani. They joined Annabel's, Mark's Club and Harry's Bar. Noemi and I used to go out with them as a foursome and I remember pushing the boat out one night and taking them all to see the Armani-clad version of *Così Fan Tutte* at Covent Garden. They wanted to experience everything that was English and exclusive. Package holiday tours of Windsor Castle and the like would be out of the question – unless of course they were going to have a private audience with Her Majesty. Robert and Sue Sangster invited them to their box at Ascot on Ladies' Day, which, for Myko, was the ultimate in excitement – the hats, the clothes, the manners and the gambling. She ate it up. We took the *Royal Scotsman,* a fabulous train with about sixteen berths and a brilliant kitchen, from Edinburgh up to Inverness and back in a weekend, stopping for meals, served in the beautiful 1930s' wood-panelled dining coach, visiting local beauty spots, castles and whisky distilleries. It was a very special weekend. Nori and Myko had the honeymoon suite, which they thought very amusing. Once Nori took us all to the fabulous Villa San Michele in Fiesole high in the hills overlooking Florence where we stayed for about five or six days. This was a high-calibre lifestyle indeed.

A less welcome intrusion into my life was a female stalker who inundated me with long incoherent letters and cards declaring her love for me, graphically describing our sexual encounters in her fantasy land. This went on for over a year and, according to her confused account, we almost got as far the altar. The letters were often accompanied by drawings of me and even once by a Polaroid of her breasts. I knew exactly who she was because she once came into the shop insisting that I read some of her 'charitable' literature before she'd leave. My eventual consent – anything to get rid of her – was obviously construed as some kind of welcome physical contact. If only I'd known what it would lead to. She would stand on a nearby street corner outside Harrods, handing out Xeroxed sheets of rambling prose, sometimes coming to watch the shop and occasionally drawing what was in the window. Apart from being a nuisance, it made both Marie (Todd), who she was convinced was my wife, and I extremely uneasy about going outside in case we bumped into her. When I reported her to the police, I was told there was nothing they could do. Eventually the letters stopped coming and she no longer appeared. I imagine the poor woman had found someone else she deemed more worthy of her attentions and had moved on to another pitch. The relief I felt was enormous.

Meanwhile business was taking that familiar cyclical turn and was picking up again. It had been a big surprise when Courtauld's pulled the plug on Arabella Pollen, the well-connected golden girl of fashion. It was yet another example of what was happening in the early nineties – you can't be big in this country because there simply isn't the support. It seemed to prove again that to survive in this world, small is better. For me, shows were back on the agenda. In 1993 *The Sunday Times* had spread the news BRUCE IS BACK. We suffered a slight setback the following year when £85,000 worth of dresses was stolen from the shop. Burglars ramraided the front plate-glass window of the shop in the small hours and grabbed everything they could, leaving a chaos of empty rails and broken glass in their wake. But the mystery was that they knew to go straight to the drawer in my office desk where I had all the takings and taken the lot. Nothing else in my office was touched. It was as if they knew exactly where to go. Who was responsible for it? We'll never know.

As a result we had no samples to show anyone. There was no point in remaking them because they'd only be ready by the end of the season. I had to go into autodrive when it came to seeing clients through the door. I suppose I can only look on the publicity we got as a result as the silver lining to an otherwise pretty black cloud. The only thing to do was to carry on and focus on the next collection, one of the best in the decade. I took a forties' and fifties' starlet theme and used accessories I had had made in Paris. We had great hair and make-up people and Michael Howells, the set designer, was superb. Working with George, he split the Claridge's ballroom into different areas with banks of seats at different angles facing a small set with a glamorous forties'-style backdrop. The models moved from one to another posing in front of the backdrops as if in a Cecil Beaton photo session. The lighting and music were particularly good too and we got a lot of excellent pictures. By having that kind of runway, I could get all of my clients, including Victoria Getty, Sue and Fi Sangster, Jessica de Rothschild, Alice Bamford, Jemima Khan, Noemi, Myko and Nori, on to the front row. It worked very well indeed.

After a few years of concentrating solely on couture, I had the idea of opening another shop, but this time one that would stock ready-to-wear. I talked to David McErlain about it and he helped me with the business plan. We talked to Noemi and Nori about backing it and they jumped at the opportunity. We found a spot in Brook Street and opened in 1996 with a spectacular party that even contained a little bit of history in the making as Cherie Blair came as well as Michael and Sandra Howard. Marie Helvin and Sue Sangster came, loyally wearing me. The shop was filled with smart day into evening wear, not too dissimilar to what I was doing as couture over in Beauchamp Place but at a third of the price. The challenge was that it was an expensive site so I would need to sell a lot of clothes each week to sustain the overhead.

Ros came back into my life to work her magic with the publicity for the opening and so did George who had continued working with me since setting up her business but on a project-by-project basis. One of Ros's wildest ideas yet was to stage a show on board a British Airways Boeing 747 between London and New York. We'd hoped to fly to JFK but, because the planes were heavily booked, we had to go to Newark, New Jersey. Fashion took the place of the in-flight film. As people were waiting to board the plane, they were given invitations to the show (not that they had much choice – talk about a captive audience), perfume samples from Penhaligon and copies of *Hello!* who were covering the event. Two stewardesses became models for the flight and joined the pros who changed on the upper deck and wandered down the aisles in suits, cocktail dresses and evening gowns from the ready-to-wear collection.

We took various fashion journalists with us together with a team from London Weekend Television. Everybody loved the show apart from one rather grumpy individual who was trying to go to sleep in Club Class. The plan was that we would transfer in New York and catch the last plane back from JFK, just giving us enough time to take the journalists to a reception at the Peninsula Hotel for a glimpse of the Big Apple. But owing to a number of cock-ups on the ground, by the time we'd found our bus there was no time for any of that. It was straight to JFK where a combination of snow and delayed flights meant we were held up till 1 a.m. I arrived back in London at 3 o'clock in the afternoon and had to appear on *London Tonight* at 5 o'clock, dazed from lack of sleep. It might have got us good coverage but it was, to say the least, a trying experience.

Later that same year, Joanna Lumley came by. She'd been a client on and off for years and banged on the window one day in Beauchamp Place to say they were filming the wedding of Sapphie in *Ab Fab* just around the corner at St Columba's church. Joanna was on her way to the set and had thought I could be her date in the scene. I agreed immediately. We did a few shots in and outside the shop with Kathy Burke, then I was dragged down to where a long line of paparazzi was waiting outside the church. Joanna planted a great big kiss on my cheek – the shot that was used everywhere including on my Christmas cards that year.

Sadly, the Brook Street shop didn't make a quick enough return on the investor's money and we wound up the whole venture the following year. I had failed to take into account that by opening there I was also cannibalising my couture business. I learned that there is a balance to be struck between ready-to-wear and couture. It's a difficult tightrope to walk. Now I look back, I realise my business has fluctuated between couture and ready-to-wear over thirty years as I currently gear up to enter the ready-to-wear market yet again, running it in tandem with couture.

Apart from that slight débâcle, there was a steady flow of good things happening in the business throughout the nineties. Two weddings stand out above the others, largely because they increased my press profile no end. This was Jemima Goldsmith's to Imran Khan in 1995. Jemima's mother, Annabel, had been a customer for some time and had introduced her daughter. I didn't go to the wedding but Marie Helvin and Jerry Hall came with me to the party in the evening where we heard how the streets near Richmond register office had been packed with photographers hanging out of the windows of the mock-Tudor homes trying to catch a glimpse of the wedding party. I was surprised at the extent of the press interest. Yes, she was a beautiful heiress without a past and he, a Pakistani, former cricketer with political aspirations and a string of well-publicised romances, but they captured the moment and for a time were the newly appointed royal couple. Paparazzi with telephoto lenses lurked around corners, snapping Jemima when she came for a fitting. We had to close the shop to anyone else when she was there. It was quite unnerving having lenses pressed against the window desperate to get *the* shot of the dress but it did no harm to the business. Jemima had been clear that she wanted something restrained but elegant, something becoming a Muslim bride. She was thinking of an outfit along the lines of the suit that Bianca wore at her wedding to Mick – only less revealing – so I designed a tailored cream day suit with a long skirt. She looked stunning.

Another equally well-publicised wedding – but for the wrong reasons – was Lisa Butcher's to Marco Pierre White. This was a *Hello!* photo opportunity. It seemed to me that the brief was to get maximum coverage from minimum coverage. The dress was beaded, off-the-shoulder, bare-backed and slashed at the waist but in the Brompton Oratory she was heavily veiled so decorum was upheld. According to press reports, the couple had a blazing row on the big day because the groom felt the dress should have been more demure. But it was exactly what the bride had wanted – a stand-out dress. She was a beautiful girl and we knew it would be a fabulous photo opportunity. The pictures outside the church should have been a pointer to how long the marriage would last. Marco's complete avoidance of me at the reception should have told me that the dress was the key to his bad humour. All that aside, Lisa was a fabulous-looking bride and that dress has proved an inspiration to many Bruce Oldfield brides since then.

Perhaps the biggest occasion of all was Rania Al-Yassin's marriage. She had come to us through Her Majesty, Queen Noor, a regular client, whose stepson she was marrying. We made her wedding dress and an off-the-shoulder evening dress for the party afterwards. Queen Noor wanted me to include a nod to Middle Eastern culture so the embroidery we used was based on a piece of Syrian embroidery I found at the V & A. It was a big, important dress that was quite over the top with glitter, gold embroidery and beading. She did look very good in it indeed. I flew out for the wedding to dress her. Prince Feisal, the bridegroom's brother, was in charge of getting her from her home to the palace where the ceremony was to take place so he took me to her. Dressing her went without a hitch although there was some discussion about her hair. She was determined to have it piled high despite the fact that it would make her even taller than her husband. She had her way. But the first problem arrived with the car that was to drive her to the ceremony – a Rolls Royce with a low roof. Try as we might, we could not get her to fit upright into the back seat without destroying her hairdo. (I was having visions of the time we had to send a bride to church standing in the back of a van for exactly the same reason.) In the end we had to manhandle her in, pushing and pulling so that she sat at an angle with her head under the slightly raised bit of roof over the back shelf – and off she went.

I was supposed to be following in another car but at the last minute protocol forbade it so I was driven all around the houses until we fetched up a little way out of town at the Hummar Palace, belonging to HRH Princess Muna, HM King Hussein's first wife and mother of the groom. It was at that point I realised the driver had no idea which palace he was meant to be taking me to. Without any Arabic, it was impossible for me to explain. Finally, after a lot of gesturing, I got him to understand that we needed to be where the actual wedding was taking place. When we arrived there eventually, the guards wouldn't let me all the way into the palace so I missed the whole thing.

However I had made it in time for the wedding celebration that took place immediately afterwards. Daylight fireworks exploded over the city during the huge reception in the palace grounds. A parachutist jumped from a plane and landed right on target in the enclosure. He was carrying a ceremonial sword that, having avoided impaling himself, he presented to the newly wed heir to the throne and his wife. Queen Noor presided over the event in a long column of shocking pink, modestly split, revealing her flat shoes. I'd never seen anyone look and walk elegantly in an evening dress with low heels but she managed it with aplomb. The image that appears regularly of that day is of Prince Abdullah standing to the right of his bride. What no one sees is that I am standing to her left. I can never figure out why I was cut from the picture!

That evening I was due to go along to HM King Hussein's palace at 7 o'clock to dress the bride for the evening party at HRH Princess Muna's. Here we were in their Majesties' dressing room when in walked King Hussein in shirtsleeves. He said immediately that he knew all about me. He'd been in

Pakistan the previous week, where he'd seen *Journey In Fashion* on TV. I couldn't believe how far the programme had travelled. He'd brought with him a diamond necklace for Rania to wear. It had been custom-made using exactly the same motif as was on her evening dress. She was thrilled.

At one point she asked me to fetch the dress. I asked her where it was.

'It's in the Queen's bedroom.'

'Well, no chance. I'm not going into the Queen's bedroom. What if the King and Queen are in it?!'

Someone else got it in the end and she was made ready. But the same thing happened again. I was driven to the party only to discover there wasn't anywhere for me to sit. I couldn't figure it out because the Jordanians are such hospitable people and I did have an invitation. They quickly found me a place on Princess Aysha's table. She was the sister of the Princes Feisal and Abdullah and I knew her as a client. The party went on into the small hours when a fleet of cars whisked us back into central Amman. I have great fondness for that family, always hospitable and courteous. Although they are the ruling family, they are surprisingly modest about how they deal with everyday life. They base themselves more on the model of the continental European royal families who work with and are very much in tune with their people.

The role of a couturier is a curious one. You inhabit such a unique place in a woman's heart. I was reminded of this recently when I had to do a fitting in New York. When I arrived I was shown into the kitchen by the maid.

'Mrs X will be here soon. Sit down. Look at the kitchen.' Puzzling.

Then my client rings from her mobile to ask if I'd arrived.

'Yes. He's the cook?'

'No, he's not the cook.'

Oh God. Panic. I'm immediately shown into the drawing room.

'Do sit down. Would you like a cup of tea? Do you smoke? Have a magazine.'

Here, I benefit from a relationship with a client whereby I'm often taken into their confidence and treated as an equal. For the amount of money they're paying, many clients expect honesty. You can't make a size 16 look like a size 10 but you can bring out the best points and minimise the worst. If, as a result of your direction, you produce a dress that flatters the client, they come back for more. At the beginning of my career, I was more hesitant and the fittings would drag on and on. Then I realised that what they want is someone in authority to take over. They're paying for my eye for proportion, my eye for detail. Now I say what I think. More or less.

When I was down in the South of France in the mid 1990s staying with Robert and Sue, I met Susan Ranouf, Robert's second wife. Through her I was invited to go to the Melbourne Cup, the Australian equivalent of Ascot, to judge the fashions in the field. It was a tremendous expenses-paid junket where all I had to do was talk to the press about what women were wearing. It's a national day in Australia and as far from Royal Ascot as you can get. The Australian sense of humour and lack of respect for *folie de grandeur* seemed to have been lost on the national press. While the women sported their tongue-in-cheek efforts to be chic, parodying elegance rather than aspiring to it, I was expected to toe the line and agree that the outfits would be winners in the royal enclosure. Naively perhaps, I fulfilled my brief and was honest about what I saw, deflecting the worst of the questions by pointing out Mrs Kerry Packer, Mrs John Magnier and Mrs Robert Sangster as being up to their usual top form. As a result, the press got out their knives.

While I was there I met Lloyd Williams and his wife, a long-standing client. They were opening Crown Casino in Melbourne, a vast complex that included luxury hotels, numerous restaurants and bars and a vast array of top-name shops. At that time there was a total confidence in the Pacific Rim and all that was happening in South East Asia. Money was filtering south into Australia, then considered to be a giant pleasure park. Barred from gambling in their Muslim countries, the high rollers would fly in with their private planes, stay at Crown Towers, the most lavish hotel, then be encouraged to spend, spend, spend. At the top end of the market they had Armani, while at the bottom of the street was an Emporio Armani diffusion outlet. The Williamses offered me a franchise for my ready-to-wear. It was easy to say yes. I spent a great deal of the year travelling between London and Australia but, sadly, once Brook Street had to go I reverted to couture again. As a result there was no future for me in Crown Casinos either.

The years were rolling by but I was as keen as ever to diversify into other areas. In 1998, I signed an extremely lucrative contract with Alexandra plc, a workwear manufacturer, as a part-time consultant. It is a completely different challenge to designing couture and great for me because the end product doesn't conflict with my own.

One unusual commission came along when I was approached by Delia Smith to design a new yellow and green strip for her football club, Norwich City. In my kitchen, cookery writers may come and cookery writers may go but Delia goes on forever. I had already been asked to design some things for her to wear on her TV show. When we met finally for a design discussion, I showed frames from the programmes which I had downloaded and printed out. I explained where she, in my opinion, looked good and where an outfit did little for her figure or was impractical. It was a sticky start. I could be a bit too forthright in my opinions. But we ended up getting on extremely well. I did more fitted clothes for her, sexy wrap tops and shirts with sleeves designed not to dangle in the gravy. When the idea of designing the strip for Norwich came up I thought it was a laugh and was keen to do it. I remember George and I flew to Huddersfield in a private plane hired by Delia where we had a meeting with one of the big sportswear manufacturers, on other occasions Sam would drive me up to Norwich for meetings and the odd fixture. Despite my lack of interest in the sport, it was all good fun, especially when I had a team to root for and could stand in the directors' box, screaming my head off, with Delia, her husband, Anne Robinson and the Bishop of Norwich.

Looking back at the nineties, despite the odd down period, it seems as if it was one big party. Usually Marie Helvin and I were on each other's arm, more often than not driven by Sam. The parties were extravagant, lavish productions that were reported in the press and, when you were snapped, were useful for keeping the profile going. There were too many to remember but two do stand out among the rest. Elton John held a fabulous party in an atmospherically lit marquee at the Greenwich Royal Hospital. Marie and I were dancing when her shoe flew off to be caught by Elton who slipped it back on her foot Prince-Charming style. On our way home much later, she tossed the unfortunate shoes out of the car window, never to see them again. They were a pair of Jimmy Choos that I'd lent her so I probably wasn't so amused. Another was the opening of Gianni Versace's shop in Bond Street. No one could believe that a designer could have a shop that big and that glitzy. The place was packed with names and faces. It was one of those occasions where you swiftly learn your place. The huge crush of photographers were clamouring for their shots and I remember being shoved to one side so they could get a shot of Elton and Versace together. I know they have a job to do, but . . .

CHAPTER TWENTY

It wasn't until the nineties that I took seriously one of those 'learn to do all the things you've been putting off for years' resolutions. I've always been a project person. Because I invariably wake up at 5 a.m. and get up soon after, I can get through my basic work by midday, so projects are what keep me going. One of the first things I did was take cookery lessons with Lyn Hall. She's run a school, La Petite Cuisine, for years and taught privately from her own 'petite cuisine' in her Kensington flat. The idea was that after slaving over the hot stove for a few hours, I should invite a couple of friends round so that I could also learn the tricks of doing everything in the right order. Food should arrive at the table unburned and at the right temperature. So I used to ask Annabel and Noemi or Lizzie and Vanessa (long-time friends in the fashion world) to dine with me. Under Lyn's watchful eye, strangely, nothing ever went wrong. I learned kitchen skills and liked the idea that I was finding out exactly how a thing should be done. It helped me to understand recipes and not to be fazed by technical requirements. I also gained the confidence not to follow the book within an inch of its life. But I have to admit that with the prospect of guests arriving in a few hours, time often tempers my desire to experiment.

My interest in interior design had begun way back when I moved into Campden Hill Square although it had never got any further than doing up my own home. When I was asked to be one of the designers to design a room for Robin Guild in The Design and Decoration Building on Pimlico Road (essentially a resource centre for the decorating trade and the public), I jumped at the chance. This was no commercial enterprise but more a chance for designers to indulge their creative imagination. We all had a free hand, which resulted in some fabulously inventive rooms: the walls of Philip Treacy's bathroom were part mirrored and part covered with collages of magazine and fashion photographs, with a ten-foot statue of a cactus gracing a corner of the room; Rifat's room was like a surreal scene from a French court set against the backdrop of a starry desert sky. I asked Tom Dixon to help make the metal sections for three chairs, abstractions of the female body. The backs and seats were heart shaped and joined at the 'waist' by two poles. One wore a bikini, with a horizontally pleated bra forming the backrest and the seat was padded and draped in silk with a trim of glass buttons. The second wore a one-shouldered dress and the third a bustier dress. They were placed at different angles in the room, lined with pleated elephant-coloured canvas and looked as if they were advancing down a catwalk. The carpet was a two-tone beige and cream slashed into shapes echoing the walls, which were hung with roughly pleated Manuel Canovas hessian, held in place with large buttons. It was a fun project and Robin Guild couldn't have been more helpful in guiding us through the process. It's a great pity that the centre eventually had to close.

One of the most momentous achievements in my life was finally giving up cigarettes. It was 28 February 28 1994, a day forever engraved on my brain. Like so many hardened smokers, I had tried to give up numerous times before and failed miserably. I'd been hypnotised twice, with very limited success. Nothing worked long-term. And then I was given a nudge by Lesley Kissin, a South African client, who gave me a copy of Alan Carr's *Easy Way to Stop Smoking*. She swore by it. I took it to Barbados that Christmas and started reading. Its message was a potent one reinforced by repetition until I reached the point where I could almost guess the next proposal. By the end, I wasn't convinced that I was going to give up but I did feel that, if I really wanted to, I had begun the necessary mental preparation. The final straw came when I was invited to New Zealand to judge a fashion competition sponsored, ironically enough, by Benson & Hedges. I couldn't find a flight that would take me there and allow me to smoke. I was sick of being ruled by the cigarette and so I decided the time had come at last to take control of things. I booked a one-to-one session with Robin Hanley, one of Alan Carr's team.

Tentatively, I stuck my head round the door of his room in a basement in Hanover Square. The first thing that struck me was the pile of cigarette packets, mostly half full, next to a selection of cigarette lighters on the mantelpiece – the tradition was that the newly converted would give their cigs and lighter to the therapist at the end of the session. But I kept hold of my gold Dupont and went straight round to Noemi afterwards. We went out, got drunk and I gave her the lighter. She lost it within a month and I haven't smoked since.

Freed from the tyranny of nicotine, I could take the first-class round trip to New Zealand. First, I flew to New York where I stayed at the Mark, a wonderful small hotel on 77th and Madison, perfectly placed for the museums. My four favourites – the Cooper Hewitt Design Museum, the Whitney, the Guggenheim and the Met – were all within spitting distance. I had tea with Liz Tilberis, the redoubtable editor of *Harpers Bazaar* who was to die from cancer shortly afterwards, and the newly arrived incoming editor, Glenda Bailey, then at *Marie Claire* US. I did some bonding with the ex-pat journalists including Hamish Bowles at *Vogue* who had been a big supporter of ours when he was on *Harpers* UK where he understood and championed couture. I wanted to get a sense of the way the fashion world was moving over there and spent some time researching a variety of hotels to see where private shows might work best. Tina Brown threw a lunch in my honour, inviting about twenty-five women to her apartment on 57th Street, so I could meet the cream of New York society. Her husband, Harold Evans, didn't show – hardly surprising in such an all-girl gathering. I was the lone male and had the good luck to be seated between Barbara Walters and Lauren Bacall who, in her seventies, retained all the presence and bearing of a legend. I was quite awe-struck but she was jokey and relaxed, pointing out to me some of the heavy hitters in the room. Thanks to Tina, I made a few new clients that day and maintained those I already knew who had also been invited to that particularly august gathering. Then it was on to LA where I was given a great fifties'-style suite at the Chateau Marmont. I hung out with Barry and his wife Jane for a few days, then took off for Bora Bora. It was beautiful with surreal sunrises, but a bit too close to the French atomic experiments for my liking. Then it was Auckland and Wellington where I judged the fashion show.

Not long after I'd stopped smoking, I was asked as Sarah Ferguson's partner to dinner with Robert and Sue Sangster, Michael and Mary Parkinson. She was very lively but I was surprised when Alan Bond came to the table and Robert said, 'Ah, Alan, let me introduce you to Fergie.' She drew herself up and said, 'Her Royal Highness, the Duchess of York.' Just like the Princess of Wales, that regal front would emerge when you least expected it. However, the dinner proceeded smoothly and she started talking about a well-known gallery owner she'd met recently.

'I think he's marvellous. I met him at a cocktail party and I said to him how much I'd like to learn about art. Do you know what he said? "Before I met you, if someone had asked me to teach you about art, I'd have said never in a million years. But now I have, I'll consider it." Don't you think that's amazing?'

'Amazingly rude. Yes,' I said.

'No, no. I love it when people speak their mind.'

We had to agree to differ. The dinner went on. Then she turned to me again to say, but apropos of what I can't imagine, 'Let me ask you a question. Why do you think the British people don't like me?'

I thought for a moment, then remembering what she had said only twenty minutes earlier, suggested, 'Well, I think, Ma'am, that perhaps they find you try too hard.'

'Hmmph. I've never heard that before.' She didn't speak to me for the rest of the evening. I'm glad to say that we have met since and, if I caused any offence, it seems to have blown over.

How could I write about this decade without mentioning the death of the Princess of Wales? Like everyone in the world, I was terribly shaken by it. We were invited to the funeral. Anita came to my flat with Caroline Charles and her husband, Malcolm Valentine, for a fortifying glass of champagne. Sam drove us through the streets of London which were absolutely empty. It must only have taken four minutes to get to Westminster Abbey. The whole affair was organised with military precision and we were seated in the nave. Facing people across the aisle made it more important to maintain composure. It was an extraordinarily sad occasion, though not enhanced for me by Elton's song or Earl Spencer's speech. The worst moment came when the procession down the aisle halted with the coffin right under my nose. The solemnity of the occasion combined with the music from the choir was enormously affecting. But a stiff upper lip was maintained. Outside the Abbey there was probably a more natural outpouring of emotion but we were completely oblivious to it.

I wasn't surprised to be invited. Although the Princess had dropped us, I had always been considered as someone who had been part of her mythology. It was widely acknowledged that I had helped define her style at a time when she was trying to establish herself, shaking off the old image. Shortly before her death, she had set a new precedent in the Royal Family by auctioning a large part of her wardrobe for charity. Seventy-nine cocktail dresses and evening gowns went under the hammer at Christies NY, causing a huge amount of international attention and raising over two million dollars. The highest bid of $222,500 went to the Victor Edelstein dress that she had worn when she famously danced with John Travolta. There were four or five of my dresses there, including the pepper-red chiffon woven with silver lame that she wore to the première of *Hot Shots* in 1992, so it all helped to keep the Bruce Oldfield flag flying. I don't believe there were any hard feelings between us and I had always refrained from jumping on the Princess of Wales bandwagon, maintaining discretion to the last. And I see no reason to change that. At one point I had asked Marie to try to wheedle out of the Princess why she wasn't visiting us any more. Marie was hosting a huge dinner at Cliveden sponsored by Tiffany's in aid of AIDS Crisis Trust whose patron was the Princess of Wales. Marie had been going out with Dodi Fayed and introduced him to the Princess in the private reception beforehand. And the rest, as they say . . . However Marie managed to ask the leading question and got the sheepish response, 'Oh I must go and see him some time.' Ah well.

The other incident that had rocked the fashion world only a month earlier was when Gianni Versace was shot dead outside his house in Miami. I had met him a few times over the years. Comparatively recently, we were standing behind one another in a queue in Loft, the sportswear store in the Faubourg St Honoré.

'Gianni, you've got a men's wear shop of your own three blocks up the street. What on earth are you doing here?'

'They make nicer T-shirts than I do,' he explained. 'Simple.'

As the cashier looked at his credit card, she looked up. 'Oh. Gianni Versace.'

Then she looked at me blankly and asked, 'Do you work for him?'

'No, I don't.' I thought it was very funny.

The nineties were particularly marked for me by the deaths of so many friends, so many of them from AIDS. Bill Reed was one of the first to go, followed by Scott. His business simply couldn't keep pace with his frenetic lifestyle and had gone belly up. He'd left America and moved to Milan where he was working freelance. It was sad to see him there back in 1982, a failed business behind him but optimistic as always about the future. He was able to gain access to a lot of the design houses whose eponymous designers had been his friends over the years. It must have been very difficult for him to make that jump from having been a real name in America to working as a second string to another designer. After running my own business for so many years I know that I wouldn't have been able to do it. Eventually, he set up a studio of his own, designing a collection with an Italian factory and things began to get better. I do not know whether he knew he was HIV positive, he certainly never discussed it with me in the intervening years, but he became very ill. A brain tumour left him prematurely senile and he began to lose his eyesight. In 1993, he was found wandering the streets of Milan and was admitted to hospital, dying a few days later. A number of us clubbed together to pay for his body to be returned to America.

Then Marion died in North Carolina. By this time I saw him infrequently, although we had kept in touch. I felt guilty that I hadn't sent him money to help but I'd left it too late. The big shock was Tina Chow. She was not the only woman I knew personally who had contracted the disease, and I had never thought of her as at all promiscuous. Not of course that you needed to be promiscuous to contract AIDS. Like a lot of things in life, it was often just bad luck or bad timing. These deaths were profoundly upsetting and of course brought with them reminders of my own mortality. I had made my decision back in the eighties when AIDS was first publicised so widely. I wasn't completely inactive sexually after that but I was very circumspect indeed. Always extremely selective and extremely careful. I did have an AIDS test after a bout of shingles when the doctor advised me it could be a result of some immuno-deficiency. I found the whole thing extremely traumatic even though I got the results in a couple of days. But it put me on edge for quite a time.

Perhaps saddest of all was Colin's death. I miss his companionship to this day. His very close friends, myself included, had to make the decision together to turn off his life-support system. I organised the service at the West London Crematorium and compiled a tape of music that I knew he liked – from Parry's 'Songs of Farewell' to Astrid Gilberto's 'Girl from Ipanema'. My cook, Sarah Ramsbottom, did the food for the wake in Colin's flat. It was a few days before Christmas 1996. Everything was more or less closed down thanks to the freezing fog that smothered London. Noemi sent a chauffeur-driven car for me. It was a huge Daimler Vanden Plas – very embarrassing. I felt more like the father of the bride than a mourner travelling to a funeral. Colin arrived very late as the hearse got lost – I remember the twenty-minute music tape was playing over and over again. As the coffin made its last journey down the conveyor belt, the automated curtains closed behind him and there was a sudden crunching sound . . . We never found out what it was and didn't enquire, but we felt that at least Colin had had the last word. One good thing to come out of the funeral was that I finally got to make up with Shelagh Sartin with whom I'd fallen out over Elm Park Gardens. I comforted her and we've patched up our differences since.

In Colin's memory, we raised quite a lot of money for a trust that we wanted to set up to help fashion illustration students at Central St Martin's. We organised groups of friends from various fields in fashion and advertising – hot, rich young people who would be interested in buying some of Colin's work that was to be shown in an exhibition at St Martin's later that year. With the executors of his estate, Judith Wicks and Roger Bull, we set up an evening in the Brook Street shop and raised about £15,000. I don't think people had realised how broad Colin's interests were and we sold as many pictures of his beloved ocean liners as of his fashion illustrations.

In 1995 I had been involved with a BBC TV programme about Barnardo's that ran for three weeks, giving them some much deserved publicity. It focused on the organisation generally but also dealt in some detail with the aftercare section and how they helped people find their parents. By this point, both Barry and George had traced their families, without suffering any great emotional traumas. I had never seriously thought of doing it myself. Violet had been like a real mum to me, and Betty Lally didn't figure. I'd also had the good fortune to know a splendid succession of mother figures who had remained with me throughout my life. I was still in touch with Edith Blair, Constance Gilbey, Judith and the rest. I had no need of a birth mother and I rarely gave her a thought. However, this programme got me thinking. In the end I concluded, Oh well. Why not? But this was no desperate emotional urge – something more in the spirit of academic enquiry.

BRUCE OLDFIELD

I wrote to Roger and sure enough, there's my letter in my file, still meticulously kept up to date even to this day.

> I feel it's time to know whether my mother is still around!
> I'm not sure what I'll do when I have the information but
> I'll deal with that if and when.

Because of the Data Protection Act, Barnardo's are unable to pass on any information they may have to the Salvation Army, whose services they use to trace people. So, having had to start from scratch, it took two years before the Salvation Army finally traced my mother on the instructions of the aftercare officer. The Family Tracing Service wrote to me to say that she had died of breast cancer in 1975, one year after Mum. She had died in St Christopher's Hospice in Sydenham. Her father had died in 1953, not long after I was born, while her mother had soldiered on to die at the age of 100 in 1989. Her sisters, Christine, Enid and Joan were all still alive. Aunt Enid was in Canada, Aunt Joan lived down Bournemouth way and Aunt Christine lived in Royal Tonbridge. More than that, it emerged that I had many cousins and two half-brothers.

I wrote to Roger:

> It appears I have three intelligent, sprightly yet elderly aunts all with families of their own and all of whom are keen to provide any information I want . . . I wasn't expecting a family reunion.

Apparently, in 1974, Betty had asked the Salvation Army to find my half-brother, David. He had an emotional reunion with her at Christmas that year, just a few weeks before she died. I remember the hesitation in the voice of the Family Tracing Service's Colonel Fairclough when he told me that my mother

324

had asked them to find her son when she was dying. 'Not you, Bruce,' he said. 'She wanted to be put in touch with David, your half-brother.' It didn't upset me. I had no previous claims on her attention or affection.

What did I feel? Very little about my mother. After all, I was nearly fifty and, as far as I was concerned, I had had a perfectly fine mother in Violet. The Barnardo's aftercare officer was assiduous in following up my case, advising me not to ignore the impact of her death on my feelings and suggesting how I might feel most comfortable about contacting the family. Apparently people often prefer to exchange letters, inform-ation and photographs before deciding whether to meet their new-found families. I was impressed with the genuine concern and thoughtfulness offered. The aftercare section employs a team of social workers and researchers who take old Barnardo's girls and boys through their records. Almost a million pounds a year goes into this work alone.

In fact, Barnardo's also approached my relatives to see whether they wanted to get in touch. After all, they might not have wanted anything to do with me. I got sweet letters from each of these three old ladies in their seventies and eighties and it turned out that Len, Joan's husband was having a big birthday party with the whole family and they asked me whether I would like to go and meet them all at once. I decided I would.

The party was at Jennifer and Stuart's (one of my new cousins and her husband) house in Hampshire. Still without a car, I got Sam to drive me in the S-class Mercedes. After making our way slowly along narrow winding roads, we pulled up outside a pleasant modern semi-detached house. I think everybody else was already there, waiting for my arrival. I guessed they'd be watching discreetly from the window so I didn't disappoint in my chauffeur-driven limo with the door opened by Sam, complete with peaked cap. I stepped out looking good in a navy suit and striped shirt.

I had already talked to my cousin Jennifer over the telephone. She, like the rest of them as it turned out, was very chatty and extremely easy-going. She greeted me and then swiftly handed me over to Joan and Len. It didn't turn out to be a melodramatic, over-emotional reunion although just about the whole family was there – three generations of aunts, cousins and step this and thats. I found it very difficult to work out my relationship with some of them as all those familial complexities had always eluded me. What was a half-cousin exactly? Nothing I'd ever had to worry about before. Jennifer's daughter, Gillian, had made me a family tree, which helped clarify things and showed that I was part of a huge family. Everyone was warm and friendly. At heart, they were just like me – ordinary. I liked the fact that they took me in their stride as someone who had done OK without being part of their orbit but were quite happy to include me if I wished – no pressure.

The house was comfortable and modern with a spacious sitting room that had large windows overlooking a mature garden. An endless stream of food was magicked from the kitchen with wine for the grown-ups and orange juice for both the very young and the very old. I mingled easily, meeting people who were about my age and had gone about their lives with varying degrees of success without any contact with me. Betty's eldest sister, Christine, was suffering from leukaemia and couldn't come. She wrote me a welcoming letter instead. She died soon after without our ever having met. However her son Christopher, a surgeon, and daughter, Sue Howells, were both there. Sue seems to have been the creative one in the family, having carved out a career as a dancer and choreographer. Sadly her obituary, less than a year later in *The Times*, spoke of a career cut tragically short by cancer.

It was a very peculiar novelty to hear them saying how much I resembled Betty or other members of the family. Actually I think I do look like her – the photo I have of her now looks something like I would look in drag.

Trying to find out what happened to Betty after she dropped from my records was too difficult, so I only have the memories of her sisters Enid and Joan. According to them, she spent some time in Mauritius and Paris with Phillipe Pinchin, my other half-brother William's father. Perhaps her interest in French was genetically passed on to me – nice idea. Speaking to the family, the party line was couched in such euphemisms as, 'She liked to have fun, loved dancing. . .'

'No, she wasn't a slapper,' said Aunt Joan firmly. 'Len, what's a slapper?'

'She liked men,' they remembered. 'No. She wasn't paid for it. She just found people she liked for a while, then moved on.'

Sounds reasonable to me – another genetic characteristic? Although she did leave something of a trail of disaster behind her, I prefer to think of her as a woman of independent spirit, looking for something that probably didn't exist, who wasn't prepared to fall in with contemporary standards. Possibly she was a little confused with her epilepsy and the medication prescribed to keep it at bay. A little bit sad, a little bit desperate, but someone who clearly had a good time when she actively sought it.

She lived in a bed-sit in Willesden, close to sister Joan (apparently sister Christine was less forgiving as her children didn't even know they had an Aunt Betty until I surfaced). Her occupations were various and decidedly unskilled. I suspect she lived on her charm. She didn't drink, couldn't have afforded nor even encountered recreational drugs (though, given her predilection for black men, she might possibly have come across weed in some form or other) so she took her pleasures where she could. If my life was a film, I'd nominate Julie Walters as the only suitable candidate for the part of Betty.

The other person who was missing from the gathering was David, my half-brother. I was intrigued that he wasn't even mentioned. I didn't meet him until some eighteen months later when I had been diagnosed with cancer. I thought I should anonymously contact him through the Salvation Army to suggest that he have a test for cancer too. One of the people in the Salvation Army office remembered being involved in the search for David twenty-five years earlier. Talk about 'degrees of separation'. They found him very quickly and I duly sent him a letter. I hadn't particularly planned to meet with him but we agreed we would. So July 1999 found me sitting in Le Caprice at lunchtime, waiting. I'd chosen the restaurant because I feel very comfortable there and it's discreet. But that day, half the press seemed to be in. Mariella Frostrup and Paula Reed came over to say hello and I whispered, 'I'm actually meeting my brother. See if you can recognise him when he walks in.' Eyes were trained on the door, but of course nobody recognised him, because he doesn't look anything like me. He has a career in computers and aviation, is divorced with two daughters, Helen and Rebecca. We got on very well. Perhaps his is the saddest story to come out of all this. He had not been told that the mother who brought him up was in fact a step-mother, so when he was contacted by the Salvation Army and subsequently confronted by a guilt-ridden, emotional woman riddled with cancer, who was, in fact his real mother, it came as quite a shock.

I don't think that I ever had the feeling, before or after our meeting, that I would suddenly be changing my lifestyle to include my new family or the other way round. They were very laid back about the whole thing, not at all pushy, which is why I liked them. I was surprised to learn from Jennifer that the family had tried to contact me in the eighties. They had seen an article that had mentioned my mother's maiden name was Lally. Putting two and two together, they had contacted Anita. Perhaps she didn't believe them – there had been a couple of men who'd popped up falsely claiming to be my father, so I don't blame her. She certainly never mentioned it.

Now I don't see them a great deal but we keep in touch. I visited Joan occasionally and I spoke on the telephone until her death in 2004 while Enid and I write to one another. I see David and his children, my nieces, quite a lot. Finding my family after all these years hasn't made a dramatic difference to my life. How could it when I've worked so hard to build my own little castle? I've always avoided emotional commitment so it could never be passionately engaging for me – I'm just not that kind of person.

CHAPTER TWENTY-ONE

As we approached the Millennium, I began to feel I had become something of an *éminence grise* of the fashion world. Already an Honorary Fellow of Sheffield City Polytechnic, I received an Honorary Fellowship from Hatfield College, University of Durham. I became a vice president of Barnardo's in 1989, and Honorary Fellow of the Royal College of Art in 1990. These were eventually complemented by an Honorary Doctorate of Civil Law from the University of Northumbria. In 2000 I was invited to be a governor of the London Institute and later a trustee of the Royal Academy and the following year I was presented with the Freedom of the City of London. Perhaps these were inevitable follow-ons from my having received an OBE when I was forty. I'd also done all those established pieces of PR too, having appeared on *Desert Island Discs,* various chat shows and been covered in generic press pieces like *A Day in the Life* or *How We Met.* I had even contributed a regular column on current London style and fashion to the German paper *Welt Am Sonntag* and written pieces for *The Sunday Times,* the *Spectator* and *Harpers and Queen.* I guess all those things and the fact I'd been trying my hand at new initiatives made me more of a rounded person than just a fashion designer and perhaps kept me cocooned from the vagaries and bitchiness of fashion as well as from bad press.

It was partly that same desire to learn more that persuaded

me to go on the Board of Governors of the London Institute. The Institute then included five art colleges under its umbrella: Central St Martin's, Camberwell, Chelsea, the London College of Fashion and the London College of Printing. Of course it was flattering to be asked but I also thought it would be interesting and that I might actually be able to do something. I was told that I was the first governor who had expressed any specific interest in student welfare and was certainly the only one who asked for a tour of the accommodation offered to the 25,000 students on courses at the time – there were only about 300 rooms available! As it turned out, I had little or no effect on anything. I was there to be a name on the letterhead, someone who was expected to read copious pages of minutes and attend numerous meetings where basically the documents were rubber-stamped by the governors. The real decisions were made by other committees, sitting separately. There's nothing unusual or sinister in that but it wasn't a culture with which I'd had any previous dealings and as I'm not a committee person I couldn't engage with my role there at all.

I was appointed a Trustee of the Royal Academy in 2000. Pleased as I was, the task was as onerous as my earlier role had been with the London Institute. The idea was for me to provide a different perspective to the board of trustees who on the whole were made up of older successful men and women largely from the world of business and politics. Though hardly in the first flush of youth, I was there to redress the balance slightly and to bring my address book to the table for fund-raising activities.

Among the highlights of being with the RA was a night at Highgrove when the Prince of Wales pointedly left a group of people and came over after dinner to thank me for coming. It was my first visit there, ferried down in a fleet of black stretch limos, carrying the great and the good, the overseas and UK trustees of the RA, for a pat on the back. Despite its grandeur, it was explained to me by a disaffected nob some weeks later that the Orangery had been built to house those functions that HRH didn't want to hold inside the mansion itself. The other memorable event was the annual dinner at Burlington Gardens (to which I have not subsequently been invited since my resignation as trustee) where I had the delightful Bjork on my right and the impenetrable Vivienne Westwood opposite. I finally felt that I'd found the 'street cred' that Katherine Hamnett had urged me to find a decade earlier during one of Mrs Thatcher's parties at Downing Street. The low point of the evening occurred when I approached a very grumpy Germaine Greer whom I had met on several occasions with Sonny Mehta, who had published my earlier book, *Season.* After receiving an initial very quizzical look, I reminded her who I was to which she sneered, 'I know exactly who you are.' Well, that put me in my place, didn't it? Not.

My position as far as fundraising for the RA was made particularly difficult as I had already embarked on a series of fundraisers for Barnardo's, firstly by putting on a £500-a-head gala at Mansion House (2000) under the patronage of the ingoing Lord Mayor, councillor Clive Martin. He had ear-marked Barnardo's as the beneficiary of his fundraising efforts in 2000. I was on his charity committee as a vice president along with Cherie Booth, the president, and others. I remember she gave a drinks party at Number 10 one evening where we all bonded. I was also helping fellow vice president Susan Bernerd with her Barnardo's Ball at the Grosvenor House Antiques Fair that year. I had also successfully negotiated with the fair's organisers that we could repeat the event the following year, again for Barnardo's when I would be chair. So I had already savaged my address book on their behalf, leaving little room for me to do anything else in fundraising circles. They wanted to have one big charity event that would crown the proceedings. We decided to put it on at Mansion House.

I wanted to instil a bit of style into the proceedings, just as we had into the 1985 Gala. The Mansion House isn't as large as Grosvenor House so we planned a high-ticket-price event that involved a fashion show with live band followed by dinner and an auction. As it was taking place mid-week and in the City, we'd forgo the dancing and allow people to get home at a reasonable hour. I assembled a small committee that included various prominent business men and social figures like Lords Astor and Bell, Arki Busson and Bernie Ecclestone. My old friend Sarah Reed was at this time working for a graphic design company, 4i, who agreed to help create a beautiful brochure that wouldn't cost any more than the usual dreary charity catalogues but would be stylish and likely to have more of an impact on the auction sales. We sourced some great items including a holiday to Machu Pichu and a William Pye water sculpture. The evening was a great success despite the some-what disappointing auction result, owing to the no-show of a couple of committee members. No names, no pack drill. Dear Joanna Lumley got up at one point, interrupting Henry Wyndham, the auctioneer, and suggested that rather than take home the commemoration bone china boxes donated by Wedgwood, that every one should buy them. Another £3,500 was raised simply by that inspirational intervention.

My brush with cancer was a wake-up call. Even when caught early by my doctor, Desmond Biddulph, and dealt with successfully, it's a frightening thing. It did give me the feeling that I wasn't necessarily going to be here for ever. As far as I was concerned, I didn't have a choice when it came to methods of treatment. I wanted to get rid of it completely through surgery that would also obviate the need for any radio- or chemotherapy. I had no doubts. Instead I had one of the best weeks of my life as

I lay in the Wellington pumped full of morphine. Lovely. At the end of it, Sam picked me up to drive me to Fi and Guy Sangster's where I was going to recuperate. It was pretty painful invasive surgery and I was still sporting a catheter, so I was far from thrilled when Sam announced near Reading that he was going to have to pull in. We reached the turning to the service station where the car sputtered on to the grass verge and stopped dead. For some reason, we couldn't get a replacement car so had to wait until George raced down the M4 to rescue me. I spent two weeks at Fresden Manor. It was a very idyllic time despite my having the wretched catheter. Fi practically had a heart attack when she caught me playing cricket with Mylo, their son, my godson. But there was no lasting damage. I fell in love with their Labrador puppy, Mole, and that's what set me off on the road to acquiring a dog of my own. Also, although I'd been keen on the idea of country life before, this fortnight really did focus my attention. I fell completely in love with the whole package.

Having set my heart on owning a dog, I spent hours poring over books of dog breeds. I wanted a sleek dog and I wanted a big dog but not unmanageably big. In the end it was the sleekness, the sensibleness and the doggy-dogginess of the Rhodesian Ridgeback that got me. The Kennel Club put me in touch with a couple of breeders, one of whom was in Suffolk. So Carol Graves-Johnson, who'd been making belts for me for about twenty-five years, invited me to stay with her in Aldeburgh. She's a very doggy person and volunteered to check out the puppies with me. It was perfect. One Saturday morning we went to find this farm where they bred Rhodesian Ridgebacks and Borzois. First of all we were shown the sire of the litter – who was as big as a Shetland pony. Carol almost had to restrain me from getting up and leaving there and then. Then the aunt was brought in as an example of the potential size of one of the bitch puppies – not so bad after all. Then the two bitches that were left from the litter were brought in. One of them was all over the place, lying on her back, peeing in the air and quite a handful. The other was much calmer altogether and she was my choice. It didn't matter a scrap to me that she was unshowable because of a barely noticeable indent in her ridge. So we took her away there and then, with her on my knee all the way back to Aldeburgh. That night, Carol, her husband Oscar, their daughters and I tried to work out what to call the puppy.

'I'm going to call her Babe,' I decided, in the end.

'You can't,' they chorused.

'Why not?'

'You can't call her Babe. It's a pig's name.'

'No. It's the Babe referred to in the Lou Reed song, *Take a Walk on the Wild Side*. It's that Babe, not a pig,' I explained.

So Babe it was. I went to bed in a room shrouded with newspaper. Babe was not house-trained yet. But she was gorgeous. When I got her home, I remembered that I'd been told that pups sometimes settled to the sound of a ticking clock, a reminder of their mother's heartbeat. The Cartier clock Noemi had given me for Christmas one year went straight into the basket. Silver spoon, or what? I haven't felt for anybody what I've felt for Babe. I was hopeless at leaving her, right from the beginning, so I have made a bit of a rod for my own back. But I don't mind. She goes almost everywhere I go and has done since the start.

Having Babe galvanised me into trying to find a country place. I was looking anywhere in the M4/M40 corridor. My old tutor, Su Suter, lives near Banbury and I liked that area very much but didn't spot anything immediately. One day I went to visit Nigel and Teresa Lawson who lived a little further north in Northamptonshire. I'd told them I was looking and they had invited me for lunch before meeting up with their estate agent,

Jane Rusham, who knew the area very well. I knew roughly what I wanted – something beautiful but not too big and not too many rooms. I'd recognise it when I saw it. Although both the Bamfords and William and Annabel Astor had suggested cottages on their estates, I knew that wasn't what I wanted. I didn't want to be part of someone else's dream. I wanted my own. After looking unsuccessfully at several places that Nigel had heard were up for grabs, a short time later I was pleased to hear that Jane had found a place she thought I might be interested in.

'It's in Wantage, quite ugly but otherwise the property is fabulous and it's a great deal.'

I didn't want anywhere ugly but decided to take a look. It was a beautiful square building that had been a mill but was spoilt by the previous owner's additions and various extensions. There was a rickety bridge leading from the road to the front door – very Disney – while inside it was all brown tongue and groove, with floors at funny levels that didn't go anywhere. In the basement there were four or five rooms that had been rented as short lets. The new owners were unsure when exactly they would want the property for themselves so we came to an agreement whereby I would redesign the interior bearing them in mind. They would pay for the works and I would put in my furniture and paintings. I went for light, airy and contemporary in a very traditional setting. Outside at the back I added a large wooden deck overlooking the millpond and the acres of land and fields beyond.

Babe and I loved that house. The only downside was the fact that we rarely had any good weather. There were a few summer days when you could sunbathe on the deck but . . . It was very private except for the nuns. They were from St Mary's Convent and had been given license by the previous owners to wander through the property whenever they liked. I had to put a stop to that. Friends would come to visit at weekends and it gave me a chance to entertain them in a way I'd never been able to before. When it came to my fiftieth birthday, apart from having a party at San Lorenzo, which I took over entirely for the evening. I also held a big lunch in the garden of the mill with all the relatives. Aunt Enid and David stayed with me. Linda and her family came, as well as Barry with his family from America.

The following year I threw another big garden party for my fifty-first. The weather was fantastic so the photographs show us all lounging round the garden, laughing and drinking. It was the last time I saw Anita. We had buried our differences long since and would see each other from time to time, though our friendship never quite regained its original intimacy. She had been diagnosed with breast cancer a few years earlier, had been in remission but was now very ill indeed. I insisted that she came and we sat together over lunch. I think she knew she was not much longer for this world. At her funeral, Annette Worsley Taylor gave an affectionate memorial speech in which she read a letter from Vicki Hamilton-Rivers with whom Anita had worked for a couple of years at Thomas Starczewski. She summed up Anita for me:

> As we all know working in the fashion industry does present its daily challenge but there was never a day when I went to work, when the prospect of seeing Anita did not fill me full of optimism . . . It was always a constant battle to get designers to be commercially creative and retailers to keep their appointments and pay their bills! Season after season though, she would get back in the ring and box cleverly. She adored fashion and the fashion industry adored and respected her . . . She showed unflagging humour, courage and determination to the

end. 'It could be worse,' she said to me when we first spoke long distance after the cancer had taken hold. 'I would have hated to have been knocked down by the number 14 bus! This way I get to plan and make preparations I want, so that those I love are equipped to carry on without me.'

Having the mill also gave me the excuse for going round all the sale rooms. At the time, I was playing the man of leisure, thinking that the business could run itself while I was out of town. It didn't take long to realise that I was wrong. Most often I would leave London on Friday morning and be back in the shop at 9 a.m. on Monday, getting up at 5 a.m. to do so. I also used the mill as a quiet place where I could work on my other projects. But a successful couturier is a couturier who sees his clients and I wasn't doing enough of that, so I gave up the mill at the end of 2002.

One of the things I wanted to use my country house for was as a showcase for my growing interest in interiors. I have always taken great care with the places in which I've lived. My environment matters a lot to me. It wasn't that I wanted to stop designing clothes, far from it, but I wanted time to indulge some of my other interests, like designing glassware and furniture. Things began to come my way in the interiors field and I was appointed consultant on the interior of several show homes in the St James Homes development at Kew Riverside. More recently I've been responsible for the interiors in the refurbishment of Carlton Terrace in Newcastle. I find interior designing a very pleasant adjunct to the fashion business and plan to expand my involvement with it over the next years.

The mill provided me with a useful breathing space. After years of being almost exclusively focused on the business and its spin-offs, I think I needed time to recharge my batteries before returning to the fray. I've become a patron of Crimestoppers (a charity founded by Lord Ashcroft to help prevent and solve crimes by setting up systems where the man in the street can give information anonymously on crime and criminal activities), and have hosted two fabulous parties for them at Spencer House. Charlotte Thomas at Aurelia Public Relations handled my PR for a few years in order to raise my profile and through them I was invited to become an ambassador for Krug champagne. I've hosted a number of tremendously lavish parties for them too – again it's good for the image, the press attention and the product. I still do as much fundraising as I can for Barnardo's. I have a lot to thank them for but I also believe in the work that they are doing for young people today. The problem they have is that the issues they tackle are very difficult to communicate to the general public in a way that will generate a positive response. Since having Babe I've also become a patron of Dogs Trust, previously the National Canine Defence League. But of course, most importantly, business goes on as ever.

To have survived for thirty years is unusual for a small British fashion company but, somewhat to my amazement, I'm still here in the fashion business and gearing up for another push forward. A couple of years ago, Vanessa Delisle introduced me to Valerie Wickes, a luxury brand consultant who has been extremely supportive and inventive in helping me evaluate the heritage of the business I've built up and deciding how to rationalise and to develop it. We've worked together to establish and promote an image of what Bruce Oldfield is about: the mix of glamour and luxury that smacks of exclusivity, intimacy and high society. We also launched a website in 2004.

I still get enormous satisfaction from knowing that a client looks great, has enjoyed the process and will feel relaxed, looking great at her 'do'. I also love it when women come in and say, 'I wore that dress you made me ten years ago and I got so many compliments.' It's a bit of a Catch 22 because although the clothes should be timeless and should last, I do want the clients to buy regularly! I also get a huge buzz when people come in off the street, find something they like and can afford and simply take it away or have a little alteration. I'm currently working on seven big weddings, including the wedding of 2004, of Lady Tamara Grosvenor, daughter of the Duke and Duchess of Westminster. The Duchess is a long-time client who introduced her daughter three years ago when we made her twenty-first birthday dress for a spectacular Russian-themed ball at Eaton Hall. HRH Princess Basma, sister of the late King Hussein of Jordan has just asked me to do the wedding dress for her daughter, Farah. The wedding will take place in Amman at the end of September 2004 and Farah will be the latest in a long line of commissions from the Royal Family of Jordan. This is the kind of continuity I value. Annabel Goldsmith introduced her daughter, Jemima. Annabel Astor introduced hers, Samantha and Emily Sheffield. Pru Horsell brought her daughter Samantha along for her twenty-first birthday dress. I may be ageing with my clientele but new blood is coming along all the time.

I'm an old optimist and see exciting possibilities emerging out of the backlash against the globalisation of fashion. If you walk down Madison Avenue, the Faubourg St Honoré or Sloane Street today, you will see the same designers with the same boutique design, the same accessories and merchandise. A lot of people are put off by the fact that what they buy that is labelled exclusive is in fact not exclusive at all. As a result, many women are now looking for something that little bit different. Exclusive, interesting and with word-of-mouth reputation. That's what I think the Bruce Oldfield label should be. I love the fact that we are able to make very beautiful clothes. The way things are finished and the care that goes into making every single garment is extremely important to me. I'm lucky not to have someone constantly looking over my shoulder, but, choosing to remain small, has meant life has been far from plain sailing.

When I look at the fashion business in Britain today, I see that nothing very much has changed. We are still the poor relation of Europe and bright young designers find the way forward is to leave the country and show their collections abroad. I have always thought of my business as a dear little English company. I have never been impressed by rapid change. I prefer the considered evolution and development of an idea to rash decisions. I found responding to the urgency of the media in the seventies and eighties and their eagerness to find and extol something new and radical was hard. Trying to force new ideas could be like forcing granite through a tea strainer. It was the antithesis to everything that I feel.

My belief is that tradition is there to be developed and expanded. It's part of our heritage and provides the boundaries within which we can create our own personal view. I have retained the idea that what I wanted to be was an English designer and I wanted to stay in England. I would rather be here than anywhere else and I like the clothes being made here. I don't do runway shows or show in London Fashion Week, preferring to stage private shows in London and 'trunk shows' to a tighter roster of private international clients in the US and Middle East. I still have no desire to produce clothes in volume. I've never wanted to work for anyone else. I've never managed to take my clothes to a wider public, having either gone too far, as in the case of the various licences where the meaning of what I do (well-made simple design) got lost in the commerciality of it all or never found the partner who could totally relieve me of the business worries and enable me to get on with the designing which is what I love to do. Of course, being so fiercely protective and independent could be a result of my fear of never wanting to lose control to anyone else and indeed why I'm still in business, self-financed and still forging forward. My aim is, as it has always been, to marry good design with commercial success. I don't relish the idea of going backwards, of ending up in a two-up two-down in a rural backwater, simply because I trusted the wrong person. It's better I shoulder the responsibility myself.

I may have adopted a lower profile but I like my privacy. I'm very happy in the company of Babe and can think of nothing I'd prefer after a day's work than settling down with my feet up and a DVD. I've usually spent so much time during the day being a salesman ten times over that by the evening I don't want to see anyone. As I write this, the pendulum is swinging back again and I'm re-introducing ready-to-wear into the shop alongside the couture. Business is good and I'm feeling optimistic about the future.

I once heard a radio interview with Joan Armatrading in the eighties in which she was asked if she was surprised by her rapid rise to stardom. Didn't she pinch herself every morning? She replied, 'No. It wasn't a big leap. It was just a series of levels. You achieve one and then move on to the next.' I identify with that, exactly.

INDEX

Abdullah, Prince, of Jordan,
    now HM King Abdullah of
    Jordan 309, 310
Aberdare, Lady 219–20
Absolutely Fabulous (TV
    programme) 307
AIDS 229, 321–3
AIDS Crisis Trust 320
Akasaka Prince Hotel, Tokyo
    266
Al-Yassin, Rania *see* Rania,
    Queen of Jordan
Alatas, Munirah 214
Albini, Walter 179
Alexander, Roger 252
Alexander Sinclair, Georgina
    'George'
  in America 265–6
  in Australia 275, 277, 278
  and Bruce's OBE party 290
  and DBH Gala Fashion
    Show 237, 238, 239, 240
  enduring friendship with
    Bruce 270
  in Singapore 264
  work for Bruce 212, 259,
    293, 305, 306, 334

Alexandra plc 313
Algonquin Hotel, New York
    143
Alia, HRH Princess, of Jordan
    262–3
Allen, Cameron 276, 278
Allen, Murray 251, 283–4,
    298
Allison, Edith 67, 76
Anderson, Alison 101, 108,
    187
Annabel's, London xii, 284
Annacat 177
Anne, Princess, the Princess
    Royal 283
Antonio (fashion illustrator)
    162–3, 191
Arias, Carlos 156, 159, 172
Armani, Giorgio 231, 249,
    253, 263, 297, 303
Armatrading, Joan 342
Ashcroft, Lord 339
Ashford and Simpson 201
Astaire, Fred ix, 125, 190–1
Astor, Lady Annabel 180,
    207, 215, 315, 336, 340
Astor, Lord William 333, 336

Atkinson, Mr (Bruce's
    headmaster) 49, 50, 67–8
Aurelia PR 339
Australia 253–6, 312–13
Australian Bicentennial Wool
    Collection Show 274–9
Aysha, Princess of Jordan 311
Azagury, Jacques 174, 270
Aznavour, Charles 166

Babe (Bruce's dog) 334–5,
    342
Bacall, Lauren 191, 318
Bach, Barbara 226
Bailey, David 191–2, 290
Bamford, Sir Anthony 287
Bamford, Lady Carol 287
Bamford, Alice 306
Banks, Jeff 223
Barbados 285–7
Barnardo's see Dr Barnardo's
    Homes
Barnes, Colin
    dies 322–3
    friendship with Bruce
        128–9, 160, 184, 185
    homes 128–9, 185
    illustration work for Bruce
        297, 300
    at Ravensbourne 119–20,
        123
Barrett, Slim 237
Barrie, Scott
    at Bruce's 40th birthday
        party 288
    dies 321

Mykonos holiday 205
    in New York 146–50, 151,
        152, 198, 201–2
    in Paris 162
Barry (Bruce's foster brother)
    in America 271, 318
    and birth family 323
    at Bruce's birthday parties
        270, 288, 337
    childhood and adolescence
        16, 21, 25–6, 29, 31, 32,
        34, 35, 38, 39, 63
    in Leeds 94–5
    in London 110, 117, 129,
        184
    and Monica Scott 87
    and music 63, 101
    Paris visit 163–4
    relationship with Bruce
        101
    in Sheffield 99, 100, 102,
        104
    T-shirt business with Bruce
        105–6
    and Violet's death 158
Bassey, Shirley xi, 236, 237,
    242
Bates, John 125, 155, 192
Bazaar 106
Beene, Geoffrey 141
Bell, Tim, Lord 296, 333
Beltrao, Anna 172, 173
Bennett, Jill 185
Bequia 302
Berkeley, Busby ix
Bernerd, Susan 332

Beverly Hills Hotel, Los
    Angeles 252
Biba 106, 123, 155
Biddulph, Desmond 333
Binding, Paul 66–7
Birger Christensen 250
Birthright Ball 256–7
Bishop, Bernadette 221
Bishop, John 221
Bisset, Jacqueline 207, 226
The Bitch (film) 224, 252
Bjork 332
Blahnik, Manolo 133, 137,
    188
Blair, Billy 153
Blair, Cherie (née Booth)
    306, 332
Blair, Edith
    Bruce keeps in touch with
        323
    on Bruce's feelings about
        his colour 93
    helps Bruce get college
        funding 109–10
    helps Bruce in West Mount
        period 48, 49, 69, 71,
        72–4, 76, 77
    letter to Bruce when he
        starts college 97
    letters to Bruce at college
        113–14, 115
    tells Bruce about
        background 95–6
Blake, Peter 189
Blass, Bill 141
Bodymap 253

Boglioni, Gael 222
Boisset, Yves 190
Bond, Alan 253, 255, 279,
    318
Bond, Eileen 'Red' 241,
    253–4, 255, 279
Bond, Susanne 253–4, 255–6,
    279
Booth, Cherie *see* Blair, Cherie
Borchgrave, Dominique de
    213, 219–20
Bosanquet, Felicity 270
Bough, Frank 238
Bowers, Mrs (DBH) 45, 48,
    49, 62
Bowles, Hamish 318
Bradley, David 125
Bravo, Rose Marie 267
Brittain, Judy 125–6
Brown, Tina 318
Browns fashion store 157, 186
Buck, Ann 172, 173
Buck, Joan Juliet 139
Buckingham Palace 282–3
Burberry 267
Burroughs, Stephen 141, 149
Burstein, Joan 156–7
Burt, Linda 63, 70
Bus Stop 106
Busson, Arki 333
Butcher, Lisa 308–9

Café Flore, Paris 163
Caine, Sir Michael 282
Callas, Maria 202, 205
Campbell, Sarah 132

Cappucine 166
Le Caprice 328
Cardin, Pierre 249
Carlton Terrace, Newcastle 338
Carr, Alan 317
Carroll, Kevin 175, 185, 264, 270
Cartmel, Adrian 186, 188
Cartridge, Miss (DBH) 74, 75
Castro's bar, Mykonos 206
Cattlin, Jane 172
Cavendish, Lord and Lady 301
CEC see Clothing Export Council
Cerruti 258
Chambers, Mr 'Chippy' (teacher) 67
Champion, David 303
Chanel, Coco 247, 301
Charisse, Cyd 191
Charles, HRH Prince of Wales 260–1, 277, 279, 281–3, 300, 331–2
Charles, Caroline 173, 239, 319
Charlie perfume campaign 130–3
Charnos 250–1
Chelsea Cobbler 132
Cheltenham Club, Harrogate 59–60, 92
Chequers 296–7
Chic, Hampstead 177
Chiles, Lois 203–4, 226

Chin, Alva 153, 186, 192
Choses 134, 138
Chow, Bonny 203
Chow, Michael 188–90
Chow, Tina 162, 163, 188–9, 190, 192, 207, 322
Chow's, London 186, 188–9
Chubb, Ann 246, 273
Cinzano, Countess Noemi 301–3, 306, 315, 317, 322
Clapperton, Mandy 179
Claridge, John 300
Claridge's 290–1, 305
Clark, Felicity 179
Clark, Ossie 105, 106, 125, 137
Cleveland, Pat 153, 162, 191, 277
Clothing Export Council (CEC) 170, 171, 172, 173, 192
Club 21, Singapore 263
Club Arethusa, London 137
Club Sept, Paris 162, 192
Cockerham, Babs 59
Coddington, Grace 133, 172, 179, 207
Cole, Michael 246
Collier, Susan 132
Collins, Hazel (model) 237, 241
Collins, Jackie 225
Collins, Joan xi, 207, 224–5, 236, 237, 238, 252
Collins, Phil 282
Comédie Française, Paris 89

Compact (TV soap) 26
Così Fan Tutte 205, 303
Cosserat, Kay 173
Cossy, Miss (DBH) 50
Coty Awards, 1973 150
Council of Fashion Designers
    of America awards 299
Country Homes and Interiors
    301
La Coupole, Paris 163
Courtauld's 305
Craig, Miss (teacher) 65
Craig Martin, Jessica 298
Craven, Miss (DBH) 68–9, 74
Creighton, George (Bruce's
    foster brother) 7, 25, 26,
    31, 34–40, 78, 323
Creole, Kid xii, 236, 237,
    238, 240
Creveling, Joanne 198–9
Crimdon Dene 35–6
Crimestoppers 339
Crolla, Scott 248, 253
Crosby-Stills-Nash and Young
    103
Crowley, Pat 177
Crown Casino, Melbourne
    313
Crowthers 106

Dagworthy, Wendy 172
D'Allesandro, Joe 103
Dark Blues 282
Davies, Tony 130
DBH *see* Dr Barnardo's Homes
Dead Sea 272–3

Delisle, Vanessa 270, 315,
    339
Dellal, Lorraine 221–2
Dellal, Suzy 221
Dellal, Zehave 224
Desert Island Discs (radio show)
    268
The Design and Decoration
    Building 316
Desmond, Dermot 287
Dewhirst 284–5
Dewhirst, Pru (née Horsell)
    284, 340
Diagonal, Guildford 177
Diamond, Anne 278
Diana, Princess of Wales
    Australian bicentennial tour
        277, 279
    at Birthright Ball 257
    and Bruce xi–xii, 222, 226,
        227–8, 233, 251, 259–62,
        293–4
    bulimia 227
    clothes auction 320
    death and funeral 319–20
    fundraising for DBH xi–xii,
        235–6, 239–40, 241–2,
        244, 281–2
    Italy trip 248
    marriage 241–2, 281–2
    personality 228, 259–60
    and Pirelli calendars 300
    at Prince Charles's 40th
        birthday party 282
    wedding dress 255
Dickinson, Howard 258

Dickinson, Sandra 59
Dior, Christian 155, 164, 171
Dixon, Tom 316
Dogs Trust 339
Donovan, Terry 285
Dr Barnardo's Homes (DBH)
  BBC programme about 323
  and Bruce: care at college
    101–2, 109–11, 113,
    126–7, 133
  and Bruce: care before
    fostering 5–8
  and Bruce: care in foster
    home 14–16, 27, 32,
    36–7, 41, 43–4
  and Bruce: care in lodgings
    80–97
  and Bruce: care in West
    Mount xiii–xiv, xv, 45–79
  and Bruce: fundraising
    xi–xii, 234–45, 281–2,
    332, 339
  and Bruce: lets him read file
    247–8
  and Bruce: makes him vice
    president 330
  and Bruce: puts in touch
    with family 323–5
  holiday camps 35
  and Janet 159
  relaunch 281
  supermarket donations to
    53
  West Mount Branch Home,
    Ripon xiii–xiv, 46–7
The Dress (film) 233

Dunaway, Faye 226
Dunn, Juliet 172

Earth, Wind and Fire 186
Eau Libre fragrance campaign
  151
Ecclestone, Bernie 333
Edelstein, Victor 213, 320
Elaine's, New York 147
Elizabeth II, HM Queen 191,
  282, 283, 290
Emanuel, David 253
Emanuel, Elizabeth 253
The Embassy, London 186
Emerson, Ted 181
Etherington Smith, Meredith
  297
Eula, Joe 150
European Union awareness
  campaign, 1992 285
Evans, Sir Harold 318
Evans, Linda 224, 225
Everage, Dame Edna xi, xii,
  236–7, 242–3
Everest, Timothy 303
Everett, Rupert 221
Evins, Reed 200
Exton, Gae 222

Fairclough, Col. (Salvation
  Army) 324
Fairfax, Lady 277
Fairley, Professor 184
Fairport Convention 101
fashion design techniques
  house blocks 122

knitted textiles 117–18
pattern making 120–2
smocking technique 130–1
fashion illustration 119–20
fashion industry
adverts 271
America 141–2, 199, 204
England 155, 170–5,
192–3, 230, 341
financing your own
company 180
franchising 263
globalisation ix–x
Japan 266–7
licensing deals 249–50
manufacturing designs
181–2
Paris 164
selling couture 212–15
fashion shows, secrets of
137–8, 197–8
Fashion Aid 253
Fay, Michael 120
Fayed, Dodi 320
Feisal, Prince, of Jordan
262–3, 309
Ferguson, Sarah 318–19
Ferry, Bryan 195–6
Field, Shirley Anne 226
Fitzgibbon, Ruth 219
Flack, Roberta 202
Flesh (film) 103
Flynt, Larry 'Hustler' 225
Ford, Oliver 218
Forrest, Robert 186
Forte, Irene 220

Forte, Lady 235
Forte, Lord 242
Forte, Sir Rocco 220, 241,
292–3
Foster, Brendan 251
Foster, Dolly 115, 124
Frances, Miss (DBH) 58
Franklin, Aretha 186, 268
Franklin, Caryn 278
Fraser, Sir Hugh 184
Fratini, Gina 125
Frazer, Keith 258
Frean, Jenny 133–4
Free 221
French, Dawn 282
Frost, Lady Carina 132
Frostrup, Mariella 328

Gairdner, Johnny 168, 237
Gaye, Marvin 131, 132, 221,
268
Getty, Lady Victoria 306
GFT 297
Gibb, Bill 125, 126, 149, 155,
192, 209
Gilbey, Ann 87
Gilbey, Constance 64–5, 76,
87, 89, 97, 99, 323
Gillian (Bruce's cousin)
326
Gilmour, Dave 222
Giovetti, Shirley 130, 192,
299
Glynn, Prudence 134
Gold, Johnny 187, 221
Gold, Suzy 176–7, 181

Goldsmith, Lady Annabel
214, 308, 340
Goldsmith, Harvey 236, 253
Goldsmith, Jemima *see* Khan,
Jemima
Graham, Penny 131, 174
Granby Hotel, Harrogate 85
Granny Takes a Trip 106
Graves-Johnson, Carol 334–5
Graves-Johnson, Oscar 335
The Great Gatsby (film) 150
Greenwich Village, New York
147–8
Greer, Germaine 332
Griffiths, Melanie 212
Grosvenor, Lady Tamara 340
Grosvenor House Hotel 235
Guild, Robin 316
Guinness, Sabrina 222
Gutteridge, Paul 104

Hagman, Larry 225
Hall, Jerry 162–3, 195–6,
207, 253, 282, 290, 308
Hall, Lyn 315
Hall, Mr (DBH) 126, 127
Halston 141, 142, 150, 200,
202
Hamaguchi, Myko 303–4,
306
Hambro, Lady Cherry 219
Hamilton-Rivers, Vicki 337–8
Hammer Horror films 103
Hamnett, Katherine 253,
265, 332
Hanley, Robin 317

Harari, Diana (Mrs Philip)
218–19
Harpers Bazaar 317
Harrogate General Hospital
95
Hartnell, Norman 119,
246–7, 267
Harty, Russell 268
Harvey, Anna 222
Havens, Richie 101, 103
Hawke, Bob 256
Hayworth, Rita 136
Hechter, Daniel 179
Heiney, Paul 233
Hello! 306, 308–9
Helvin, Marie
and Bailey 191–2, 290
and Bruce 207, 224, 290,
306, 308, 314
and Dodi Fayed 320
modelling 151, 162, 195,
282, 290
social life 163, 308, 314
Henri Bendel, New York x,
139–45, 152–6, 291
Herbert, Michelle 299
Herbert, Victor 116–17, 123,
125, 130, 131, 133–4,
178–9, 195
Hett 11–12
Hicks, Sophie 219
Highgrove 331–2
Hilditch and Key 251, 283,
284
Hill Samuel bank 181
Hill Vellacott 176

Hilson, Bobby 129
Hobbs, Lyndall 222
Hobbs, Romilly *see* McAlpine,
    Lady Romilly
Hobday, Dave 114
Hockney, David 264–5
Holker Hall, Cumbria 301
Hong Kong 217
Hopkins, Gerard Manley xiv,
    67, 301
Hornois, Jacques de 164
Horsell, Pru *see* Dewhirst, Pru
Horsell, Samantha 340
Hossak, Rick 60
Howard, Michael 306
Howard, Sandra 306
Howells, Michael 256–7, 305
Howells, Sue 326
Howstan, Miss (teacher) 65
Humphries, Barry *see* Everage,
    Dame Edna
Hurd, Miss (teacher) 65–6
Hurt, Nick 288–9
Hussein, HM King, of Jordan
    311
Huston, Angelica 133, 189
Hutchins, Roger 131, 174

Illsley, John 276
Imperator, Arthur 203
In at the Deep End (TV
    programme) 233
International Design
    Conference, Aspen,
    Colorado 264–5
Interview magazine 160

IRA 184
Iredale, Jennifer (Bruce's
    cousin) 325, 328
Iredale Stuart 325
Irwin, Miss (DBH) 50–1,
    53–4, 56–7, 68–9, 69–70,
    74
Ishiguro, Kazuo 269
Iveagh family 216

Jackpot (film) 160, 165–7
Jagger, Bianca 136–7, 165,
    185, 187, 202, 207, 220,
    226, 308
Jagger, Sir Mick 290, 308
James, Charles 200
Janet (Bruce's foster sister)
    17, 43, 66, 159, 182–3
Japan 266–7
Le Jardin, New York 145
Jarre, Jean Michel 191
Jaya, Edmund Surya 203
Jenners 177
Jill (Oldfield production
    manager) 259
Jiricna, Eva 265
João (friend) 127
John, Sir Elton 314, 319
Johnson, Betsy 145
Jones, Annabel *see* Astor, Lady
    Annabel
Jones, Grace 162–3, 186
Jones, Tim 69
Jordan (country) 272–3,
    309–11
Joseph 253

Jourdan, Charles 237
Juarez, Bianca 220–1

Kamali, Norma 145
Kanawabo, Rei 266
Karan, Donna 258, 274, 277
Katherine, Princess of
    Yugoslavia 241
Keating, Billy 276
Kensington Market 106
Kensington Palace 260
Kent, Roger 69
Kent, Rosemary 160
Kenzo 122, 162, 274
Khalifa, Ahmes 214
Khan, Imran 308
Khan, Jemima (née
    Goldsmith) 306, 308,
    340
Khomo, Ninivah 174, 186,
    188, 228, 270
Kid Creole and the Coconuts
    xii, 236, 237, 238, 240
Kiehls, New York 148
King, Larry 212
Kirk, Neil 271
Kirke, Simon 221
Kissin, Lesley (client) 317
Kjeldsen, Mr (DBH) 74–6,
    91–2
Klein, Calvin 202, 249, 253
Knight, Mr (Nike CEO) 252
Knowland, Viv 237
Koltai, Chrissie 276
Kotler, Maurice 164
Krug 339

LA County Museum of Arts
    Costume Council 225–6
Labelle, Patti 168
Lagerfeld, Karl 162, 189,
    230, 301
Lally, Betty Eileen see Oldfield,
    Betty Eileen
Lally, Christine (Bruce's aunt)
    324, 326, 327
Lally, Enid (Bruce's aunt)
    324, 327, 329, 337
Lally, Joan (Bruce's aunt)
    324, 327, 329
Lamb, Tim 297
Lambert, Alistair 13, 17
Lambert, Christine 17, 23,
    29, 30, 31, 35–6
Lambert, Marie 11–12,
    17–18, 23, 35–6, 61, 158
Lambert, William 12, 17,
    29
LaMonte, Carla 204–5
Langan's, London 186
Lange, Jessica 163
Lanvin 171
Lanzarote 268
Lartigue, Jacques-Henri 191
Lauren, Ralph 150, 198
Lawrence, Lynne 240
Lawson, Lord and Lady
    335–6
LDC see London Designer
    Collections
le Bon, Simon 290
le Bon, Yasmin 290
Leser, Bernie 277

Lett-Haines, Arthur 269–70
Liberty 125, 134, 138
Linda (Bruce's foster sister)
  childhood 17, 20–1, 29, 30,
    33, 34
  French holiday with Bruce
    289–90
  marries 157
  to Palace with Bruce
    289–90
  socialising with Bruce in
    London 129, 270, 288,
    337
  and Violet's death 158–9
Little, Debbie 258
A Little Black Dress, Leeds
  177
Little Nell 222
Littmann, Marguerite 219
Logan, Phyllis 233
Lomas, Jane 288–9
London
  club scene 137, 186, 187
  fashion scene 155, 170–5,
    192–4
  gay scene 220
  restaurants 186, 188–9
London Collections 175, 192
London Designer Collections
  (LDC) 173–5, 192–4
London Designer Collections
  Association 175
London Institute 331
Los Angeles 203–4, 224–6,
  252
Lumley, Joanna 307, 333

Luther, Mary Lou 203

Magnier, Mrs John 312
Major, John 296–7
Marcella Borghese cosmetics
  192
Margaret, HRH Princess 223
Marion (model)
  dies 321–2
  in London 186
  in Los Angeles 225–6
  in New York 150–2, 153,
    154
  in Paris 161–2, 163
Mark hotel, New York 317
Marks, Anna 164
Marks, Monty 164
Marks & Spencer 273–4
Martin, Sir Clive 332
Massin, Sidney 130
Masters, Violet
  appearance 17–19
  background 9–13
  Bruce's 'home visits' to
    61–3, 70–1, 72, 78, 82–5,
    91, 108–9, 129
  Bruce's presents to 66, 158
  character 19
  dies 158–9
  fosters Bruce xiii, xiv, 7–8,
    14–44, 48
Matthews, Vincent 277
Maunkberry's, London 186
McAlpine, Lord Alistair
  217–18, 254–5, 270,
  292–3

McAlpine, Hamish 220–1
McAlpine, Lady Romilly, (née Hobbs) 217–18, 241, 270
McCannell, Ursula 269
McCardell, Claire 141–2
Mcleod, Lis 94
McDonald, Billy 287
McDowell, Colin 279
McErlain, David 292–3, 306
McErlain, Susan 292
McKinney, Shona 218–19
McPhail, Douglas 57, 74, 75
McPhail Mr (DBH) 47, 48, 51, 53–4, 62, 67–8, 69, 70, 74–5, 76, 77, 94
McPhail, Mrs (DBH) 47, 51, 53–4, 77
McPherson, Elle 275
Medway, Wendy 237
Mehta, Sonny 332
Melbourne Cup 312
Melchett, Lady Sonia 219–20
Menkes, Suzy 248, 279
Mercury, Freddie 253
Minelli, Liza 150, 191, 202
Missoni 179, 274
Mitchell, Joni 101, 221, 225, 268
Mitsui 266–7
Miyake, Issey 253, 266
Modlinger, Jackie 273
The Mojo, Sheffield 92
Monroe, Marilyn 301
Montcalm Hotel, London 174
Montana, Claude 274

Montlake, Ivor 157
Mori, Hanae 266
Morris, Bernardine 153
Morris, Cedric 269
Morrison, Guy 215
Mortimers restaurant, New York 202–3
Morton, Peter 224–5
Morton's restaurant, London 288
Morton's restaurant, Los Angeles 224
Mosimann, Anton 301
Mr Freedom 125, 142
Mucha, Pauline 130
Muir, Jean
    and Australian Bicentennial Wool Collection 274, 278–9
    and Bruce's OBE party 290
    and Fashion Aid 253
    sales in America 145
    shows 192
    status as designer 125, 155
    style of clothes 194
Muna, HRH Princess, of Jordan 310
My Favourite Things (TV programme) 268
Mykonos 205, 206

National Portrait Gallery, London 270
Neiman Marcus 130, 141
Nemoto, Nori 303–4, 306
Nesbitt, Carol 37–9, 51

Nesbitt, Noel 37–9, 51
Neville, Angela 276
Neville, Bernard 125
New Wave fashion shows
    170–3, 192–4
New York
    fashion scene 199
    nightlife 145–8, 150–2,
        201–3
    shopping 140–2, 148
Nicholson, Jack 189, 282
Nike 251–3
No Scruples 221
Noiret, Philippe 166
Nolan, Sidney 255
Nolan, Viv 237
Noor, HM Queen, of Jordan
    309, 310
Norwich City football strip
    313–14
Novak, Kim 225

O'Connell, Mimi 138
Oldfield, Betty Eileen (née
    Lally; Bruce's mother)
    xiii, xiv, 1–9, 248, 324–5,
    326–7, 328
Oldfield, Bruce
    and art 269–70, 317
    and cinema 101
    and cooking and
        entertaining 117, 185,
        228–9, 315
    and family background
        xii–xv, 1–4, 73–4, 95–7,
        248, 323–9

and French culture 64–5,
    87–90
friendships 270
fundraising xi–xii, 234–45,
    281–2, 332–3, 339
and gardening 29
and holidays 206–7
home likes and dislikes
    23–4, 228–9
honours and awards 267,
    288–90, 330–3
icons and influences 105,
    106, 124, 141–2, 191,
    195
and money 27–8, 272
and music 30, 58, 99, 101,
    103, 131, 186, 187, 205
and racism 39–41, 92–3,
    149, 187–8, 222–3
and reading 30, 66–7
relationship with Barry 101
secrets of his success 126,
    128, 132, 157
and sport 32, 52
TV appearances 233–4,
    268
and women 63, 104, 187,
    203–4
working methods and habits
    156, 177–9, 226–7, 315
Oldfield, Bruce: EVENTS
birth 1
postnatal illness 4
in DBH home 5–7
fostered by Violet xiii, xiv,
    7, 9, 14–17, 18–44

early interest in
dressmaking and clothes
20–2, 26
rescues childhood pet 24–5
early creativity 25–7
schooldays in Hett 29–32,
41–2
early stammer 31–2
life in the country 32–3
going to church 33, 58
early Christmases 33–5
early holidays 35–6
early hobbies 36–7, 52–3
foster 'aunts' and 'uncles'
37–9
childhood accidents 39
passes eleven-plus 41
moves back to residential
care 42–4
life at West Mount xiii–xiv,
45–58
homesickness 48–9
schooldays in Ripon 49,
64–8, 76
teenage outings and
holidays 58–63
'home visits' to Violet 61–3,
70–1, 72, 78, 82–5, 91,
108–9, 129
teenage interest in clothes
61–2
teenage behaviour gets him
into trouble 67–71, 74
career plans 71–2, 76, 87
asks about his background
73–4

moves into lodgings 76–86,
95–6
'unreliable' with money
82–6, 90
in sixth form 86–7, 90–1
first trip to Paris 87–90
interest in clothes continues
90–1
teenage social life 92–4
disappointing A levels 95
gets more information on
background 95–7
accepted at Sheffield
Teachers Training
College 97
at college in Sheffield
98–111
becomes Chairman of
Social Committee 102
sets up T-shirt business
105–6
gives up teaching 106–8
accepted at Ravensbourne
College of Art and Design
109–10
at Ravensbourne 112–23
photo shoot at Biba 123
at St Martin's School of Art
124–35
makes costumes for dance
company 127
wins Saga Mink
Competition 129–30
designs for Revlon 130–3
leaves college 133–5
meets Bianca Jagger 136–7

collections for Liberty and
  Choses 138
goes to New York to design
  for Bendel's 139–54
New York social life 146–50
starts relationship with
  Marion 150–2
dropped by Bendel's 153
collections for Tsaritsar
  155–7, 159–60, 169
Violet dies 158–9
moves temporarily to Paris
  160–4
makes costumes for *Jackpot*
  165–7
exhibits at New Wave shows
  170–3
helps set up London
  Designer Collections
  173–5
sets up own business
  175–83
business moves to Walton
  Street 183
at home in Campden Hill
  184–5
London social life 185–90
makes costumes for *Le Taxi
  Mauve* 190–1
visits to France 191–2
business grows 192–8
first solo show 192
breaks with New Wave
  designers 193–4
sales visits to America
  198–205

New York social life 200–2
in Los Angeles 203, 224–6
holidays 205–7
diversifies designs 207–8,
  209–10
moves to couture 209–15
business moves to
  Beauchamp Place 211
moves in high circles
  216–28
meets Princess of Wales
  222
judges fashion design
  competition in South
  Africa 222–3
moves to Redcliffe Gardens
  228–9
opens ready-to-wear shop
  230–3
business anecdotes 231–3
puts on Gala Fashion Show
  for DBH xi–xii, 234–45
discusses joining Hartnell
  246–7
reads DBH file xii–xiii,
  247–8
goes into licensing 249–53
shows at Fashion Aid 253
makes dresses for Bond
  wedding 253–6
attends Birthright Ball
  256–7
moves office and workshop
  to Argon Mews 258–9
work for Princess of Wales
  259–62

shows in Singapore 263–3
invited to International
Design Conference
264–5
tries to get into Japanese
market 266–7
public recognition 267–9
collecting paintings 269–70
advertises in *Vogue* 270–1
moves to Elm Park Gardens
271
as consultant for M&S
273–4
shows at Australian
Bicentennial Woollen
Collection Show 274–80
another gala for DBH
281–2
goes to Prince Charles's
40th birthday party
282–3
more licensing deals 283–5
business problems 284–5
Christmas with the
Sangsters 285–7
40th birthday party 288–9
receives OBE 288–90
show at Claridge's 290–1
takes over sole ownership of
business 291–4
dropped by Princess of
Wales 293–4
reinvents business 295–301
supports Tories in 1992
election 296–7
attempts to get into men's

wear 297–8
shoots own collection for
Sunday Telegraph 298–9
attends Council of Fashion
Designers of America
awards 299
designs clothes for Pirelli
calendar 299–300
new friendships 301–4
female stalker 304
business picks up again
304–12
robbery at shop 305
opens and closes Brook
Street shop 306–8
more society weddings
308–11
works with Delia Smith
313–14
nineties social life 314
ventures into interior
design 315–16, 338
gives up smoking 316–17
goes to New Zealand to
judge fashion competition
317–18
goes to Princess of Wales's
funeral 319–20
loses friends to AIDS
321–3
traces birth family 323–9
brush with cancer 333–4
acquires Babe and moves to
country 334–8
recent and future business
ventures ix–x, 339–42

Oldfield, David (Bruce's half-brother) 2, 96, 324, 328–9, 337
Oldfield, Lawrence (Eileen's husband) 1–2
Oldfield, William (Bruce's half-brother) 2, 4, 96, 327
Ong, BS 263–4, 290, 303
Ong, Christina 263–4, 290, 303
O'Neal, Ryan 136
Oranmore & Browne, Lady Oonagh 166
Orde, Cuthbert 269
Originelle 176
O'Sullivan, 'Lunchtime' 287
O'Sullivan, Margie 287
Outram, Frances 269
Ozbek, Rifat 174, 186, 206, 253, 316

Packer, John 223
Packer, Mrs Kerry 312
Palmer, Adèle 278
Pantone 299
Paragon 148
Paris 87–90, 161–4, 190–1
Parkinson, Mary 318
Parkinson, Michael 278, 318
Parkinson, Norman 166, 281, 300
Pateras, Mrs Chrysanthy 213–14
Pateras, Nini 214
Patrick (Linda's husband) 157, 270
Patrique (friend) 191
Paula Marie (friend) 161
Pavarotti, Luciano 223
Pearls restaurant, New York 147
Pemberton, Miss (head of St Martin's) 124
Perth, Australia 254–5
La Petite Cuisine 315
Philip, HRH Prince, Duke of Edinburgh 282
Picasso, Paloma 162–3
Pierce, Eileen 39
Pierce, Neville 39
Pilkington Products 251
Pinchin, Philippe 327
Pinky and Diana (designers) 199
Pirelli calendars 299–300
Plaza Hotel, New York 142–3, 152–3
Polizzi, Olga 239, 292–3
Pollen, Arabella 305
Ponting, Joan 177
Portanova, Baroness de 220
Porter, Thea 155
Porter, Tony 173
Powers, Stefanie 226
Price, Anne 210
Price, Anthony 253
Puccini, Giacomo 205
Puttnam, Lord David 265
Pye, William 333
Pyrah, Gail 92
Pyrah, Judy 92

Quant, Mary 155

Racine, Jean 64–5, 89
Raines, Christina 200
Rampling, Charlotte xi, 160,
    165–7, 190–2, 207, 236,
    242
Ramsbottom, Sarah 322
Rania, HM Queen of Jordan
    (née Al-Yassin) 309-11
Ranouf, Susan 279, 312
Ravensbourne College of Art
    x, 112–14, 115–20, 123
Rayne 251
Raywood, Craig 200–1
Reed, Bill 185, 321
Reed, Paula 328
Reed, Sarah 122–3, 133, 226,
    333
Reeson, David 168–9, 270
Reeve, Christopher 222, 242
Reid and Taylor 223
Renta, Oscar de la 274
Revlon 130–3
Rhodes, Zandra 110, 125,
    149, 155, 253
Ricci, Nina 171
Richardson, Anita: EVENTS
    goes into business with
        Bruce 175–83, 197, 198
    personality 176, 227
    goes to a party at Bruce's
        185
    New York social life 200–1
    keen on wholesale market
        210–13
    goes to Hong Kong 217
    reluctant to go into ready-
        to-wear 229
    finds PR agent 230
    and DBH Gala Fashion
        Show 236, 237, 240
    and Hartnells 246–7
    seeks out licensing deals
        249, 250, 251, 252
    at Birthright Ball 257
    finds new office and
        workshop 258, 259
    shouts at Princess of Wales
        by accident 260
    goes to Singapore 264
    tries to get into Japanese
        market 266–7
    goes to a Bruce birthday
        party 270
    attempts to curtail Bruce's
        spending 272
    cracks in relationship with
        Bruce 280
    goes to Prince Charles's
        40th birthday party 282
    works with licensors 285
    and Bruce's OBE 288, 290
    leaves business 291–3
    goes to Princess of Wales's
        funeral 319
    contacted by Bruce's birth
        family 329
    dies 337–8
Ridley, Jane 87
Rifai, Alia 273
Ripon 45–6

Ripon Grammar School
    49–50, 64–8
Ritchie, Hon. Teresa 116
Robbins, Bruce 258, 259
Roberts, Michael 137, 187,
    188, 195, 200, 270
Roberts, Tommy 142
Roberts Memorial Home,
    Harrogate 5–6
Robinson, Anne 314
Rogers, Ginger ix, 125
Ronson, Gail 219
Rosen, Michael 236, 239,
    241
Ross, Diana 201–2, 253
Rothschild, Jessica de 306
Rothschild, Lady Victoria de
    207
Royal Academy 330–3
Royal Scotsman (train) 303–4
Rusland Hall, Cumbria 301
Rykiel, Sonia 145, 274

Sagrani, Minal 214
St Jacques, Stirling 162
St James Homes development,
    Kew Riverside 338
St Laurent, Yves 119, 122,
    162, 164, 253
St Martin's School of Art x,
    124–7, 133–4
Saks 141
Salvation Army Family Tracing
    Service 324, 328
Sam (Bruce's driver) 296,
    314, 319, 325, 334

Samuel, Kathryn 298
San Lorenzo restaurant,
    London 186, 197, 227,
    337
Sangster, Fiona 219, 287,
    306, 334
Sangster, Guy 287, 334
Sangster, Mylo 334
Sangster, Robert 264, 279,
    285–8, 303, 312, 318
Sangster, Susan 262, 264,
    285–8, 303, 306, 312, 318
Santana 103
Sartin, Shelagh 271, 323
Saunders, Jennifer 282
Savage, Percy 171–2, 173,
    174, 175
Savary, Peter de 246
Scott, Fifi 87
Scott, Monica 86–7
Scott, Selina 238
Season (book by Bruce) 291,
    332
Secombe, Sir Harry 283
The Sentinel (film) 192,
    199–200
Seymour, Jane 207, 226
Shandwick Communications
    230
Sheffield, Emily 340
Sheffield, Samantha 340
Shiner, Lorette 176
Shingler, Tina 87
Shirley, Liz 156
Simone, Nina 101
Sinclair, Serena 156

Singleton, Roger xii–xiii, 247, 323–4
Smith, Delia 313–14
Smith, Liz 273
Smith, Richard 189
Smith, Tony 65, 90–1
Smith, Willi 149
Soames, Emma 219
Sombrero club, London 186
Soskin, Kira 175
Soskin, Tania 155–6, 159, 169
Souissi, Neila 231
South Africa 222–3
South African Breweries 222
Spago restaurant, Los Angeles 225
Spencer, Earl 319
Stack, Robert 84
Stanley Creek, Braida 269, 301
Starczewski, Thomas 337–8
Stassinopoulos, Arianna 202–3
Stassinopoulos, Mrs 202
Statton, Candy 186
Stefanides, John 302
Stephanie, Princess, look-alike 270–1
Stone, Paulene 224
Streisand, Barbra 226
Stringfellow, Peter 92, 242
Strong, Sir Roy 265
The Stud (film) 224, 252
Studio 54, New York 201–2

Stutz, Geraldine x, 139, 140, 144–5
Sue and Helen (designers) 172
Sumaya, Princess, of Jordan 272–3
Sunday Bloody Sunday (film) 205
Sunday Telegraph 298–9
Surya, Los Angeles 203
Suter, Elizabeth 'Su' 119, 335
Sweeney, Oliver 303
Sydney 275–80
Sydney Opera House 276

Talley, André Leon 187, 190, 201
Tate, Sharon 203
Tavares 186
Le Taxi Mauve (film) 190–1
Taylor, Liz 202
Taylor, Mr (DBH) 76
Temptations 58
Ten Years After 103
Tennant, Pat 143, 144, 154
Tester, Sonia 127
Thatcher, Baroness Margaret 296, 332
Thompson, Robert 64
Tilberis, Liz 317
Todd, Marie 231, 304
Tojo, Shuji 173
Tramp 187, 220
Travolta, John 320
Treacy, Philip 316

Tsaritsar 139, 155–7, 159–60, 165, 169, 173, 175
Underworld coffee bar, Ripon 58–9

Valentine, Malcolm 319
Valentino, Mario 164, 193, 297
Vanvelden, Jan 248
Variety Club 267
Varty, Keith 134
Versace, Gianni 274, 277, 314, 320–1
Viera, Andrea 187
Viera, Christina 187
Vogue 132–3, 179, 222, 270–1
Vreeland, Diana 189

Wainwright, Janice 105
Walker, Catherine 277
Walker, Lizzie 270, 290, 315
Walters, Barbara 318
Wan, Barney 126
Ward, Rachel 180
Wardrobe 176–7
Warhol, Andy 103, 160
Warn, Kerry 186
Watson, Adrian 81, 84, 86
Watson, Anna 113, 114, 115, 117–18, 157
Watson, Mr (Bruce's landlord) 78–9, 81–2, 95
Watson, Mrs (Bruce's landlady) 78–9, 80–6

Wattenphul, Juju 301
Watts, Winnie 13
Wedgwood 333
Weekes, Mr (bank manager) 176
West Mount Branch Home, Ripon xiii–xiv, 46–7
Westminster, Duchess of 340
Westwood, Vivienne 332
Wetton, Sheila 179
Whitbread Literary Award, 1988 268–9
White, Marco Pierre 308–9
White, Michael 222, 290
Whiteman, Smudge 177
Wickes, Valerie 339
Wicks, Judith 323
Wilder, Billy 225
Williams, Lloyd 312
Winner, Michael 193, 199–200
Wintour, Anna 299
Wolkenfeld, Felix 177–8, 259
Wolkenfeld, Judith 177–8, 258–9, 260, 289–90, 293
Women's Wear Daily 199
Wood, Jo 221, 290
Wood, Ronnie 221, 290
Woodhead, Lindy 179–80
Woodstock music festival 103
Woolfson, Ros 230–1, 233, 236, 237, 238, 246, 250–1, 268, 306

Worsley Taylor, Annette 139,
    155–6, 168, 169–72, 173,
    175, 194, 337
Worth, House of 130
Wyman, Astrid 220, 222
Wyman, Bill 222
Wyndham, Henry 333

Yamamoto, Yohji 266
Yeo, Mrs Tim 297
Young, Terence 160
Yuki 155, 172

Zuma restaurant, London
    290